I0119420

MATTERING PRESS

Mattering Press is an academic-led Open Access publisher that operates on a not-for-profit basis as a UK registered charity. It is committed to developing new publishing models that can widen the constituency of academic knowledge and provide authors with significant levels of support and feedback. All books are available to download for free or to purchase as hard copies. More at matteringpress.org.

The Press' work has been supported by: Centre for Invention and Social Process (Goldsmiths, University of London), European Association for the Study of Science and Technology, Hybrid Publishing Lab, infostreams, Institute for Social Futures (Lancaster University), OpenAIRE, Open Humanities Press, and Tetragon, as well as many other institutions and individuals that have supported individual book projects, both financially and in kind.

MAKING THIS BOOK

Mattering Press is keen to render more visible the unseen processes that go into the production of books. We would like to thank Natalie Gill and Uli Beisel, who acted as the Press' coordinating editors for this book, Julien McHardy for design, the two reviewers John Law and Mario Blaser, Steven Lovatt for the copy editing, Jenn Tomomitsu for proofreading and formatting, Alex Billington and Tetragon for the typesetting, and Will Roscoe, Ed Akerboom, and infostreams for their contributions to the html versions of this book.

COVER

Cover image by Francisco Navarrete Sitja: Devices for a soft territory: Alto Patache coastal fog oasis (Atacama, Chile).
Cover art by Julien McHardy.

ENVIRONMENTAL ALTERITIES

EDITED BY
CRISTÓBAL BONELLI
AND
ANTONIA WALFORD

Mattering Press

First edition published by Mattering Press, Manchester.

Copyright © Cristóbal Bonelli and Antonia Walford, chapters by respective authors, 2021.

Cover image © Francisco Navarrete Sitja, 2021.

Cover art © Julien McHardy, 2021.

Freely available online at https://www.matteringpress.org/books/environmental-alterities

This is an open access book, with the text and cover art licensed under Creative Commons By Attribution Non-Commercial Share Alike license. Under this license, authors allow anyone to download, reuse, reprint, modify, distribute, and/or copy their work so long as the material is not used for commercial purposes and the authors and source are cited and resulting derivative works are licensed under the same or similar license. No permission is required from the authors or the publisher. Statutory fair use and other rights are in no way affected by the above.

Read more about the license at creativecommons.org/licenses/by-nc-sa/4.0/

ISBN: 978-1-912729-14-2 (ppk)
ISBN: 978-1-912729-15-9 (pdf)
ISBN: 978-1-912729-16-6 (epub)
ISBN: 978-1-912729-17-3 (html)

Mattering Press has made every effort to contact copyright holders and will be glad to rectify, in future editions, any errors or omissions brought to our notice.

CONTENTS

SECTION 3: COLLECTIVITIES

LIST OF FIGURES

CONTRIBUTORS

LYS ALCAYNA-STEVENS is a visiting research fellow in the Anthropology Department at Harvard University and a postdoctoral researcher at the London School of Hygiene and Tropical Medicine. She received her PhD in Social Anthropology from the University of Cambridge in 2017 and was a Fondation Fyssen fellow at the Institut Pasteur and Laboratoire d'Anthropologie Sociale (Collège de France) in Paris from 2016–2018. She has worked extensively in rural Democratic Republic of Congo since 2012, conducting research on health and environmental politics.

CRISTÓBAL BONELLI is a psychologist, psychotherapist and anthropologist currently based at the department of Anthropology of the University of Amsterdam. He is the principal investigator of the ERC project 'Worlds of Lithium', in which he and his team study the socio-ecological disruptions emerging around decarbonisation strategies in Chile, China and Norway. He has conducted long-term ethnographic research in southern and northern Chile, where he collaborates with the Center for Integrated Research on Disaster Risk Reduction (CIGIDEN) and the Center for Intercultural and Indigenous Research (CIIR).

MAGNUS COURSE teaches anthropology at the University of Edinburgh. He has carried out research in southern Chile, the Scottish Outer Hebrides and southern Italy. He is the co-producer of *Iorram*, a feature-length documentary on Gaelic imaginings of the sea and is currently starting work on a book about the disappearance of Purgatory.

MARISOL DE LA CADENA has worked as an anthropologist in Peru, England, France and the USA. She teaches at UC-Davis. Her most recent book is *Earth Beings. Ecologies of Practice Across Andean Worlds* (2015), which is based on decade-long conversations with Mariano and Nazario Turpo, Andean *runakuna* from Cuzco. She co-edited (with Mario Blaser) *A World of Many Worlds* (2018.) Currently she works on what she calls 'cow-forming livescapes' in Colombia.

MARIANNE DE LAET is professor of anthropology and STS at Harvey Mudd College in Southern California. Her work on knowledge practices is concerned with the ways in which knowing and sensing together craft the known/sensed object. A psychologically trained anthropologist of science, she is interested in the self as a distributed subject, mediated by the company it keeps with animals and materials. She is currently writing about water and sustainable water technologies; taste and tasting; and living and dying with dogs.

DEHLIA HANNAH is a philosopher and curator and postdoctoral fellow of the Royal Danish Academy of Art and Arken Museum of Modern Art, Copenhagen. She holds a PhD in Philosophy from Columbia University with specialisations in philosophy of science, aesthetics, and philosophy of nature. Her recent book *A Year Without a Winter* (2018) reframes contemporary imaginaries of climate change by revisiting the environmental conditions under which *Frankenstein* was written and the global aftermath of the 1815 eruption of Mount Tambora.

PENNY HARVEY studies infrastructures to explore the material and social relations of modern statecraft, knowledge practices and the politics of value. She has conducted long-term ethnographic research in Peru and is currently researching nuclear power in the UK. She is Professor of Social Anthropology at the University of Manchester, and author of *Roads: An Anthropology of Infrastructure and Expertise* (with Hannah Knox), *Infrastructures and Social Complexity* (edited with Casper Jensen and Atsuro Morita) and *Anthropos and the Material* (edited with Krohn-Hansen and Nustad).

STEFAN HELMREICH is professor of anthropology at MIT and author of *Alien Ocean: Anthropological Voyages in Microbial Seas* (University of California Press, 2009) and of *Sounding the Limits of Life: Essays in the Anthropology of Biology and Beyond* (Princeton University Press, 2016). Helmreich's essays have appeared in *Critical Inquiry, Representations, Public Culture, The Wire, Cabinet* and *American Anthropologist*.

CASPER BRUUN JENSEN is an anthropologist of science and technology currently residing in Phnom Penh, Cambodia. He is the author of *Ontologies for Developing Things* (Sense, 2010) and *Monitoring Movements in Development Aid* (with Brit Ross Winthereik) (MIT, 2013), and the editor of *Deleuzian Intersections: Science, Technology, Anthropology* with (Kjetil Rödje) (Berghahn, 2009) and *Infrastructures and Social Complexity* with Penny Harvey and Atsuro Morita (Routledge, 2016). His work focuses on climate, environments, infrastructures, and speculative and practical ontologies.

STINE KRØIJER is associate professor in Anthropology at the University of Copenhagen. Her research interests span climate, nature, cosmology and political activism in the Amazon Basin and Northern Europe.

ANNET PAUWELUSSEN works as assistant professor in Marine Governance with the Environmental Policy group of Wageningen University and as Ocean Nexus research fellow with the University of Washington. Her anthropological research explores epistemological and ontological complexity in marine conservation and restoration, with a particular focus on gender, more-than-human relations and environmental care in indigenous and scientific practices. It builds on over a decade of ethnographic engagement with coastal and maritime communities, sea people and marine scientists in Southeast Asia.

BRONISLAW SZERSZYNSKI is professor of sociology at Lancaster University. His research seeks to situate social life in the longer perspective of human and planetary history, drawing on the social and natural sciences, arts and humanities. He is co-author with Nigel Clark of *Planetary Social Thought* (2020), author of

Nature, Technology and the Sacred (2005), and co-editor of *Risk, Environment and Modernity* (1996), *Re-Ordering Nature* (2003), *Nature Performed* (2003) and *Technofutures* (2015).

MANUEL TIRONI is associate professor and co-convener of the Critical Studies on the Anthropocene group at the Instituto de Sociología at P. Universidad Católica de Chile. He is also a principal investigator at the Center for Integrated Research on Disaster Risk Reduction (CIGIDEN). He is the author of *Disasters and Politics: Materials, Experiments, Preparedness* (edited with Israel Rodríguez-Giralt and Michael Guggenheim). His latest projects have engaged with issues of toxicity, environmental justice, politics of care and geological knowledge. He is currently conducting a four-year ethnographic project on modes of attention to geo-climatic disruptions.

ANTONIA WALFORD is a lecturer in Digital Anthropology at UCL. Their work explores the effects of the exponential growth of digital data and algorithms on social and cultural imaginaries and practices, centring on the data infra-structures of climate science, and with an ethnographic focus on Brazil. They have published in journals such as *Social Analysis, Cultural Anthropology,* and *Environmental Humanities,* and recently co-edited (with Nick Seaver and Rachel Douglas-Jones) a special issue with *JRAI* on the Anthropology of Data.

ACKNOWLEDGEMENTS

WE THANK ALL THE PARTICIPANTS OF THE WORKSHOP 'ENVIRONMENTAL Alterities' held in Amsterdam in September 2016. We kindly thank Annemarie Mol for having made this workshop possible and for having generously supported its realisation through her NWO Spinoza Prize. The editors wish to thank Arianna Injeian for her dedicated formatting of every essay in this book before submission, and Alejandra Vergara and Sofia Valdivieso for transcribing the conversations.

At Mattering Press, we thank our editors, Uli Beisel and Natalie Gill, and our copy editor Steven Lovatt. Many thanks to the two non-anonymous reviewers Mario Blaser and John Law. We also want to thank Casper Bruun Jensen for reading and commenting on an earlier version of the introduction. Last but not least, we thank all the authors who responded to our call, for the enthusiasm, patience and commitment they brought to this project.

This book has received funding from the European Research Council (ERC) under the European Union's Horizon 2020 research and innovation programme (grant agreement No. [853133])

Part of the writing up of this book was also supported by Cristóbal's Marie Curie Global Fellowship 'Invisible Waters' (n. 706346), funded by Horizon 2020. We would also like to express our gratitude for the support provided by the Center for Integrated Research on Disaster Risk Reduction (Cigiden-Conicyt/Fondap/15110017) and the Center for Intercultural and Indigenous Research (CIIR-Conicyt/Fondap/15110006).

ENVIRONMENTAL ALTERITIES

Cristóbal Bonelli and Antonia Walford

THIS BOOK IS ABOUT EVERYDAY ENVIRONMENTAL ENGAGEMENTS IN A TIME that has been framed through and with environmental crisis. It is intended as a means of slowing down the speed with which a discourse of 'Anthropocene collapse' is employed and circulated (see Stengers 2018). As scholars have pointed out (see for example Haraway et al. 2016), one of the problems with public and policy discourse around the Anthropocene is that it *collapses* all sorts of differences – cultural, political, social, racial, cosmological – into one linear trajectory encompassed within a 'future perfect continuous' tense (see Stengers in Davis and Turpin 2013), hurtling towards a common catastrophe. This collapse is refracted in various registers – environmental, conceptual, political – and it obscures the possibility of making room for other ways of living and thinking (Viveiros de Castro 2019; see Povinelli 2012). The 'Anthropocene collapse' eclipses the acknowledgement that the concept of the Anthropocene is a deeply depoliticising Western invention (Swyngedouw and Ernston 2018) with aspirations of universality (Hecht 2018). It also obscures the fact that the destructive effects of climate change are distributed unequally along fault lines that were laid down in colonial times and continue through capitalist and racialising systems to this day (Davis and Todd 2017; Yusoff 2018). Even more profoundly, in so doing, it negates the constitutive possibility of difference, the partiality, heterogeneity, multiplicity and alterity of its own existence.

In this book we develop this critique by exploring what we call 'environmental alterities'. Environmental alterities is used here to signal a sensitivity to aspects such as the uncertainty and unknowability, edges and limits, excess, overflow and extremes that characterise environmental engagements. Rather than trying to overcome environmental alterities in and through our knowledge practices, focusing on them demands that we actively elicit them as crucial to learning from mundane, experiential and grounded environmental engagements (see Latour 2018). This sensitivity also presents us with the possibility that, far from being features only of extraordinary environmental crisis, we encounter these aspects all the time in our relations with the environment. In this book we take it for granted that in very mundane ways, we still do not know what 'the environment' is and what it does (Deleuze and Guattari 1987). As Gayatri Spivak has argued, we need a language to try to take account of the alterity of the planet in ways that do not reduce it to the singular encompassing 'globe' of globalisation; on the contrary, '[T]he planet is in the species of alterity, belonging to another system; and yet we inhabit it, on loan' (Spivak 2003: 72).

Scholars in anthropology and STS, as well as in many other disciplines such as geography, philosophy of science, literature studies, environmental studies and cultural studies, have laid a solid and inspiring base from which to start and further expand this exploration of environmental alterities. In this introduction, we lay out three different epistemic paths that emerge from this critical scholarship.

The first is what we gloss as 'limits'. Here, we see scholars developing theoretical approaches to the edges or limits of human relationality with the environment. Important questions posed here are: what escapes our means of counting and knowing the environment? How does the earth act in our absence? In what ways is the planet more than the scale of the human? The second sensitivity is to 'heterogeneities'. Here, rather than focusing on a kind of environmental 'outside', we see scholars drawing out the differences internal to presumed unities and homogeneities, multiplying the possibilities for relationality and existence. Important questions here are: how to make room for ways of living that are not responsible for the Anthropocene collapse, and that have persisted at the margins of the modern constitution? How to design possible and multiple lines of thought and action that are not destructive but rather have the potential to trigger ontological openings in the ways we relate to our immanent environmental surroundings?

It is easy to see how these two approaches might rub each other the wrong way. One seems to be directed at what lies beyond relationality – human, or (more radically) otherwise (see for example Clark 2010, or Meillasoux 2006 respectively); from the other's perspective, there is no such thing as 'beyond relationality'. However, the third mode we want to explore, which we call 'heterogeneous limits', is a sensitivity which attempts to countenance both these positions, including the paradoxes and contradictions that this presents. Such an attempt can be understood, in part, as a continuous movement *between* these previous two epistemic paths. This sensitivity is to unexpected figure–ground reversals and self-contradictions which entail a shift between relationality and non-relationality, between the internal and external, between knowledge and its excesses. Rather than oppose the two previous approaches, this mode thus offers an interstitial space between environmental relationality and its limits as a fertile source of environmental thinking, turning the contradiction of such a perspective into a virtue. In this way, this third mode is an attempt to explore the extent to which these two sensitivities can engage in a relation of 'disjunctive synthesis' (Deleuze and Guattari 1983) capable of producing a series of generative explorations of differences that subsequently make new differences (Bateson 1972).

It is this third mode that the chapters in this book develop and explore, suggesting in so doing that to focus exclusively on either what we are calling 'limits' or on 'heterogeneities' is to obscure the extent to which environmental engagements are dynamic and shifting, and often circumscribed within a realm of figure–ground reversals, self-contradictions and 'in-betweens'. Each chapter brings different notions of alterity into relation with each other; the chapters range over different settings, mostly if not all ethnographic; and each chapter differs in its approach – but all share a commitment to dwelling, more or less uncomfortably, in this space of heterogeneous limits when it comes to trying to understand environmental engagements, be that with the sea, the forest, animals, spirits or planets. In this introduction, we will first elaborate on the three different positions we have outlined above, before introducing the chapters and other content in the volume.

WHAT COMES AFTER AFTER-NATURE?

We want to start by returning briefly to the idea of Anthropocene collapse. We use the idea of collapse to refer to the way in which the Anthropocene works to erase differences (see Harvey et al. 2019). But perhaps the defining collapse of the Anthropocene – the collapse of the distinction between nature and culture – was also one of the most important theoretical moves of the twentieth century across the humanities and social sciences. Drawing from the disciplines that we know best, science and technology studies (STS) and social anthropology, this 'after nature' movement has been characterised by an analytical focus on anti-essentialism, emergence, relationality, contingency and enactment. Some arguments aimed at destabilising Eurocentric 'nature/culture' divides have been based in indigenous lifeworlds (for example Viveiros de Castro 1998; de la Cadena 2010; Cruikshank 2012), while others draw inspiration from scientific or technological practices that are often set in Europe or the US (Mol 2002; Law, Lien, and Swanson 2018; Latour 1991). In both, it has become almost taken for granted that there is no natural world separate from culture or the social, and vice versa; and it is now commonplace to talk of multiple 'worlds' or 'ontologies', which are emergent from practices that simultaneously enfold and co-construct both what we might think of as 'nature' and 'culture' – hence the popularity of the neologism 'naturecultures' (coined by Donna Haraway in her *Companion Species Manifesto* of 2003). The subsequent realisation that we have thus limited our social and political worlds through a focus only on culture or humans has meant that several influential versions of this after-nature thinking – such as the multispecies turn (Kirksey and Helmreich 2010; Tsing 2015) – have pushed for an expansion of our horizons of relationality beyond the human, and beyond only human relations, to include all sorts of sundry entities, from dogs to coral to fungi to salmon, in our configurations of sociality (Haraway 2003; Hayward 2010; Tsing 2015). Again, this is also a collapse of sorts, in so far as it is an argument about how the 'natural' is inherently 'social' (Tsing 2013). The Anthropocene thus seems to provide inescapable proof of the claim that there is no Nature 'beyond' the cultural, the social, the political:

we all live in hybrid and heterogeneous realities that are socio-material and natural-cultural in multiple ways.

However, there is also a slippage occurring here, as contemporary Anthropocenic discourse becomes interwoven with earlier after-nature arguments. If in earlier after-nature scenarios, scholars revelled in pushing back against the determinism of nature in the name of non-deterministic emergence, in the Anthropocene version what is notable is that the environment is increasingly described in relationship to its destruction by (white Western capitalist) humans. In this sense, recognising the after-nature status of 'the environment' is no longer just an emancipating commitment to hybridisation over purification, but an acknowledgement of the historically destructive effects of social or human relations, and a realisation that there is no part of what we thought of as 'nature' that is uncontaminated by capitalist, colonial effluvia of some sort or another, be it plastics, radioactive isotopes or heavy metals (Liboiron 2018). The socialised 'nature' of post-nature becomes the damaged 'environment' of environmental crisis. From this perspective, the expansive relationality of post-nature approaches collapses into the dystopian framing of anthropogenic environmental degradation, leading to 'the sense of undoing that many call the Anthropocene' (Hetherington 2019: 2). In our reading, it is this slippage that has in turn led to what might be called a reappraisal of nature, with several scholars resisting the idea that the earth is in fact exhausted by humans' relations to it and pushing for a means of re-asserting the earth as a domain at least in part independent from the humans it hosts (see for example Clark 2010). This is where we locate one juncture that characterises the broad spectrum of after-nature approaches today; the question then becomes, what comes *after* after-nature? [1]

ENVIRONMENTAL ALTERITY 1: LIMITS

Two sets of scholars can be summoned here to guide us in thinking about an answer to this question. One set helps us consider what comes after after-nature in the sense of an (autonomous) outside. The second set of scholars inspires us to think about the potential for expansive relationality to generate difference not sameness, such that 'after-nature' contains its own potential for transformation.

In the first broad set of scholars, we see how people are pushing back against Anthropocene collapse by thinking about the limits, edges and endpoints of human relationality. A strand of argument to this effect has emerged across various disciplines. It stresses – directly or indirectly – the need to take into account something that is 'beyond' humans: something of the world which exceeds human relations. Perhaps the clearest example of this is geographer Nigel Clark's book, *Inhuman Nature: Sociable Life on a Dynamic Planet* (2011), in which Clark makes a case against the relational encompassment that charac- terises many after-nature approaches. He calls for a return to what he calls a sort of 'ground' to critical analyses, arguing against the symmetry which characterises co-constructivism, on the basis that we are dependent on an earth that is, to all intents and purposes, not dependent on us – and in fact supports us. He suggests therefore that radical asymmetry is a better way to think about the relationship we might have with the earth and argues that science provides a way to access the 'world in our absence'. In the terms we employed previously, Clark is in this way refusing the easy mapping of the 'nature' of post-nature critical thought onto the 'environment' of environmental crisis.

Another geographer, Kathryn Yusoff, also asks how to think about the world in the absence of humans – or what she terms the 'insensible' (2013); that is, that which is 'beyond me' (ibid.: 209), that which is not, and will never be, categorised and named by scientific (or any other) systems of meaning and ordering of nature. Her enquiries are ethically motivated, directed at trying to become 'responsible' for the loss of species that humans will never know: 'how to be responsible to that which disappears without a trace?' (ibid) she asks. Yusoff seeks a way to 'recognise' these as-yet unknown entities by thinking along what she calls the 'the edges of the insensible':

> There exists an urgent need to find modes of recognition beyond 'our' abilities
> to make non-human worlds intelligible if biodiversity loss is, for the most
> part, lost to sense. (This is not just a problem of recalcitrance or immanence,

but of a radical non-relationality.) This is difficult work, because ... it involves a modality of thought that moves against the priority of our senses to attempt to release other modalities of being that are not our own and will never be fully sensible to us.' (ibid)

Here Yusoff is interested in the limits of knowledge, what can by definition never be included in our accounting for and of nature. She questions the common equation, in new materialism and cognate approaches, of the non-human with the material. What if 'these other worlds that occasionally graze 'ours' perhaps do not leave anything so pronounced as a material trace?' (ibid.: 216)

Both Clark and Yusoff are explicitly concerned at the incapacity of contemporary forms of social scientific and critical thought to deal with those parts of the world which, they argue, are by definition beyond 'us', beyond material semiotic relations; Clark takes social constructivism as the exhausted paradigm, while Yusoff (perhaps more subtly) points to the inadequacies of new materialist approaches. Although we would take issue with the idea that scientific practice is a privileged means to access the 'world in our absence' as Clark seems to suggest,[2] both Clark and Yusoff highlight that the Anthropocene confronts us with the limits of the human, *including* scholarly attempts to overcome those limits (through, for example, the inclusion of the putatively 'non-human'). Clark and Yusoff have subsequently gone on to develop these ideas together through an enquiry into what they call 'geosocial formations' (Clark and Yusoff 2017). They point out that human social life is literally dependent upon the ground beneath it, but they also trace out the historical intertwining of the geological sciences and social thought, from Marx to Deleuze and Guattari – hence the 'geosocial'. However, they do so in order to argue that 'what is at stake is an inhuman agency that is not and cannot be fully co-extensive with the human domain, however inclusively this is imagined' (ibid.: 16).[3] The geological does not only appear simply as a lively material in their analysis, to be included in social reckonings. Rather, they emphasise the impossibilities of this inclusive aspiration: 'what is at issue is not only how to extend or enrich the composition of shared worlds but what to make of forces capable of interrupting, undermining or overwhelming the very conditions of doing politics or being social' (ibid.: 15).

The capacity of the world to escape or overwhelm our means of knowing it has also recently engaged literary theorists concerned with themes of ecological disaster. In his recent book *The Great Derangement: Climate Change and the Unthinkable* (2016), Amitav Ghosh is interested in the failure of another social practice, this time the literary novel, to tackle climate change. Ranging over different times and places, Ghosh traces how writing the improbable was entirely neglected in modern fiction, the early writers of which were more interested in the mundane, everyday and predictable, than the violent and unpredictable (Jane Austen's treatment of the Napoleonic War only through the mundanities of the rural English drawing room is perhaps one infamous example of this). This narrow solipsism, Ghosh argues, has meant that fiction has shied away from dealing with the inhuman 'uncanniness' of climate change. But, he argues, 'we are confronted suddenly with a new task: that of finding other ways in which to imagine the unthinkable beings and events of this era' (ibid.: 45). He presents us not only with the limits of the literary imagination, but also the narrowness – indeed the 'derangement' – of historical thinking and political action when faced with 'the unthinkable'. In a rather different tone,[4] literary theorist Timothy Morton (2013), inspired by the philosophers who espouse Object Oriented Ontology (or OOO as it is known), has coined the term 'hyperobjects' to try to take account of global warming as a phenomenon that exceeds the human. Drawing extensively on philosopher Graham Harman's investigations of objects[5] – specifically the Heideggerian idea of objects being 'withdrawn', such that there is a part of every object (a category which includes all manner of humans and non-humans) which is not available for relationality at all – Morton seeks to account for how hyperobjects, like climate change, are fully independent of, and transcend, human cognition: 'The transcendental gap between things and thing-data becomes quite clear when we study what I like to call *hyperobjects*: things that are huge and, as they say, 'distributed' in time and space – that take place over many decades or centuries (or indeed millennia), and that happen all over Earth – like global warming. Such things are impossible to point to directly all at once' (Morton 2018: 22; see also Morton 2013). Hyperobjects are beyond the human exactly because they provoke 'scalar dilemmas' (Morton 2013: 19) in which they cannot be thought of as occupying a 'series of now-points in time and space' and in which they 'confound the social and psychic instruments we use to measure them' (ibid.: 47); and yet at the same time, you cannot extricate yourself from them: hyperobjects are 'viscous' (ibid.: 30).

Finally, and in a different vein to the previous approaches, we have already briefly mentioned Spivak's work on post/de-colonial comparative literature, and in particular her concept of 'planetarity'. Unlike Morton, her challenge to re-think what the 'planet' is through its alterity captures the *political* necessity of this form of environmental alterity, which understands the Anthropocene collapse as a legacy of colonialism. Spivak writes: 'if we imagine ourselves as planetary subjects rather than global agents... alterity remains underived from us; it is not our dialectical negation, it contains us as much as it flings us away' (2003: 73); it is 'mysterious and discontinuous' with us (ibid.: 102). She urges us to make the familiar unfamiliar, to render 'our home uncanny', riffing on Freud (ibid.: 73–74), as a necessity for addressing the pervasive eurocentrism and orientalism that characterises literary studies. Thinking in terms of planetarity, for Spivak, is confronting the ways in which we must accept the 'untranslateable' without translating it into 'acceptance' (2015: 291) and realising how we must be open to a difference that exceeds the tolerance of liberal multiculturalism (2003: 100) and is instead an 'experience of the impossible' (2003: 102).

Here then we present one form of environmental alterity which lies at the edges of, or even beyond, the human. The forms it might take vary considerably depending on the author, but there is a sense in which we have reached the edge or the limits of our knowledges and practices – as both 'humans' and as critical scholars – and that those edges or limits are *generative* exactly because they challenge us, confound us and escape us. What lies beyond those limits? For Clark, it is a ground that 'supports us', that carries on independently of us. For, Yusoff, it is something like the 'insensible' (Yusoff 2013).[6] For Spivak, it is alterity that is not caught in an exoticising dialectic but encompasses it. For Ghosh, it resides in the uncanniness of earthly violence and the reluctance of literature, history and politics to engage it. But all of these authors ask us, in different ways, to think about the limits of the collapse between humans and the world, and about the world as excessive of human thought and practice.

ENVIRONMENTAL ALTERITY 2: HETEROGENEITIES

The second set of scholars we want to highlight is pushing back against Anthropocene collapse by making room for heterogeneous ways to live in our critical times – but without relying on an autonomous ground existing beyond human relationality. As such, these authors have been trying to make room for a kind of alterity that, rather than being concerned with an 'outside' emerging at the edges of human relationality, focuses on the generative force of immanent and relational difference.

Notable in this respect has been the invitation made by Donna Haraway (2016) to explore unforeseen connections and rebuild lively, sympoietic assemblages in a historical time she calls the *Cthulucene*, a concept that revitalises the ancient Greek term *khthonios*, roughly translated as 'of the earth'. Haraway's intervention problematises the centring of the human in the Anthropocene by offering the idea of the *humus*, a take on the human understood as inherently pertaining to the 'biotic and abiotic working of the Earth' (Haraway and Franklin 2017: 2). In doing so, Haraway develops an imagination which allows us to realise that unities do not precede their heterogeneous relatings. This is an imagination that challenges the sciences of the 'modern synthesis', which tend to be based upon competitive unities and relations 'whose actors and stories are mostly described mathematically in competition equations' (2016: 62). Etymologically, *sympoiesis* means 'making-with', a concept that Haraway mobilises in order to state that no living entity is really auto-poietic, nor fully self-organised: 'Critters interpenetrate one another, loop around and through one another, eat each another, get indigestion, and partially digest and partially assimilate one another, and thereby establish sympoietic arrangements that are otherwise known as cells, organisms, and ecological assemblages' (Haraway 2016: 58).[7]

In a similar critical relational vein, Marisol de la Cadena has recently noted that the Anthropocene obscures engagements that might be taking place within 'heterogeneous worlds that do not make themselves through practices that separate ontologically humans (or culture) from non-humans (or nature)' (de la Cadena 2019). In contrast to this, de la Cadena proposes we make room for the *anthropo-not-seen*, a kind of cosmo-political sensitivity that considers the *anthropos* as always partial and radically situated. By telling us the story of Massima, a peasant woman who refuses to leave her lands to extractivist mining corporations in Peru – as her existence is inherently *with* the land – de la Cadena offers us an example of a radical and immanent relationality working at the core of extra-modern populations. Somehow, de la Cadena's sympoietic imagination (and not only this!) allows us to deploy and push forward what Helmreich (2014) has coined as 'symbiopolitics', that is, a 'politics of living things coexisting, incorporating, and mixing with one another' (2014: 56), a politics whose understanding of relations as emerging outcomes of sympoietic perceptions might be an inspirational source.

Haraway's and de la Cadena's work strongly resonates with other more-than-human conceptualisations of relationality in South America that have offered us understandings of kinship (in general), and affinity (in particular), as going beyond inter-species borders to involve relations between humans and animals, plants and spirits. Indeed, in a way which resonates with one of the slogans proposed by Haraway for the Cthulucene *'Make Kin Not Babies!'*, Amerindian ethnographic work has revealed how affinity is the generic mode of relatedness in South America, a mode of relatedness that prevails over consanguinity and its subsequent understanding of kinship limited by biological premises (see Viveiros de Castro 2001, also Bonelli 2019). For this post-natural conceptualisation of relatedness, the Other, and the outside, are conceived of as a constitutive relation.

Through all these post-natural sensibilities, the possibility of the kind of 'ground' understood by Clark is made relative, as it depends on the particular positionality of, for instance, Massima and her situated becomings. As far as the Anthropocene trope is concerned, these relational conceptualisations of 'difference from within' resonate with recent and growing attempts to think about our planet 'from the inside', a move with the capacity to reveal the complex, dynamic and heterogeneous aspects of the Earth (Arenes, Latour, and Gailladert

2018, see Szerszynski in this volume). Challenging the modern imagination of environmental transformations as if they were taking place in a given 'container universe' (Latour 2004; Law 2015), and as Jensen and Blok (2019) have recently argued, this sensitivity towards heterogeneous worlds pushes against theoretical tendencies that solely focus on how developments in the natural sciences can inform and explain emerging ecological material-transformations (Bennett 2010; Coole and Frost 2010). At the same time, it also challenges the equally reductive theoretical formulations of eco-Marxist approaches that seek to explain ecological transformations solely as an expression of the history of capitalism (Malm and Hornborg 2014; Moore 2015; Wark 2015).

Complicating theoretical tendencies that construe responses to ecological crisis as dictated either by natural scientists or by social scientists, scholars supporting this heterogeneity have underlined the richness of attending to the juxtaposed knowledges and practices at stake in different divergent environmental settings, making explicit that we cannot understand our environmental engagements only by relying on scientific practices or secular politics. Broadly conceived, this scholarship concerned with heterogeneity has shed light on how differentiating among dissimilar co-existing configurations of practices allows us to learn what is at stake in each empirical transformative environment, and to generate new conceptual tools to better account for the 'arts of living' on our damaged planet (Tsing et al. 2017). Here, we consider the allusion to 'art' as being not only metaphorical but literal: the arts of living on a damaged planet entail the continuous creative development of particular skills that emerge in very situated practices linked to very particular problems, thus making explicit that coping with environmental transformation does not imply the existence of a unified or transcendental domain.

ENVIRONMENTAL ALTERITY 3: 'HETEROGENEOUS LIMITS' OR DIFFERENCE AS A KIND OF TABAPOT

All the chapters in this book draw on and enter into generative dialogue with the sets of scholars we have introduced above, and the broader constellations of ideas they propose. Thus, Marianne de Laet's chapter on the concept of 'the pack' takes up Haraway's provocation to 'think with' other species and draws on Tsing's work on multispecies anthropology. We see Bronislaw Szerszinski in his chapter drawing on the related notion of Latour's Parliament of Things. Both Stine Krøijer and Magnus Course engage directly in Amerindian relational anthropology, Course in the context of proposing an ethical mode of the human for fishermen in Scotland, Krøijer in order to explore the multiplicity of alterities in the forests of the Sieko-pai people in Ecuador. Annet Pauwellusen troubles the nature/culture binary by building on the work of scholars such as Descola and, again, Haraway, in order to think about the alterity of the sea for the people of the Massalima Archipelago in Indonesia. Lys Alcayna-Stevens, inspired by Yusoff's work, presents the edges of scientific understandings of the forest.

However, by attending to questions of both 'heterogeneity' and 'limits' as outlined above, the chapters in this book in fact collectively start to flesh out what we think of as a third position, by focusing our attention on the space *in-between* these sensitivities, 'not-quite' one nor the other. And in fact, since the first time we met most of the book's contributors in Amsterdam in 2016 in a workshop we called 'Environmental Alterities', we have been continuously tinkering with how best to frame this provocation in a way that does not end up triggering further irresolvable oppositions, or immediate gut reactions against either limits *or* heterogeneity. Indeed, what we and the authors ended up doing throughout this long process was to experiment exactly with the continuous movement *between* these positions, searching for unforeseen ways to create inter-theoretical alliances between scholarships and scholars that are strongly moved by partially connected after 'after-nature' concerns. Therefore, rather than being simply the *means* by which different positions are assumed, the relation between what we are calling heterogeneity and limits can, we argue, be the *ends* as well. That is, it is precisely holding both of these positions together, and the movement *between* these two positions, that emerges as the generative dynamic – not one or the other. This means that the conceptual yields of environmental alterities, understood as the exploration of heterogenous limits, lie not in differentiating heterogeneous relationality from external autonomous alterity, but in making room for thinking of and with the alterity of relationality, and the relationality of alterity, at the same time.

We have drawn on two scholars in particular to guide us in trying to think through this third mode. The first is Isabelle Stengers, who has worked extensively on the philosophy of science from what we have called an 'after nature' perspective. Here, we are particularly inspired by her recursive and paradoxical formulations of scientific practice. Through such formulations, she works within an after-nature or co-constructivist paradigm, and nevertheless manages to simultaneously subvert it. For example, in her early work on particle physics, taking the neutrino as an example, she tells us that the neutrino 'exists simultaneously and inseparably "in itself" and "for us"', an 'apparently paradoxical mode of existence' which is populated by *factishes* that are both dated and transhistoric' (2010a: 22). Although Stengers' argument here dovetails with those of Latour and other co-constructivist approaches to scientific knowledge, for Stengers it is not so much the hybridity of these entities, but their paradoxicality that needs to be taken seriously and sustained; unlike Latour, with Stengers the issue is never 'resolved' or, indeed, 'collapsed' – she does not allow the reader to rest on one side or the other but keeps both sides of the relation in constant question.

This becomes clearer in relation to our notion of environmental alterities through her distinction between the experimental and the field sciences. Stengers distinguishes explicitly between what she calls the experimental or laboratory sciences (of which physics is exemplary) and the field sciences, such as the Earth Systems sciences. According to Stengers, whereas the experimental sciences aim to create the world in the laboratory (as with the neutrino), the field sciences go outside and 'follow' the world. This endeavour to follow the world does not bring 'stable proofs', as laboratory practices do. Rather, 'irreducible uncertainty is the mark of the field sciences' (1993: 144). Whereas laboratory sciences produce 'factishes' which are real exactly because they have been constructed (as Bruno Latour has also written about extensively (Latour 1993), Stengers invokes the notion of the 'terrain' (ibid.: 144) as the peculiar object of the field sciences. Unlike the factish of the experimental laboratory, which by definition 'explains itself', the terrain 'induces and nurtures questions, but does not supply the ability to explain the answer that will be given to them' (2010b2: 230). The terrain cannot be taken into a laboratory, and nor can it be made to represent any other terrain. It demands that those who study it follow it at its own pace in order to 'bring it into existence' (1993:145). It thus emerges from, but is in no way determined by the practice of those who follow it; on the contrary, it can 'object' – and, as she says in her later writing on the concept of Gaia, 'intrude' (Stengers 2015: 137; see also Jensen and Blok 2019). Further, the terrain must in a sense 'pre-exist the one who describes it' (Stenger 1993:144). The natural entities of the experimental laboratory are determinate entities with the power to create a clear cause and effect relation and can be made to speak for entities like them everywhere. The 'field' of the field sciences, on the other hand, is a specific terrain that is neither willing nor able to offer guarantees of causal certainty or represent other places.

Stengers develops these ideas even further in her recent engagements with the Anthropocene (2015a, 2015b, 2017), and her cosmopolitical proposal around the figure of Gaia, the latter understood as an unruly, disruptive, ominous being that intrusively demands unexpected ways of thinking and acting around and throughout entangled practices in times of environmental crisis.[8] On the one hand, Gaia is a new kind of being, 'existing in its own terms, not in the terms crafted to reliably characterise it' (Stengers 2015: 137). It is neither living nor non-living but, Stengers writes, requires instead that we 'complicate the divide between life and non-life, for Gaia is gifted with its own particular way of holding together and of answering to changes forced on it (here the charge of greenhouse gas in the atmosphere), thus breaking the general linear relation between causes and effects' (ibid.). Here Stengers stresses the ways in which Gaia is excessive to the binaries themselves – between knowledge and world, life and non-life, phenomena and model, and is therefore new, or at least difficult to recognise. At the same time, Gaia pays tribute to the diverse and many times divergent worldings (see Omura et al. 2019) and entanglements between people and untamed earthly forces. This attention to the relational existence of Gaia then produces an ethical imperative that multiplies the myriad configurations of thought and action needed to articulate a political positionality in times of environmental crisis: ecological responses should be multiple, pragmatic and experimental, so the way we design and think about them should resist any tendency towards totalising generalisation.[9] We argue that Gaia reformulates the space between limits and heterogeneity as we have defined them earlier in the text. As Jensen and Blok put it, '[G]iven Gaia's indifference to human pleas, it is indeed possible to speak of an asymmetric relation to a new 'ground', of the kind that held Clark's (2011, 2014) attention. For Stengers, however, Gaia does not designate a set of inhuman materials forming autonomous worlds' (Jensen and Blok 2019:). Which is to say, Gaia seems to unapologetically suggest an outside, in Clark's terms, that is nevertheless thoroughly 'inside'.

We can follow the thread of Stenger's paradoxical formulations through many of the chapters in this book, several of which focus empirically on different scientific practices. In her examination of living with dogs, Marianne De Laet puts Haraway's notion of species companion into conversation with ethological ideas of dog behaviour, in order to ask of *both* how humans might be able to 'speak for' dogs if we have no access to their *umwelt*. If Stine Krøijer is interested in her chapter in the possibility of non-relationality in the context of Sieko-pai understandings of the relational emptiness of palm oil plantations, it is a non-relationality that unabashedly points to how, paradoxically, it can only be sustained in relation to other forms of relationality, be they shamanic, historical or political. In Lys Alcayna-Stevens' description of primatologists' experiences of the forest, where their scientific work gets endlessly interrupted by losing their research subjects (bonobo chimps) altogether, and they spend periods of time wandering the forest lost in thought, we see clearly, if indirectly, an evocative description of Stengers' notion of the 'terrain' and indeed Gaia, intruding and demanding, both produced by the field sciences and pre-existing them. And in Bronislaw Szerszynski's exploration of planetary existence, he draws directly not only on the planetary sciences, but also on Stengers's work with Ilya Prigogine in order to point us towards the possibility of planetary 'becoming', a sort of intensive planetary alterity in which planets differ not just from each other, but also from themselves (this volume, p 203). In all cases, the paradoxical and often recursive shapes that emerge from the chapters' analyses are sustained and curiously explored, rather than refused or resolved. Neither 'heterogeneities' nor 'limits' alone quite capture what the authors assembled here are trying to describe.

There is another scholar whose work has also inspired us to think about the generative potential of indeterminacies, albeit in a different idiom to that of Stengers: anthropologist Roy Wagner, who interrogated the anthropological concepts of nature and culture by experimenting with the paradoxical essence of meaning in his work with the Daribi of Papua New Guinea and the Usen Barok of New Ireland (although always in relation to Western, anthropological, forms of meaning). Although Wagner's work is prolific and full of tropes and images which complicate and involute the opposition between what we have called 'limits' and 'heterogeneities' – like his infamous idea of 'symbols that stand for themselves' (Wagner 1986) – here we want to draw specifically on his later work on chiasmatic relations and what he called the 'reciprocity of perspectives'. In one of the last articles to be published before his death in 2018, entitled *The Reciprocity of Perspectives* (2018) Wagner makes a case for an analogical chiasmatic understanding of nature and culture, working through a series of different examples in typically heterogeneous fashion. Drawing on thinkers from Wittgenstein to Einstein, he evidences his own argument in the article by demonstrating the creativity and generative function not so much of thinking *through* self-contradiction but thinking itself *as* self-contradiction. In his rendering, meaning is always becoming something else: 'it is neither exclusively subjective nor objective, but rather a continuous dialogic transition between the two' (ibid.: 506). It is this transition itself which is the ever-shifting locus of meaning, rather than the poles it transits between; so 'metaphor' Wagner writes, the bridge between the signifier and signified, 'is language's way of figuring out what we mean by it' (ibid). Energy, likewise, is not of one kind or the other, but only the 'generic 'kind' of its transformation from one specific kind to another' (ibid.: 505). The 'chiasmus' at the heart of this form of relationality is the shift of perspectives that allows, for example, as Marilyn Strathern writes in a commentary on Wagner's 2018 article, '[A] symbol that (in one mode) stands for itself' to 'also (in the other) stands for something else' (see Wagner 1986), as in a Barok ritual feast: 'where you see a male youth you also see a female ancestress; where you see a nubile girl you also see an out-marrying clansman' (Strathern 2018: 511–512). Here we see the way that the invention of meaning, its extension into the world, is simultaneously 'mined – 'elicited' – out of its own resources' (Holbraad and Pedersen 2017: 89).

Wagner provides us with another evocative image from the Tolai peoples of East New Britain, in Papua New Guinea. In the words of one of Wagner's Tolai friends, cognition and perception might be summarised with the following figure of the *tabapot*:

> Imagine a tree whose top foliage cuts the shape of a human face against the sky and fix the shape of that face in your mind, so that it appears as a real face, and not just a profile. When you have finished, turn back to the tree, and imagine it as a free-standing object without reference to the face. When you have both images firmly fixed in your mind, just hold them in suspension and keep shifting your attention from one to the other: tree/face, face/tree, tree/face, and so on. That is what we call a *tabapot* (Wagner 2018: 502).

Wagner's development of this idea of 'chiasmatic thinking' then complements, to our mind, the elicitation of recursive and paradoxical formulations of knowledge and truth that we drew from Stengers. Where in the latter, we are asked to hold contradictions together and 'follow' what happens when we do so, in the former we are pointed towards what you might call a particular 'chiasmatic skill' of shifting our attention between what we might think of as mutually opposed intellectual positions, in a series of figure-ground reversals between knowledge and its limits and excesses; between practice and its exhaustion; and, in this case, between ever-expanding heterogeneous relationality and a grounded non-relationality.[10] Again, as a tactic we can borrow, we can see how thinking through such a *tabapot* form can be traced out in several of the chapters of this book. Annet Pauwellusen's investigation of the notion of 'twinship' between humans and sea creatures that she encountered in the Masalima Archipelago argues that twinship expresses 'co-existence' between humans and the non-human realm of the sea, but also simultaneously indexes an 'excess' that forces us to think 'in-between' the categories that we might be accustomed to draw on as anthropologists (this volume, 63). As she traces out the complexities of this notion, she shows how the amphibious sea twin also has a figure-ground reversal at its heart, such that it can be both the sea and a part of the sea; but this also shows us that twinship 'liquefies' figure and ground, turning the ground into fluid that will not hold steady for analysis (this volume, 77). Course's analysis starts by demonstrating how the 'structural isomorphism' (this volume, 36) of the land and the sea in Gaelic poetry also contains within it a moral asymmetry and contradiction, such that the sea is both a danger and a refuge, both Other and familiar. His chapter tacks between these two ideational formations, one symmetrical, one asymmetrical, in order to develop a parallel argument that flips the figure-ground relation of ontology to ethics in Amerindian perspectivism, urging us to re-centre the figure of 'the human' in the process. In a very different vein, Alcayna-Stevens' chapter switches back and forth stylistically between semi-fictional reflections, primatalogical observations, ethnographic data and anthropological theory, constantly destabilising the perspective of the reader, but nevertheless adding up somehow to an evocative description of a 'sylvan thinking' as a thinking with and through the failure and partiality of meaning (this volume, 151).

Here, and across the chapters more generally, we are reminded of the generative potential of the edges and limits of our own conceptual apparatuses as Anthropocene scholars. Kim Fortun's (2012) characterisation of the Anthropocene as a time of 'exhausted paradigms' neatly captures the imbrication of environmental collapse with a feeling of conceptual fatigue; just as the resources of the earth are running out, so too are 'our' conceptual resources. As a result, the Anthropocene literature has been replete with calls for new approaches, from radical interdisciplinarity to eco-modernism to science fiction (for example, Tsing et al. 2015). However, as several of the authors here emphasise, another question might be whether, alongside new paradigms, we also need simply to acknowledge the edges of our current knowledge-practices without immediately posing new, more encompassing, ones; that perhaps we need also to dwell on exactly the in-betweens, the not-quites, the self-contradictions and the impossibilities of the environmental contexts we are working in, as themselves generative of a form of political, intellectual and ethical engagement.

THIS BOOK

We have organised this book around three key loci of environmental engagement. The first section is Sea; the second section is Forests; the third is Collectives. In the spirit of chiasmatic thinking, and in order to create some sort of fidelity with our attempt to identify conceptual, ontological, and ethical openings, we have also invited different scholars to discuss these chapters in a conversational format, based on a previous, critical discussion about the central arguments made in this introduction. Each section therefore includes a commentary on the chapters in that section, in the form of a conversation. These conversations are integral aspects of the book; we hope in this way to keep the idea of 'environmental alterities' *chiasmatic*, continually shifting and turning. Here, we present the chapters in relation to each other and those conversations, in order to explain the structure of the book.

The first section includes the chapters by Magnus Course and by Annet Pauwelussen, which both focus on a particular aspect of 'the environment' – the sea – and on a particular kind of category – the human. Course picks up directly on the question we posed in this introduction, of what comes after after-nature; his answer is, contrary to a post-human intuition, a 'humble anthropocentrism'. In order to develop this, Course draws on Scottish Gaelic folk tales, in which seals appear as both socially continuous but morally discontinuous with humans. Humanity emerges from these tales in two distinct modalities: one can be understood through tropes of domestication and colonisation, but there is also another way that centres the human as part of a much wider web of affective attachments. This multiplies the possibility of what being human might mean, yet also circumscribes a limit to what a human can be. Turning subsequently to his ethnographic work with fisherman in Scotland, Course argues that being human is an ethical, rather than an ontological condition. The oscillatory uncertainty of humans' relations to seals, and to the sea that both exceeds and constitutes humanity, resolves itself into a question of ethical decision-making – what sort of human do we intend to be?

Pauwelussen also picks up on the idea of the 'human' as it appears in her ethnographic work in the Indonesian islands of Masalima, among a very different set of seafarers. Also interested in exploring the limits of the human, Pauwelussen develops this in relation to the concept of 'twinship', which offers itself as a fertile idea to think with: twins are the same but also not the same. This appears in her material as twinship not between humans, but between humans and octopuses and crocodiles. Tracing out these connections and disconnections through rich ethnographic detail, Pauwelussen shows us a complex relationship that signals both an otherness and a likeness; the term for what we could call 'human' – *manusia* – is a term for personhood that exceeds the people from Masalima as it also embraces the sea, without however, fully capturing it. *Manusia* thus emerges as a means not to make a distinction between humans and animals, nature and culture, but focuses our attention on what escapes conceptualisation, indexing an in-between space that, as we have remarked, evokes the *tabapot* as a pivotal ethnographic figure at the centre of environmental engagements.

In both Course and Pauwelussen's analyses, difference resides in making heterogeneous that which might be presumed to be 'the same' – in these cases, the 'human'. But both also point to the difficulty of holding still the relation between people and the sea; particularly in Pauwelussen's piece, we are left with a social theory and practice that both encompasses and exceeds human rela- tionality, thus ethnographically revealing that the sea is an autonomous alterity which is at the same time immanent to/with the people of the sea. This section of the book is concluded with a conversation between Stefan Helmreich and Penny Harvey, who in their discussions of the chapters and the introduction, point to the role of kinship in manifesting forms of environmental relations of alterity, and remind us among other things of the importance of remembering the heterogeneous histories and uneven distributions and intensities of these environmental forms of relating and belonging.

The second section, 'Forests', takes us to two very different forest settings; one forest of Ecuador with the Sieko-pai people; the other the forest of pri- matologists in DR Congo. If both Course and Pauwelussen are interested in 'different kinds' of humans and forms of extensive relationality, both Stine Krøijer's and Lys Alcayna-Stevens' chapters focus on 'different kinds' of natures. In her chapter, Krøijer turns our attention towards the environmental alterity of what she explicitly calls 'non-relationality'. Investigating the ways in which trees are understood in the indigenous Sieko-pai's world, Krøijer examines two different forms of environmental alterity. One of these is recognisable from the anthropological literature arising out of the multi-natural landscape of the forest, but the other, surprisingly, emerges from the unlikely place of an intrusive plantation. Refusing, along with Sieko-Pai, to see plantations only as spaces of monoculture and extractivist colonialism, the plantation becomes a source of a particular kind of environmental alterity, 'a wild and uncontrolled realm that escapes human attempts at knowing and owning it' (this volume, 106) – and one which the Sieko-pai do not recognise and are unsure how to relate to. Krøijer thus argues that plantations are relationally multiple, and far from being forms which anthropologists might think they recognise, offer the chance to re-examine our presumptions about ever-expanding relationality. In her use of the nature/culture binary to understand these environmental alterities, Krøijer also raises the question of the adequacy of our linguistic frameworks to adequately grasp what is at stake, an issue picked up by several of the chapters (Alcayna-Stevens, de Laet).

Also starting with the problem of 'Nature', Alcayna-Stevens opens her chapter by asking what is to be done when the primatologists with whom she works seem to romanticise Nature or the forest. In thinking through this, she starts to assess what she calls the 'edge work' or 'cusp work' that goes on in scientific practice. In part pushing back against various ideas of science as disembodied and detached, she points to all the moments of waiting, searching and wondering. Employing what she calls 'ethnographic fiction' as an experimental device to explore the unanswerable, unfathomable and indeterminate grounds of the forest, her piece exemplifies exactly the sort of meandering day-dreaming that she is describing, interweaving the journey of a 'composite character' on a search for bonobos, with primatological theories about bonobo social life, with ethnographic observation from her field-site and her own personal experiences of being in the forest. Evoking the interstitial spaces of an embodied relation to the forest, Alcayna-Stevens goes well beyond a critique of romanticisation to show how paying attention to these 'in between' moments can generate further appreciation and respect for alterity, asymmetry, indeterminacy and the unknowable. This section of the book is concluded with a conversation between Casper

Bruun Jensen and Marisol de la Cadena, who ask us to consider, among other things, whether the concerns of the two chapters and the introduction in fact point to the impossibility of pure relationality or pure non-relationality, and whether there is not more than one way of doing both environmental politics and environmental alterity.

The third section of the book we have called 'Collectivities'. This is to signal how these chapters confront one of the overarching challenges of environmental alterities, that is, how to compose an after-nature world? In this section, Marianne de Laet presents us with three evocative auto-ethnographic stories around living with dogs as a form (or not) of alterity. Tacking between a series of positions of sameness and difference between herself and her dogs, de Laet's three stories address issues around subjectivity, species-thinking and ethology, and anthropocentrism, eventually proposing 'the pack' as a way to try to grasp 'a language for togetherness' that also pushes back 'against the fantasy that dogs are with us, naturally, all the way' (this volume, 178). As a form of an unsteady, shifting collective, the pack also, we suggest, indexes a *tabapot* figure for learning from human-animal collaborations that exceeds alterity while at the same time resisting a sort of generic, natural intra- or inter-species harmony. De Laet's piece also makes explicit one of the underlying questions of the book – what to do with the realisation that language fails us in our descriptions, if we are simultaneously 'after' a post-modern response to such a realisation? Working around essentialist language, she refuses to 'reify alterity', instead presenting a shifting terrain of differences in which relationality is nevertheless very possible; where 'living together', as a form of 'fidelity' emerges as a direct antidote to any sort of post-modern ennui.

If, as Clark and Yusoff have suggested (2017), the multi-species thinking that characterises de Laet's chapter has failed to take the non-organic into account, then in our last chapter Bronislaw Szerszynski does just that by asking how planets come to matter when thinking about cosmopolitical collectives. Equally concerned as de Laet with the question of non-human compositions, Szerszynski however introduces a very different tradition, that of geophilosophy, drawing on Deleuze, Guattari and Simondon. Planets emerge from his description not as the stable background to human dramas, but engaged in their own forms of relating, creating and differentiating. Grafting Latour's concerns around the Parliament of Things onto a planetary scale, Szerzynski argues that in order to answer Latour's question – how many are we and how should we live together – we need to understand planets as being in a constant process of becoming, of being not just different to each other, but different internally to themselves. This section of the book concludes with a conversation between Dehlia Hannah and Manuel Tironi, who begin by drawing on their personal experiences of political upheaval and recent parenthood to reflexively re-think their relation to their work on environmental crisis. Part of their conversation critically considers the role of interdisciplinarity in the Anthropocene discourse, and the way in which the arts and social sciences could or should relate to the natural sciences, in order to invent new forms of disciplinary collective.

END?

Crisis stories surround the Anthropocene, and for good reason: the news is filled with extreme weather events caused by global warming, toxic spills, bio-diversity decimation and, more recently, global pandemics. Despite the fact that it seems impossible to untangle the human from the non-human in the face of the distributed effects of such catastrophes, this thoroughly socialised nature – polluted nature, damaged nature, feral nature – is simultaneously characterised as 'terrifyingly antisocial' (Hetherington 2019: 4). It feels like something has been unleashed: scientists talk of tipping points and runaway processes; our climate predictions fail, as do our political apparatuses. As we were in the middle of writing this introduction (May 2019), the UN released an urgent warning about environmental destruction; school children were strik-ing from school to protest the lack of political action on climate change; there were massive protests in London and other major cities by activists under the banner 'Extinction Rebellion'; and various environmental activist movements were contesting the violent extraction of natural resources in South America and elsewhere. As we finalise it (January 2021), we are caught up in the Covid-19 pandemic that has infected 92 million people, and killed 2 million people, around the world and will make its effects known for a long time to come. The times feel extraordinary and urgent.[11]

It may seem counterintuitive at a time like this to suggest that we slow down our critical thought. Nevertheless, with this book, we do want to shift attention to the generative potentials of lingering with the limits of our conceptual tools, and to point to the challenges that this moment poses for our presumptions about environmental relationality. What we do not know matters too, and uncertainty is not scepticism. Although the background to this book is one of political urgency, it remains the case that negotiating heterogeneous limits is also part of the everyday of environmental engagement. In this book, the contributors focus on the edges and limits of mundane negotiation implied in the way different people relate to the excesses of their everyday existences in different contexts. We see this as presenting a hopeful ethics of possibility, concerned with practices of care for a myriad of environments that are shaped by, but not fully encompassed by, the catastrophic spirit of our historical era.

NOTES

1 As Marilyn Strathern predicted (1992).

2 As if scientists were not also humans, and science not also a social endeavour; see Jensen and Blok 2019.

3 The geological sciences, they argue, might in fact provide a different sort of image to collapse: 'the very configuration of the earth into a single, integrated system in the newly dynamic earth sciences has been the condition of a more dis-integrated, fractious and multiple vision of the planet (N. Clark, 2016). p10' (Clark and Yusoff 2017).

4 Though Ghosh does cite Morton.

5 Harman was one of the main proponents of OOO, which became very popular in the early 2000s, and spawned a large online discussion and following.

6 See also Waterton and Yusoff's notion of 'indeterminacy', which captures a space that 'exceeds classification' (2017: 9).

7 Strongly inspired by the symbiogenetic theory proposed by the American biologist Lynn Margulis (1991), Haraway builds upon the term *symbiogenesis* and its capability to capture the notion that evolutionary biological novelty arises not just from Darwinian descent with modification, but also through the symbiotic fusion of diverse types of cells and organisms (see Helmreich 2014).

8 Here we do not intend to discuss Gaia scholarship in detail. For further recent discussions about it see Jensen and Blok 2019, Latour et al. 2019, among many others.

9 See also Viveiros de Castro 2019 for an interpretation of Amerindian thought in this vein.

10 It should be noted that this shift presupposes a reciprocal, generative self-contradiction between the two, rather than a renewed opposition between nature-culture divides. As Wagner writes, 'Nature… is a cultural concept, but culture itself is a natural fact. All this means, however, is that culture is a self-differentiating variable; in chiasmatic terms the contradiction is revealed; culture is the difference between *itself* and nature; nature is the similarity between the two (2018: 508).

11 As we revise this introduction (January 2021), our planet has dramatically changed due to the emergence of Covid-19. This introduction, as well as the chapters and the conversations, were written before this pandemic moment. In this context, we have witnessed the rise of anti-scientific thinking, which has subsequently triggered diverse pro-science mobilisations. As scholars inspired by anthropology and science and technology studies, we feel the urgency of not going back to holist understandings of Science, with a capital S, but to reveal, once again, the relevance of the situatedness of scientific practices. Even if an exploration of this new planetary scene goes far beyond the aims and the scopes of this book, we hope that the 'chiasmatic' spirit of our intervention, instantiated in the concept of 'environmental alterities', can potentially contribute to keeping in circulation the fact that science is a set of situated practices, continuously and *chiasmatically* evolving.

REFERENCES

Arènes, A., B. Latour, and J. Gaillardet, 'Giving Depth to the Surface: An Exercise in the Gaia-graphy of Critical Zones', *Anthropocene Review*, 5 (2018): 120–135.

Bateson, G., *Steps to an Ecology of Mind: Collected Essays in Anthropology, Psychiatry, Evolution, and Epistemology* (Chicago, IL: University of Chicago Press, 1972).

Bennett, J., *Vibrant Matter: A Political Ecology of Things* (Durham, NC: Duke University Press, 2010).

Bonelli, C., 'On people, Sensorial Perception, and Potential Affinity in Southern Chile', *Social Analysis*, 63.2 (2019): 66–80.

Clark, N., *Inhuman Nature: Sociable life on a Dynamic Planet* (London: Sage, 2011).

——, 'Geo-politics and the Disaster of the Anthropocene', *The Sociological Review*, 62 (2014), (S1), 19–37.

Clark, N., and K. Yusoff, 'Geosocial Formations and the Anthropocene', *Theory, Culture and Society*, 34. 2–3 (2017): 3–23.

Colebrook, C., T. Cohen, and J. Miller, *Twilight of the Anthropocene Idols* (Ann Arbor: Open Humanities Press, 2016).

Coole, D., and S. Frost, eds., *New Materialisms: Ontology, Agency, and Politics* (Durham, NC: Duke University Press, 2010).

Cruikshank, J., 'Are Glaciers 'Good to Think With'? Recognising Indigenous Environmental Knowledge', *Anthropological Forum*, 22.3 (2012): 239–250.

Steffen, W., P. Crutzen, and J. McNiell, 'The Anthropocene: Are Humans Now Overwhelming the Great Forces of Nature', *AMBIO: A Journal of the Human Environment*, 36.8 (2007): 614–621.

Davis, H., and E. Turpin, 'Matters of Cosmopolitics: On the Provocations of Gaïa. Isabelle Stengers in Conversation with Heather Davis and Etienne Turpin', in E. Turpin, ed., *Architecture in the Anthropocene: Encounters Among Deep Time, Design, Science & Philosophy* (Ann Arbor: Open Humanities Press, 2013), pp. 171–182.

de la Cadena, M., 'Indigenous Cosmopolitics in the Andes: Conceptual Reflections Beyond Politics as Usual', *Cultural Anthropology*, 25.2 (2010): 334–370.

——, 'Uncommoning Nature: Stories from the Anthropo-not-seen', in Penelope Harvey et. al., eds., *Anthropos and the Material* (Durham, NC: Duke University Press, 2019), pp. 35–59.

Deleuze, G., and F. Guattari, *Anti-Oedipus. Capitalism and Schizophrenia* (Minneapolis: University of Minnesota Press, 1983).

——, *A Thousand Plateaus*, trans. By B. Massumi (Minneapolis: University of Minnesota Press, 1987).

Deleuze, G., and F. Guattari, *Kafka: Toward a Minor Literature* (London: University of Minnesota Press, 2003).

Fortun, K., 'Ethnography in Late Industrialism', *Cultural Anthropology*, 27.3 (2010): 446–464.

Franklin, S., 'Staying with the Manifesto: An Interview with Donna Haraway', *Theory, Culture & Society*, 34.4 (2017): 49–63.

Green, S., and others, 'A celebration of Roy Wagner and "The reciprocity of perspectives"', *Social Anthropology/Anthropologie Sociale*, 26.4 (2018): 511–518.

Ghosh, A., *The Great Derangement: Climate Change and the Unthinkable* (University of Chicago Press, 2016).

Haraway, D., *The Companion Species Manifesto: Dogs, People, and Significant Otherness.* (Chicago: Prickly Paradigm Press, 2003).

——, *Staying with the Trouble: Making Kin in the Chthulucene* (Durham, NC: Duke University Press, 2016).

Haraway, D., and others, 'Anthropologists Are Talking – About the Anthropocene', *Ethnos*, 81.3 (2016): 535–564.

Harvey, P., C. Krohn-Hansen, and K. G. Nustad, *Anthropos and the Material* (Durham, NC: Duke University Press, 2019).

Hayward, E., 'FINGERYEYES: Impressions of Cup Corals', *Cultural Anthropology*, 25.4 (2010): 577–599.

Helmreich, S., 'Homo microbis: The Human Microbiome, Figural, Literal, Political', *Thresholds*, 42 (2014): 52–59.

Hetch, G., 'Interscalar Vehicles for an African Anthropocene: On Waste, Temporality, and Violence', *Cultural Anthropology*, 33.1 (2018): 109–141.

Hetherington, K., ed., *Infrastructure, Environment and Life in the Anthropocene* (Durham, NC: Duke University Press, 2019).

Holbraad, M., and M. A. Pedersen, *The Ontological Turn: An Anthropological Exposition* (Cambridge: Cambridge University Press, 2017).

Hulme, M., *Can Science Fix Climate Change? A Case Against Climate Engineering* (Cambridge: Polity Press, 2014).

Jensen, C., and A. Blok, 'The Anthropocene Event in Social Theory: On Ways of Problematizing Nonhuman Materiality Differently', *The Sociological Review*, 67.6 (2019): 1195–1211.

Kirksey, E., and S. Helmreich, 'The Emergence of Multispecies Ethnography', *Cultural Anthropology*, 25.4 (2010): 545–576.

Latour, B., *We Have Never Been Modern* (Simon and Schuster (England), Harvard University Press (United States), 1991).

——, *Politics of Nature: How to Bring the Sciences into Democracy* (Cambridge, MA: Harvard University Press, 2004).

——, *Facing Gaia. Eight Lectures on the New Climatic Regime* (Cambridge: Polity Press, 2017).

——, *Down to Earth: Politics in the New Climatic Regime* (Cambridge: Polity Press, 2018).

Law, J., 'What's Wrong with a One-World World?', *Distinktion: Journal of Social Theory*, 16.1 (2015): 126–139.

Law, J., M. Lien, and H. Swanson, 'Modes of Naturing: Or Stories of Salmon', in T. Marsden, ed., *Sage Handbook of Nature* (SAGE Publications, 2018), pp. 868–890.

Liboiron, M., 'How Plastic Is a Function of Colonialism', *Teen Vogue* (21 December 2018), < https://www.teenvogue.com/story/how-plastic-is-a-function-of-colonialism> [accessed 1 January 2020].

Malm, A., and A. Hornborg, 'The Geology of Mankind: A Critique of the Anthropocene Narrative', *The Anthropocene Review*, 1.1 (2014): 62–69.

Margulis, L., ed., *Symbiosis as a Source of Evolutionary Innovation: Speciation and Morphogenesis* (Cambridge: MIT Press, 1991).

Mol, A., *The Body Multiple: Ontology in Medical Practice* (Durham, NC: Duke University Press, 2002).

Moore, J. W., *Capitalism in the Web of Life: Ecology and the Accumulation of Capital* (London: Verso, 2015).

Morton, T., *Hyperobjects: Philosophy and Ecology after the End of the World* (Minnesota: University of Minnesota Press, 2013).

——, *Being Ecological* (London: Penguin, 2018).

Nadim. T., 'Blind Regards: Troubling Data and Their Sentinels', *Big Data & Society,* 3.2 (2016): 1–6.

Omura, K., and others, eds., *The World Multiple: Everyday Politics of Knowing and Generating Entangled Worlds* (New York: Routledge Advances in Sociology, 2019).

Povinelli, E., 'The Will to Be Otherwise/the Effort of Endurance', *South Atlantic Quarterly* 111.3 (2012): 453–475.

Spivak, G., *Death of a Discipline* (New York: Columbia University Press, 2003).

——, 'Planetarity', in B. Cassin, ed., *Dictionary of Untranslatables: A Philosophical Lexicon* (Princeton, NJ: Princeton University Press, 2015).

Stengers, I., 'Accepting the Reality of Gaia: A Fundamental Shift?', in C. Hamilton, C. Bonneuil, and F. Gemenne, (eds.), *The Anthropocene and the Global Environmental Crisis: Rethinking Modernity in a New Epoch* (Abingdon, UK: Routledge, 2015a), pp. 134–144.

Stengers, I. *In Catastrophic Times: Resisting the Coming Barbarism* (Ann Arbor, MI: Open Humanities Press, 2015b).

——, 'Autonomy and the Intrusion of Gaia', *South Atlantic Quarterly,* 116 (2017): 381–400.

——, *Another Science Is Possible. A Manifesto for Slow Science* (Cambridge, UK: Polity Press, 2018).

Strathern, M., *After Nature: English Kinship in the Late Twentieth Century* (Cambridge: Cambridge University Press, 1992).

Swanson, H. A., N. Bubandt, and A. Tsing, 'Less Than One But More Than Many: Anthropocene as Science Fiction and Scholarship-in-the-Making', *Environment and Society,* 6:1 (2015): 149–166.

Swyngedouw, E., and H. Ernston, 'Interrupting the Anthropo-obScene: Immuno-biopolitics and Depoliticizing Ontologies in the Anthropocene', *Theory, Culture & Society,* 35.6 (2018): 3–30.

Tsing, A. L., 'More-Than-Human Sociality: A Call for Critical Description', in K. Hastrup, ed., *Anthropology and Nature* (London: Routledge, 2013), pp. 27–43.

——, *The Mushroom at the End of the World: On the Possibility of Life in Capitalist Ruins* (Princeton, NJ: Princeton University Press, 2015).

Tsing, A. L., H. A. Swanson, E. Gan, and N. Bubandt, *Arts of Living on a Damaged Planet: Ghosts and Monsters of the Anthropocene* (Minneapolis, MI: Minnesota University Press, 2017).

Viveiros de Castro, E., 'Cosmological Deixis and Amerindian Perspectivism', *Journal of the Royal Anthropological Institute,* 4 (1998): 469–488.

——, 'GUT Feeling about Amazonia: Potential Affinity and the Construction of Sociality', in L. Rival and N. Whitehead, eds., *Beyond the Visible and the Material* (Oxford University Press, 2001).

——, 'On Models and Examples: Engineers and Bricoleurs in the Anthropocene', *Current Anthropology,* 60 (2019): S296–S308.

Wagner, R., 'The Reciprocity of Perspectives', *Social Anthropology*, 26.4 (2018): 502–510.

——, *Symbols That Stand for Themselves* (Chicago, IL: University of Chicago Press, 1986).

Wark, M., *Molecular Red: A Theory for the Anthropocene* (New York: Verso, 2015).

Waterton, C., and K. Yusoff, 'Indeterminate Bodies: Introduction', *Body & Society*, 23.3 (2017): 3-32.

Yusoff, K., 'Insensible Worlds: Post-Relational Ethics, Indeterminacy and the (K)nots of Relating', *Environment and Planning D: Society and Space*, 31.2 (2013): 208–226.

SEAS

THE WOMAN WHO SHED HER SKIN

TOWARDS A HUMBLE ANTHROPOCENTRISM IN THE OUTER HEBRIDES

Magnus Course

> *Except for the point, the still point,*
> *there would be no dance, and there is only the dance.*
>
> T. S. Eliot, Burnt Norton

DRIVING SOUTH ACROSS THE CAUSEWAY THAT LINKS THE HEBRIDEAN ISLANDS of South Uist and Eriskay, one can sometimes observe a seal walking on the water. Or perhaps waddling on the water is a more accurate, if less elegant description. This surprising vision is easily explained: at a certain point of the tide's turning, the rocks where this particular seal likes to lie become submerged just below the Atlantic's surface and the seal basks along the top of them until finally slipping away under the waves. The first time I saw this miraculous seal, it caught my attention to the extent that I almost crashed my car. And ever since, I've looked at seals with a mixture of bewilderment and suspicion. There is undeniably something about seals that draws deeply on some inner urge to anthropomorphise them, to look into their deep, dark eyes and see them as 'friendly', or 'grumpy' or 'angry'. To understand seals as blurring the boundary between the human and beyond is not simply my own personal idiosyncrasy, but a phenomenon widespread around the globe. From the indigenous Mapuche communities of southern Chile where I lived for many years, to the west coast of Scotland where I've been working more recently, the idea that seals might live as humans under the waves, and can indeed become humans on land, is present in one form or another.

In this essay, I use both archival material on the seal-people tradition and my own ethnographic work with Gaelic-speaking fishermen in the Outer Hebrides to provide an answer to the question posed by the editors of this volume: what comes after after-nature? The answer I suggest is that what comes after after-nature is the same thing that came before after-nature and indeed could be said to have created nature as an ontologically distinct category in the first place: the human. To make this argument I'll be drawing on material which, at first glance, might lead us in a very different direction. For the songs and stories of the seal-people at the heart of this essay correspond to what is often referred to as animism, and animism in turn is often understood as a way of conceptualising the world which challenges and disrupts the anthropocentrism of what Philippe Descola has called the 'naturalism' of the Enlightenment thinking to which we in Europe and elsewhere often imagine ourselves to be heirs (2013). What does all this 'animism', so frequently martialled to argue for a variety of versions of post-humanism, look like when we approach it, not as a series of closed propositions, but as open-ended invitations to reflect upon what it means to be human? In what follows, I bring my own ethnography into dialogue with some of the insights of both feminist STS studies and anthropology from beyond Europe to demonstrate how these seal stories foreground an ethics of care predicated on and constitutive of the human position, an ethics of care which clearly resonate with contemporary fishermen's commitment to sustainability. In doing so, I aim to recast the human from an unquestioned ontological state to a contingent ethical one. For what I want to suggest is that although the lesson of the seals does indeed challenge and disrupt the dominant configuration of anthropocentrism, it doesn't do away with the centrality of the human. It leads us instead to a human refigured, a human centred in and constituted through relations of care and compassion with the world around her: a 'humble anthropocentrism' to use Georges Canguilhem's concept (1994; 2008).

THE PEOPLE OF THE SEA

The Sea itself

In the Gaelic tradition of Scotland and Ireland, as in many other traditions around the world, the sea is understood to constitute a kind of mirror of the land. As the great Gaelic poet Sorley MacLean notes in his essay on sea-imagery in Gaelic poetry, 'Gaelic folklore ascribed to the sea the counterpart of everything on land' (1985: 99). So, we find accounts of the entire range of social forms: hierarchy, as marked by the 'kings' and 'queens' of all of the sea creatures – 'They say all the creatures of the water do have their own king' – a man in South Uist relates (Thomson 1954: 32); a division of labour, as marked by the existence of 'herdsmen' of 'sea-cattle', of villages surrounding castles; and so on. At first sight then, we seem to be dealing with a classic case of animism, a projection of earthly human sociality onto the marine world. Yet this broader structural isomorphism between land and sea fails to account for a key difference: that when viewed from a moral and religious viewpoint, the sea appears fundamentally different to the land. Thus Father Allan MacDonald, a priest and folklorist in Eriskay at the turn of the nineteenth century, was told that: 'The sea is considered much more blessed than the shore [...] the sea is holier to live on than the shore' (Gregorson Campbell 2005: 513). This notion was widespread in the Gaelic world: John Gregorson Campbell notes the saying '*Cha d'thig olc sam bith on fhairge*', 'Evil comes not from the sea' (Gregorson Campbell 2005: 272), an idea which seems to be linked to the notion that neither ghosts, fairies nor demons could come below the high-tide line. Thus, a common strategy for evading pursuit by these supernatural creatures was simply to sprint for the beach (Gregorson Campbell 2005: 29). It is hard here to unravel the theological from the cosmological. There is certainly a tradition in Christianity which goes in quite the other direction, against the divinity of the sea: St Paul famously prophesises a paradise in which 'the sea was no more' (Revelation 21:1). And to this day, there is still a strong taboo in South Uist against letting a priest onto a boat, or even to touch a boat, despite the necessity of having a boat blessed by the priest at the Fishermen's Mass. And likewise, we encounter the seemingly contradictory idea that, despite the idea that 'evil comes not from the sea', witches frequently go to sea or manipulate the sea in order to drown their victims (see Gregorson Campbell 2005: 179).

Despite its frequent association as a refuge from evil, the sea was certainly not seen as a refuge from danger. There exists a substantial number of charms against drowning, as well as a wide variety of taboos to be upheld while at sea. Many of these taboos are linguistic. For example, while at sea seals are referred to as *bèist mhaol* (bald beast) rather than *ròn*, the usual term for seal, and drowning is referred to as 'travelling', *siubhail* rather than by the usual word *bàthadh*'. Some of these taboos are still present among the Gaelic-speaking fishermen of Uist with whom I worked. In particular, the injunction never to turn back once you have set your course, as well as the idea that if possible, one should always avoid turning a boat anti-clockwise, but rather *deiseal*, clockwise in the direction of the sun. And the danger of the sea is also a central trope in centuries of Gaelic song and prose. The image of a loved-one's body beneath the waves, hair tangling with the seaweed, is one of the stock images of Gaelic poetry from at least the seventeenth century to the present (MacLean 1985). Take for a recent example, a stanza from the lament 'S daor a cheannaich mi an t-iasgach, 'I paid dearly for the fishing':

> *Tha do bhreacan ùr uasal*
> *Ann an ùrlar an aigeil,*
> *'S tha do lèine chaol bhòidheach*
> *Aig na rònaibh ga sracadh.*

> *Tha do ghàrtanan rìomhach*
> *Air ìnean nam partan,*
> *'S tha d' fhaltan donn dualach*
> *Na chuachaibh 's na phreasaibh.*

> Your proud fresh plaid
> Is spread out on the sea-bed,
> Your fine handsome shirt
> Is being torn by the seals.

Your handsome garters
Are on the crabs' claws
And your brown curly locks
Are tangled and matted.[1]

In Kenneth MacLeod's famous essay, *Duatharachd na Mara*, 'The Dark Mystery of the Sea', he notes that 'the old people would speak about the dark mystery of the sea, and with that they meant that there were things associated with it that were not at all associated with natural things such as stones or soil, that she had virtues that even the Seed of Adam could not fathom' (1910: 242).[2] The figurative depth of the sea is beyond fathom and I do not pretend to do anything other than dip my toes in it here. I want simply to make two related points: that while at one level there exists a certain symmetry between the sea and the land, this symmetry must always be understood within the context of asymmetry when viewed in moral or religious terms. And secondly, that this moral and/or theological asymmetry is not given or pre-determined in its content or direction; in some cases, the sea is a place of refuge against evil, in others, it is a realm untouched by God.

Good seals, bad seals

So, what place do seals have in all this? I want to suggest that in line with the sea itself, they display both a social continuity with humanity (as in a paradigmatic case of animism) but also, (and perhaps more importantly for the people who told and sang of them), a moral discontinuity with humanity. I will argue that it is this shifting combination of continuity and discontinuity, symmetry and asymmetry that allowed the people engaging with seal stories to reflect upon and reconsider, and ultimately, recentre, the relational parameters of what it means to be human. A good place to start is David Thomson's 1954 compendium of seal stories from Scotland and Ireland, tellingly entitled *The People of the Sea*. Let me quote at length Thomson's account of a South Uist man endowed with 'vision', speaking after an incident in which four fishermen drowned and one young boy survived:

And I saw two seals come ashore to him, swept in by the same waves. And the two seals did take off their skins and, when they did, two young women stood by this boy. And they went one either side of him. And they made to shift a coffin each. But the strength of the sea carried those coffins from them. So they went to another two coffins and this boy was between them looking on to the coffin in the centre. And the two seal women tried to draw these coffins back away from the waves. But it was no use again, for didn't an awful size of a wave come and swamped them and left them there out of their hands. And I couldn't see the boy. But when the wave drew back I saw the boy standing there half-drowned, and he holding on to this last of the coffins with every bit of strength he had left in him [...] And that was the last of it. I saw the two seal women sit down on the coffin and weeping by it. And I saw this boy go down on the shore and gather up the two sealskins and bring the two to them. And the two seal women stopped weeping then, and they took the skins from the boy and went back into the sea.

(Thomson 1954: 40–41)

Another well-known tale within the Gaelic tradition is that of the origin of Clan MacCodrum of North Uist. A fisherman sees and then seizes a sealskin left on a beach. No sooner does he do so than a beautiful woman appears at his side demanding the return of her 'clothes'. The fisherman refuses, takes the woman home with him, eventually marries her and has children with her. He is always careful to hide her skin/clothes, and constantly shifts their hiding place to prevent her returning to the sea. Eventually, one of their children accidentally reveals that the skin is hidden in a haystack (what better emblem of agrarian patriarchy?), and the woman is thus able to return to her life as a seal. She promises to greet her children from a rock in the bay, 'and early the next morning the children went down to the sea and there they found every kind of fish on the rock and their mother came and waved to them and called to them and she went on giving them fish until they grew up and prepared for marriage. Her sons and daughters married and that is how the Clan MacCodrum came to this earth'. (Thomson 1954: 198) An alternative account of this same tradition can also be found in John Gregorson Campbell's collection: 'There is a sept in North Uist known as *Clann 'ic Codrum nan ròn*, 'the MacCodrums of the seals', from being said to be descendants of these enchanted seals. The progenitor of the family, being down about the shore, saw the seals putting off their coverings and washing themselves. He fled home with one of the skins and hid it above the lintel of the door. The owner of the covering followed him. He clad her with human garments, married her, and had a family by her. She managed ultimately to regain possession of her lost covering and disappeared' (Gregorson Campbell 2005: 156).

These stories of the seal people are not confined to the Gaelic tradition, but exist in one form or another all around the coasts of northwest Europe. A paradigmatic seal-people or 'selchie' story recounted to Thomson comes from the Shetland Islands to the north of Scotland: a seal-hunting trip encounters, kills then skins a group of seals. A storm grows, and one of the hunters remains stranded on the rock in the middle of the ocean. As night closes in, a group of seal people move up onto the rock, and 'he could hear a wailing, a kind o'singing, like the voices o' the selchies. It was a lament he made out, when he made out the words, a lament for the loss o' their skins, for now they sang i' the lament that they could swim no more; they must live on land like men and women, they would ne'er again see the city o' coral and pearl that lies below the waves' (Thomson 1954: 153). Eventually one of the seals approaches the stranded hunter and agrees to return him to the shore in exchange for return of the skin of her son, the skin which will enable him to return to his life at sea.

Stories of seal-people saturate the folklore archives of both Scotland and Ireland, although frequently in a more fragmentary manner than those col lected by Thomson and Campbell. A quick example in Gaelic comes from the School of Scottish Studies at the University of Edinburgh, archived under the title *Na Ròin a bha a Tilgeadh nan Clach*, 'Seals Throwing Stones'.[3] The teller, Archibald MacInnes of Eriskay was repairing fishing gear on the uninhabited small island of Fuday: 'This great roar was to be heard behind us and when we looked down there was a group of these seals rolling around on the beach as if they were going mad with laughter, and others with stones ready to throw at us. First one stone came, then two, then three until at last there was a shower of them falling around my ears. We stood up lest we were killed and headed for the vessel as fast as our feet could take us. We piled into it and we pulled away from the shore and we were definitely in time. The seals were not able to throw the stones as far as our boat, which was just as well. [...] Iain turned to me, and he said: 'If I was', he said, 'to believe that such a thing as spells existed I would say that those seals are people that are under a spell, being as clever as they were'. 'Smart or not', I said, 'I will no longer approach them so boldly' (Fomin & Mac Mathúna 2016: 56).

A seal morality

The stories above illustrate a degree of social continuity between humans and seals. Seals have, or at least had, the power of speech. They live in communities, towns and cities under the sea. They are bound by both kinship and friendship, and they possess social institutions such as marriage through which kinship emerges. They practise recognisably human ways of making a living: tending herds, hunting and so on. They, like us, mourn the dead. It is this basic continuity of social forms which allows the worlds of the seal and of the human to continually interpenetrate, to mingle, to flow together: seals and humans do deals, betray each other, marry, fall in love, save each other, have children and so on. We might be tempted then, to argue that in line with the contemporary focus on the post-human, the source of difference between seals and humans, their physical bodies, can simply be shrugged off as skin, as clothing; that what distinguishes 'us' from 'them' is nothing more than a superficial layering obscuring our fundamental unity.

Some readers may already have noted certain striking parallels between the stories of the seal-people and what has become known as Amerindian perspectivism. So, what is this perspectivism? Put simply, it is the observation that in many Indigenous American configurations different kinds of beings see different worlds in the same way. A couple of examples will make this clearer: in an Amazonian context, it is common to hear that peccaries see each other as human and that they see humans as jaguars. Jaguars, on the other hand, see each other as human but see humans as peccaries. These perspectival ideas are not confined to South America but are widespread throughout the Americas as a whole. Thus, for example, among many indigenous peoples of the northwest coast of North America it is said that salmon see each other as humans, they see humans as bears, and they see the leaves on the bottom of the river as salmon (Guédon 1984). The Brazilian anthropologist Eduardo Viveiros de Castro has described this phenomenon of Amerindian perspectivism in terms of deixis (1998). In a conventional use of the term, deixis refers to the referential meaning of an utterance being dependent on the spatial, temporal or personal position from which it is emitted. Yet in the deixis characteristic of perspectivism it is the world itself which is dependent on the position from which its perception emanates, hence Viveiros de Castro's label of 'cosmological deixis'. A key point is that in perspectival ontologies not only do all beings appear human to themselves, but, as with the seal-people, they act towards one another as humans would – in other words they all possess human 'culture'. For example, peccaries see themselves as living in villages, having shamans and frequently holding manioc beer parties (although what constitutes manioc beer for peccaries appears to humans as mud, while what constitutes manioc beer for jaguars appears to humans as human blood). The crucial point is that 'Amerindian ontological perspectivism proceeds along the lines that *the point of view creates the subject*; whatever is activated or 'agented' by the point of view will be a subject' (Viveiros de Castro 1998: 476, emphasis in original). And it is the occupation of this subject position, rather than any 'natural' essence, which defines one as 'culturally' human.

Having spent many years working and living with indigenous South American people whose outlook is distinctly 'perspectival', I'm often surprised when anthropologists see some kind of natural affinity between post-humanism and perspectivism. For what always struck me was that when presented in their full ethnographic context rather than abstracted as philosophical propositions, these perspectival narratives were ultimately a kind of hyper-anthropocentrism; because anything could be human it was even more important to define what was *really human*. This point emerges most clearly in Carlos Londoño Sulkin's important work among Muinane people in Colombia which describes how while other species may see themselves as human, they are actually always ethically flawed (2006). So, peccaries see themselves as human, but are incestuous; jaguars see themselves as human, but are cannibals, and so on. The thrust of perspectivism, then, if we follow Londoño Sulkin, could potentially be understood not so much as ontological, but ethical. And it is this understanding of the human as a contingent ethical position which I wish to take forward from these discussions of perspectivism into our consideration of the seal-people.

Perhaps a good place to start is with the recurring, central motif of the theft of the skin, a theft that is perhaps key to revealing a fundamental discontinuity between humans and seals. Let us take, for example, the figure of the fisherman in the story recounted above, of the founding of Clan MacCodrum in North Uist: it is his theft and hiding of his seal-wife's skin that binds her, unwillingly, to him. Without her skin, she cannot return to the sea, to her people, to her true identity. It is only through her child's unintentional revelation of the location of her skin that she is able to escape and return to the sea. This story seems to tell us a lot about 'Man's' mastery over nature. It speaks to us about gender, about the difficulties of virilocal post-marital residence in Gaelic areas of the time, of a woman's continuing bond with her children, even across the species divide, but perhaps most importantly, it reveals a particularly gendered version of a possible relationship with the non-human. As a vibrant line of feminist scholarship has pointed out, the traditional phrasing of 'Man's dominion over nature' is not coincidental but reflects a particularly patriarchal 'dominion' constituted through tropes of conquest, theft and rape. The story also tells us about possibility, about the possible fecundity and fertility of cross-species relationships. The couple have children, they are happy, and even after recovering her skin and returning to the sea, the seal-wife continues with her relationship of responsibility and care towards her children, visiting them daily and providing them with food until their marriage. The children of Clan MacCudrum are still present today and would have been known to the people among whom these stories circulated. We can perhaps see in this aspect of the story a different vision of a human/

non-human relationship, one premised not on 'dominion' but on an ethics of care, a point to which I shall return. This relationship is contrasted with the previous relationship based upon patriarchal domination, one initiated through a theft and a betrayal, and maintained through an enslavement. And the consequences of this? The misery of all parties: the sadness of the seal-wife and the eventual abandonment and loneliness of her human husband. These stories seem to be somewhat reminiscent of those Western Apache stories documented by Keith Basso (1996) as moral correctives, but rather than being tied to the topography encountered every day, they are tied to the creatures encountered every day, a point made in the context of Amerindian perspectivism by Londoño Sulkin (2006).

It seems to me that what is at stake is two versions of anthropocentrism, both of which place the human centre stage, but within very different kinds of relationship with the non-human. In the figure of the husband, we see the classic figure of an arrogant, patriarchal anthropocentrism which seeks to dominate, control and subjugate the seal-wife. Yet we are also offered a version of a humble anthropocentrism in the figure of the children who care for and are themselves cared for by their non-human mother, without ever losing their own humanity (remember they are the first generation of Clan MacCodrum, an indisputably human clan).

Yet while in the cases discussed above, the moral failing is on the human side, there are also tales of the moral failing being on the side of the seals. The ideas that seals can become angry and attack people indiscriminately is also present, as in the example from Eriskay of seals pelting unsuspecting fishermen with rocks. And within the Irish Gaelic tradition, there are several accounts of people being killed or lured to their deaths by seals, or at least, supernatural deaths attributed to the volition of seals. We cannot simply say, then, that seals serve as rhetorical exemplars of moral goodness against which human failings stand out in stark relief. The asymmetry is not consistent, but it is always present. This argument can be extended from the ethical to the political. For example, we learn from a man in County Mayo, that the seals meet once a year to elect their king. 'There is one day in the year, you understand, when they send the seals in thousands from along the coast to choose their king. And they disperse to their own places after' (Thomson 1954: 141). Like the Scottish and Irish people of the time, the seals lived under a king. However, unlike the people of the time, this was a king of their choosing, chosen on an annual basis. A bit like Clastres' famous Indian chief, the seals offer an image of an alternative society, a different way of living and of organising power, but one which for a variety of reasons seems to fall apart when applied to human society. The seal-human relationships seem so full of potential for imagining alternative forms of life, yet so doomed to failure, that the stories seem to reverse Donna Haraway's prior reversal of Lèvi-Strauss: seals are so good to think with, that we can't possibly live with them (see Haraway 2003: 5)

The idea which I want to take away from these ethnographic and archival fragments is that of a continual process of rethinking and recentring what it means to be human. It is precisely the continuities between people and seals which allow the discontinuities their discursive force. Discontinuity and continuity, difference and similarity, are not fixed relationships but in continual movement, shaping and re-shaping what it means to be human. To quote Maria Puig de la Bellacasa, 'Ontology grounded in relationality and interdependency needs to acknowledge not only an essential heterogeneity, but also 'cuts' out of which heterogeneity can flourish' (2012: 204). Perhaps the 'human' is just such a cut, for these stories surely (to steal a phrase from T. S. Eliot) dance around a point, a point that is the human. The key idea is that the human is neither abandoned nor diluted; it is reflected upon and critiqued but it does not disappear; it is, I argue, recast in a humbler light constituted by and constitutive of, not a fixed ontological state, but a contingent ethical position. But what might this humble anthropocentrism look like in practice? What place might it have in a world in which our relationship with the 'Parliament of Beings' can so often seem broken beyond repair? To answer this question, I want to turn now to my own ethnographic work with contemporary Gaelic-speaking fishermen in the Outer Hebrides to see how the particular ethic of care continues to resonate in their relationship with the sea.

THE CARE OF THE SEA

Hebridean inshore fishing

Dòmhnall pauses from his focus on the winch, to observe the strange creature's progress across the deck. Its colours shift almost imperceptibly at first, like an hour hand watched, but as it moves from the red of the gunwales to the blue of the non-slip mat laid across the deck floor, an indigo tinge grows and spreads across it. Dòmhnall can't resist; he scoops up the creature by its forlornly waving tentacles and places it on his fluorescent plastic jacket, exclaiming 'Gibealach bochd!', 'Poor octopus!' in his native Gaelic. But before we can ascertain whether its colour-shifting abilities are up to the challenge of hi-viz yellow, we're called back to attention by the crewman, Stephen, that the next lobster creel, cliabh-giomaich, is in sight. Dòmhnall peels the octopus off his jacket and throws it back into the sea. Some fishermen invert the octopuses that come up in their creels; a quick flick turns them inside-out, killing them and revealing their organs to the world. For they are great raiders of both prawn and lobster creels, entering and devouring all within, leaving only husks. But Dòmhnall lets this one go.

We're on a smallish, 30-foot boat – the Azalea – with a small cabin, a small diesel engine, an open deck and a winch to the starboard side. It is captained by its owner, Dòmhnall, and has a single other crew member, Stephen. It is typical of the inshore fishing fleet of the southern Outer Hebrides, fishing for langoustines ('prawn' as they are known locally) and both brown and velvet crab off the calmer eastern side of South Uist, Eriskay, and Benbecula in the autumn, winter and spring, and then moving around to the west, to the open Atlantic for the more lucrative lobster fishing of the summer.[4] The entirety of the catch is pooled in oxygenated tanks at the shellfish cooperative in South Uist, and then shipped, live, to Spain on a weekly basis and sold in a colossal fish-market just outside Barcelona. None of the fishermen is rich, but they do earn a living – an increasingly difficult achievement in a region with one of the lowest average incomes in the British Isles.

On a nice sunny day like today, I like being out here. Dolphins, porpoise and seals abound. Previous visits have revealed basking sharks and killer whales, and the most bizarre of the ocean's wanderers, the sunfish, laid out lopsided on the choppy surface like a punctured beach-ball. The breeze is fresh, and the spray casts rainbows with each crash of the bow. There have also been less pleasant days, days with grey, overcast skies, cold, cold winds, and creeping damp, days when the seasickness pills that I take each morning are pushed to their limits. But even these days are good, for there is something irresistible about watching a creel emerge from the sea, a shape and form coalescing in the deep and then bursting through the surface as the winch hauls it through. I'm here with not one, but two ulterior motives: the first is my interest in the sea, and more specifically, my inchoate attempt to understand what the sea is from the perspective of Gaelic culture; the second, and more concrete motive, is to gather data for a report I'm preparing on behalf of the Western Isles Fishermen's Association. The remit of the report is to illustrate the deep and enduring connections between Hebridean fishing and the Scottish Gaelic language. Its purpose is to broaden the scope of the current political debate about the imposition of Marine Protected Areas (MPAs) by the Scottish Government around parts of the Hebrides and elsewhere in Scotland.[5]

The goal of the report I completed on behalf of the fishermen was to illustrate that the cultural and linguistic values of fishing had been completely overlooked by and omitted from the various impact assessments carried out, and thus was in breach of both national and European legislation, in particular the *European Charter for Regional or Minority Languages*, which clearly placed member states under an obligation to take these values into account. My primary focus was on language, and it soon became clear that fishing played a fundamental role in the maintenance and transmission of Scottish Gaelic.[6] But it also gradually became apparent to me that fishermen's insistence on the importance of Gaelic could not be extricated from a broader commitment to a particular relationship with the sea. In what follows, I seek to describe their engagement with the sea, not simply as a means to achieve an economic end, but as an end in itself.

The health of the sea

At the heart of fishermen's relationship to the sea is the claim that the fecundity and vitality of the sea does not exist despite human engagement but because of it. Contrary to the stereotypical stance – which one fisherman referred to as 'the demonisation of fishermen' – by environmental lobbyists, the fishermen's relationship with the sea is not limited to a concern with stock levels of target species but concerns the marine environment as a whole. Their measure of the 'health' of the sea refers to several factors: the quantities of species observed, the diversity of species observed and the range of size of individuals within a species. Fishermen are concerned if only small or only large exemplars of a particular species are encountered. For example, while we were out just off the southeast corner of Uist, fishing with rods for mackerel to bait his prawn creels, Pàdraig was concerned that all of the mackerel seemed to be particularly large, 'Where are all the young ones?' he wondered. This constant concern with diversity both within and across species was not limited to life below the surface. All of the fishermen with whom I worked had a deep and intimate knowledge of creatures of air, land and sea. Sailing out of Eriskay in search of prawns, Calum explained to me how you could tell the age of both herring gulls and common gulls by the differing patterns of their plumage; just north of Barra, Alasdair expounded his theories on the relation between sea eagles and wader populations; while back on land in Ludag, Angus somewhat sheepishly offered me a small net bag of carrageen, a seaweed used as a traditional gelatin substitute for a sweet milk pudding. This intimate knowledge of the marine environment as an integrated and interconnected whole certainly has pragmatic elements. As is well known, clusters of certain 'indicator' species serve to identify the location of target species. And what constitutes a 'target' species is itself constantly shifting as tastes and prices, and thus the economic viability of fishing, change. For example, nobody in Britain eats velvet crab, but it commands a high price in Spain. Over the years, the nature of fishing has changed dramatically, from domestic to commercial, and across a wide variety of target species (Coull 1996). Yet despite these factors, fishermen's knowledge of and concern for the sea cannot be reduced to pragmatic considerations alone. Even the oldest fishermen retain a sense of surprise and wonder, marvelling at creatures such as basking sharks and killer whales, and even the everyday meetings with octopus and lobster. As Dòmhnall explained to me, 'I've been fishing every year of my life since I was eight. Now I'm 52 and I've never seen an identical year'.

Yet fishermen are not simply external observers looking in at the life of the sea; their presence, their engagement, their acts of care, constitute a part of that life. For at the centre of the complex webs of exchange which constitute marine life, are the fishermen themselves. It is through their selective 'harvesting' or 'hunting' of certain species that a certain balance, and therefore fecundity, is maintained. As one Benbecula fisherman put it to me, 'If we stop, the sea will die'. A widely cited example is Broad Bay off the coast of Lewis, where a blanket ban was placed on fishing around twenty-five years ago. A recent survey of the bay revealed a seafloor covered in nothing but starfish, a 'dead' sea from the fishermen's perspective. Here it is worth noting Stefan Helmreich's distinction between 'life forms' and 'forms of life' in contemporary limit biologies (2016). No fishermen would deny that the starfish are alive (a 'life form') but all would concur that their blanket monopoly of the sea bed does not equate to life (a 'form of life'). The latter is always both relative and holistic, always premised on relations between a multiplicity of species. One could take this observation down the path of a post-humanist critique of anthropocentrism, that the relativity of life and the irreducibility of life, always relativise the role of the human. However, the fishermen with whom I worked take this observation in the opposite direction, one which follows the stories and songs of the seal-people which they grew up listening to, one in which the human plays a central role.

For if the difference between a dead sea and a living sea is nothing more nor less than people's engagement with it, what is it about human engagement that makes a difference? More specifically, why do fishermen claim that their practices constitute care of the sea? The practices they mention in this regard are all oriented towards sustainability. Such practices include self-imposed voluntary closures of certain fishing grounds during spawning seasons of certain species, the return of 'berried' (i.e. egg-bearing) female lobsters to the sea, the imposition of minimum size limits for both crab and lobster and the return of all non-target or undersized catches to the sea. The fishermen emphasise, firstly, that these are traditional practices that have been carried out for centuries, and secondly, that these are self-imposed restrictions emerging from their own knowledge of the sea and from their own duty of care as 'custodians' or 'guardians' of the sea. They demonstrate what to the fishermen at least, is the self-evident truth that, as Pàdraig commented to me, 'The people that should manage the sea are the people that are working the sea, that live in that fishing community'. Sustainability is, and always has been, necessarily part of their practice, as Dòmhnall noted, 'We're not going to cut our own throats now and in the years to come'.[7] Moreover, as we shall see, the sustainability they practise is not rooted solely in economic self-interest; rather they feel it is the necessary ethical stance which humans must take. Whereas some proposed solutions to environmental crisis seek to remove humans from the equation – indeed, this is precisely what Marine Protected Areas aim to do – fishermen see the best way forward as one which places them and their constitutive ethics of care centre-stage.

Generations of care

I've described above fishermen's understanding of themselves as the 'guardians' or 'custodians' of the sea, as the element which ensures and maintains a sea full of life. However, at the heart of my argument is not ecology, but what fishermen say in other registers, in the inter-linked registers of ethics and kinship. I seek to describe here how and why the value of their role in the sea cannot be exhausted by the scientific, economic, or any other paradigm. They fish the way they do because it is the right thing to do. Their knowledge of the sea cannot be extricated from their ethical stance towards it. Care, knowledge and labour go hand in hand, resonating with Puig de la Bellacasa's statement that 'Care is more than an affective-ethical state: it involves material engagement in labours to sustain interdependent worlds, labours that are often associated with exploitation and domination' (2012: 198). As Angus, the manager of the shellfish co-op, explained to me, 'Small boats support more people, they give more people a go at the fishing. It's the big factory trawlers from elsewhere that do all the damage. We could go down that road, but it wouldn't be right'. The benefits of fishing are seen as extending beyond the immediate interests of fishermen to the communities – both human and non-human – which fishing sustains.

Not just the forms of their practice, but also the ethical rationale for their practice is inherited from previous generations. All of the fishermen with whom I worked were themselves sons of fishermen. As one Uist fishermen commented to me, 'You've got generations and generations of experience passed down. My father would say to me, "You've got to go to this place at this time and there'll be lobsters there." And I did that, and I'm doing that, and that's the way it works, and my grandfather did that as well'. The various traditional sustainable practices described above – the avoidance of spawning grounds, the return of egg-bearing females and undersized catch – were acquired not through external legislation, but from fathers and grandfathers, from cousins and uncles. Likewise, knowledge of the best fishing areas for particular species, and the changing of these areas during seasonal or meteorological shifts are all acquired from prior generations. Use of technological innovations such as GPS, fish finders, etc. is seen as supplementing but never replacing this knowledge. An example provided by several fishermen was the use of 'marks', geographical reference points for particular areas of the sea bed, so, for example, when the summit of a particular mountain comes in line with the end of a particular island, you know you're over an area of raised, rocky seabed particularly good for lobster in late summer after heavy winds, and so on. Techniques of material culture are also inherited; for example, Dòmhnall makes his own lobster creels, with a wooden bottom and hoops wrought from discarded broadband cabling. He learnt this technique from his grandfather (minus the broadband cable!) and shows me the catch records to prove that these wooden-bottomed creels are twice as effective as the commercially produced steel creels. Much of this continuity with prior generations is expressed through fishermen's particular commitment to the Gaelic language. Whereas 61% of the population of South Uist speak Gaelic, 83% of fishermen do. As one Benbecula fisherman told me, 'It's [Gaelic] been nurtured in fishing more than anywhere else. There's very few jobs where you speak Gaelic all day; just fishing, so it's being strengthened all the time'.

In practising fishing, fishermen are not simply earning a living. They understand themselves to be both maintaining and transmitting a particular relationship with the sea, a relationship which sustains both fishermen and the sea itself. In doing so, they are also constituting a link between generations in the sense used by Pogue Harrison when he says that 'there exists an allegiance between the dead and the unborn of which we living are merely the ligature' (2005: ix). Without the sustainable practices and knowledge inherited from fishermen in previous generations, and without the transmission of this to future generations, there would be no fishery in Uist. The sea would be as dead as the communities which it supports. As Calum tells me as we grade prawn for size, 'If we go out of it, well, that's going to be a major loss I would say. We keep these islands well populated; we keep up their culture and their language'. There is a deeply held concern that young people are struggling to enter fishing, that previous government schemes to subsidise them starting out in fishing are under threat, and that the younger generation will have little choice but to leave the islands.

Whereas some environmentalists entertain a utopian post-human vision of 'a world without us' (see Weisman 2008) and in this case, 'a sea without us', such a vision is nothing but dystopic for the people with whom I worked.[8] For them, 'a sea without us' can be nothing other than a dead sea, a sea deprived of its vital – in both senses of the word – element: us. The fore-fronting of this concern occurs in a historical and political context in which people are haunted by the spectre of their own future absence. Human dwelling in the southern Outer Hebrides is not and cannot be taken for granted. Current pressure from reduced council services, from a lack of infrastructural investment and from high levels of unemployment have led to an ever-worsening trend of depopulation. These pressures coalesce in the widely held idea that many people 'in government' would – despite 8,000 years of continuous human habitation – like to see Uist turned into a conservation park, a place in which the human no longer has a place. As one crofter exclaimed to me, 'The most endangered thing here is us!' Although the loss of the human presence here may seem unlikely for now, it is precisely what happened to prior generations during the infamous Clearances of the mid-nineteenth century, when landlords across the Highlands forcibly evicted thousands of people in a process of 'rationalisation' and 'improvement' of their estates (Hunter 1976). The historical legacy of the Clearances, when the majority of the population of South Uist was forcibly exiled to Canada to make way for sheep farms, is still bitterly recalled in song and poetry, both in Uist and in those communities in Cape Breton where the exiles ended up (Stewart 1998; Campbell 1990).

TOWARDS A HUMBLE ANTHROPOCENTRISM

Anthropocentrism, it would seem, is not exactly hot stuff in social theory right now. The idea that the human perspective is, or even should be, necessarily central is under attack from all sides. For some, it underlies an intellectual configuration which portrays an external 'nature' as a resource to be conquered. For others, it is simply a dangerous remnant of a very particular genealogy of Western thought that should be 'provincialised' (see Chakrabarty 2007) to allow other non-anthropocentric understandings to flourish. Both of these overlapping critiques see going beyond the human as a necessary step, both intellectually and practically, as we struggle to deal with environmental carnage on every side. It is hard to disagree. For the discipline of anthropology, a discipline which as its name suggests has placed the anthropos at centre-stage, this is something of a challenge. As Bruno Latour noted at a recent American Anthropological Association conference – with some irony and a smattering of glee – anthropology is rushing to abandon the anthropos, just as the rest of the world is seeking to place it full centre-stage through the now ubiquitous references to the Anthropocene. Calls to expel the human from our thinking don't just come from without, but from within anthropology. Take for example Margaret Weiner's remarks in a collective essay on the relation between STS and anthropology: 'Could anthropology be other than anthropocentric? What would a nonanthropocentric anthropology look like, in the Anthropocene? All those anthropos seem an exercise in human narcissism!' (in de la Cadena & Lien 2015: 468). Nevertheless, here I have argued that we should pause, that we should not exile the anthropos quite so eagerly or hastily, and even that we should return to the human as the central point of our endeavours. The basis for this pause is simply an acknowledgement both of the wide variety of forms that anthropocentrism takes, and of its inevitability. There are, for sure, the arrogant, hierarchising and colonialising forms, which have been so rightly critiqued. But there is also anthropocentrism in a more subtle key, one which understands the human to be as much an ethical position as an ontological one, one form of which I hope to have described in this paper.

At the centre of this essay – in both the stories of the seal-people and the concerns of contemporary fishermen – stands the figure of the human. But is this human the much-maligned Enlightenment 'anthropos' whose tragic self-exile from the 'Parliament of Things' (Latour 1993) has led to environmental catastrophe? Well, not exactly. In the stories of the seal-people we see an alternative conceptualisation of the human, one which undeniably places the human at centre-stage, but which does not extract the human from life. In the particular Gaelic context I have been describing, this understanding of what it means to be human stems from a cosmological outlook in which the capacity to be 'as human' is not restricted to humans alone. In exploring what is sometimes, rather dismissively, referred to as Gaelic 'folklore' – a wealth of oral and written material dating back as far as the seventh century – I have described a relationship between human and non-human which is highly porous and malleable.[9] We learn that to fail to respect the seal-people, to see them as 'just' animals, would lead to vengeance and disaster. At the centre of these stories, then, is a recognition of not just the relational quality of human life, but also of the ethical responsibilities that constitute it. Tempting as it might be, it would, I think, be profoundly distorting to claim that the fishermen with whom I worked are some strange anachronistic enclave of European animism (see Candea & Alcayna-Stevens 2012). They are not. They are, as already mentioned, well-versed in the registers of science, but they are also the heirs to and participants in a religious tradition which has a profoundly developed understanding of both life and the human. I think it would be distorting to ignore or dismiss this cultural background, for the fishermen with whom I worked all grew up hearing these stories of the seal-people and listening to their songs. While I doubt any of them would concede to a belief in seal-people, they all recognise what is at these stories' heart: that humans stand within, not outside, the web of life.

In describing the values and practices of Hebridean inshore fishing as a kind of humble anthropocentrism, I have sought to delineate a particular view of the human. To say that the human is the point from which life is measured is not to commit to a static, universalising or essentialising understanding of the human. As Monica Greco puts it, 'the fact that the individual, the organism, and indeed the human form, should be regarded as ontologically contingent, does not contradict the perspective that might place the living being at its centre' (2005: 20). I think this is a point with which the Hebridean fishermen described in this paper might concur. Perhaps most importantly, Greco, following Canguilhem, imagines an anthropocentrism which 'rather than affirming a right of supremacy, suggests a kind of humility, an acknowledgment of (inevitable) partiality or, to use Canguilhem's own expression, a form of "honesty"' (2005: 20). I think the Hebridean version of humble anthropocentrism that I have described here resonates with such a project. It is simply an honest acknowledgment that we are not aloof spectators, but players in the game. Much contemporary writing in a post-human vein imagines, both literally and rhetorically, a world without us. Building on what I've learnt from fishermen in Uist, I've suggested that maybe this is not the most productive line of thought regarding our editors' question of what comes after after-nature. Rather, I would suggest that the measure of life, like the measure of anything in a post-Einsteinian world, must come from a point. For better or worse, we are this point; both the measure of life, and life itself.

NOTES

1 This song was sung in 2018 by Margaret Campbell of South Uist and recorded by Gillebride MacMillan as part of our ESRC project, *Sustainability, Culture and Language in Hebridean Fishing.*

2 From a draft translation by Micheal Newton.

3 This story, and several others, were transcribed and translated as part of Fomin and Mac Mathúna's Stories of the Sea project: http://arts.ulster.ac.uk/storiesofthesea/index.html

4 'Inshore' fishing refers to boats operating within six miles of the coast, primarily to catch shellfish. According to Scottish Government statistics, 1,431 out of a total of 2,206 registered Scottish commercial fishing boats are inshore vessels.

5 For important discussions of the impact of the new 'enclosure of the oceans' see Bresnihan 2016 and McCormack 2017.

6 Scottish Gaelic, *Gàidhlig*, is a Goidelic Celtic language related to, but not mutually intelligible with Irish Gaelic. The 2011 census revealed 57,375 speakers, all of whom are

bilingual with English. The Outer Hebrides is the only place where Gaelic is spoken by a majority of the population.

7 See Nightingale 2013 and McCall Howard 2017, for further ethnographic data on sustainability among Scottish fishermen.

8 See, for example, debates around the John Muir Trust's attempts to designate large chunks of Scotland as 'wilderness' (MacDonald 2013).

9 A full account of this relationship is beyond the scope of this paper but see Bateman 2009; Hunter 1995; Newton 2009.

REFERENCES

Basso, K., *Wisdom Sits in Places: Language and Landscape among the Western Apache* (Santa Fe, NM: University of New Mexico Press, 1996).

Bateman, M., 'The Landscape of the Gaelic Imagination', *International Journal of Heritage Studies*, 15 (2009): 142–152.

Bresnihan, P., *Transforming the Fisheries: Neoliberalism, Nature, and the Commons* (Lincoln, NE: University of Nebraska Press, 2016).

Campbell, J. L., *Songs Remembered in Exile* (Aberdeen: Aberdeen University Press, 1990).

Candea, M., and L. Alcayna-Stevens, 'Internal Others: Ethnographies of Naturalism', *Cambridge Anthropology*, 30 (2012): 36–47.

Canguilhem, G., *A Vital Rationalist: Selected Writing*, trans. by A. Goldhammer (New York: Zone Books, 1994).

——, *Knowledge of Life*, ed. by P. Marrati and T. Meyers. Trans. by S. Geroulanos and D. Ginsburg). (New York: Fordham University Press, 2008).

Chakrabarty, D., *Provincializing Europe: Postcolonial Thought and Historical Difference* (Princeton: Princeton University Press, 2007).

Coull, J., *The Sea Fisheries of Scotland: A Historical Geography* (Edinburgh: John Donald, 1996).

de la Cadena, M., and M. Lien, 'Anthropology and STS: Generative Interfaces, Multiple Locations', *HAU: Journal of Ethnographic Theory*, 5 (2015): 437–475.

Fomin, M., and S. Mac Mathúna, *Stories of the Sea: Maritime Memorates of Ireland and Scotland* (Berlin: Curach Bhán Publications, 2016).

Greco, M., 'On the Vitality of Vitalism', *Theory, Culture and Society*, 22 (2005): 15–27.

Gregorson Campbell, J., *The Gaelic Otherworld*, ed. by R. Black (Edinburgh: Birlinn, 2005).

Guédon, M-F., 'An Introduction to the Tsimshian World View and Its Practitioners', in M. Seguin, ed., *The Tsimshian: Images of the Past, Views for the Present* (Vancouver: University of British Columbia Press, 1984), pp. 137–159.

Haraway, D., *The Companion Species Manifesto: Dogs, People, and Significant Otherness* (Chicago: Prickly Paradigm Press, 2003).

Helmreich, S., *Sounding the Limits of Life: Essays in the Anthropology of Biology and Beyond* (Princeton: Princeton University Press, 2016).

Hunter, J., *The Making of the Crofting Community* (Edinburgh: John Donald, 1976).

—, *On the Other Side of Sorrow: Nature and People in the Scottish Highlands* (Edinburgh: Mainstream, 1995).

Latour, B., *We Have Never Been Modern*, trans. by C. Porter (Cambridge, MA: Harvard University Press, 1993).

Londoño Sulkin, C., 'Inhuman Beings: Morality and Perspectivism among Muinane People (Colombian Amazon)' *Ethnos*, 70 (2006): 7–30.

McCall Howard, P., *Environment, Labour and Capitalism at Sea: 'Working the ground' in Scotland* (Manchester: University of Manchester Press, 2017).

McCormack, F., *Private Oceans: The Enclosure and Marketisation of the Seas* (London: Pluto Press, 2017).

MacDonald, F., (2013) 'Against Scottish Wilderness', *Bella Caledonia*, 17 July. <http://bellacaledonia.org.uk/2013/07/17/against-scottish-wildness/> [accessed 28 March 2019].

MacLean, S., 'Notes on Sea Imagery in Seventeenth Century Gaelic poetry', in W. Gillies, ed., *Ris a' Bhruthaich: The Criticism and Prose Writings of Sorley MacLean* (Stornoway: Acair, 1985), pp. 83–105.

MacLeod, K., 'Duatharachd na Mara', *The Celtic Review*, 6 (1910): 241–257.

Newton, M., *Warriors of the Word: The World of the Scottish Highlanders* (Edinburgh: Birlinn, 2009).

Nightingale, A., 'Fishing for Nature: The Politics of Subjectivity and Emotion in Scottish Inshore Fisheries Management', *Environment and Planning A*, 45 (2013): 2362–2378.

Owen, N., M. Kent, and P. Dale, 'Ecological Effects of Cultivation on the Machair Sand Dune Systems of the Outer Hebrides', *Journal of Coastal Conservation*, 6 (2000): 155–170.

Pogue Harrison, R., *The Dominion of the Dead* (Chicago: University of Chicago Press, 2005).

Puig de la Bellacasa, M., 'Nothing Comes without its World': Thinking with Care', *The Sociological Review*, 60 (2012): 197–216.

Roberts, C., *The Ocean of Life: The Fate of Man and the Sea* (New York: Penguin, 2012).

Stewart, J., 'The Jaws of Sheep: The 1851 Hebridean Clearances of Gordon of Cluny', *Proceedings of the Harvard Celtic Colloquium*, 18/19 (1998): 205–226.

Thomson, D., *The People of the Sea* (Edinburgh: Canongate, 1954).

Viveiros de Castro, E., 'Cosmological Deixis and Amerindian Perspectivism', *Journal of the Royal Anthropological Institute*, 4 (1998): 469–488.

Weisman, A., *The World Without Us* (London: Virgin Books, 2008).

VISITS FROM OCTOPUS AND CROCODILE KIN

RETHINKING HUMAN-SEA RELATIONS THROUGH AMPHIBIOUS TWINSHIP IN INDONESIA

Annet Pauwelussen

INTRODUCTION: AMPHIBIOUS TWINS IN THE MASALIMA ARCHIPELAGO

> My father's name is Hamma. He was Bajau. Others call us sea people. My father was born together with an octopus. They were siblings (saudara), so the octopus is my uncle (om). (Hamma Ali, 28 March 2013, Pamantauan)

I had come to Hamma Ali's house to learn about the man's seafaring skills. It was dark outside; waves were rumbling below his house on stilts. We were on Pamantauan Island, part of the Masalima Archipelago, where the currents of the Makassar Strait converge with the Java Sea. Scattered on five tiny islands (Pamantauan, Sabaru, Saleriang, Masalima and Pamalikkan), a population of several thousand lives here, mostly from fishing and trade. As is common practice in rural Indonesia, our meeting started with an explanation of how Hamma Ali, his household and more distant kin were all related. Hamma Ali's cephalopod kin came as a bit of a surprise to me. Prompted by questions, he elaborated on how the octopus was born and cared for as a full member of the family:

> The octopus was still a baby. After he was born, my grandparents couldn't just release him in the sea right away. They first built a basin for him and filled it

with seawater. They kept the baby for three months. Then they considered him mature enough to be brought to the sea. When they did so, they gave him provisions (*bekal*): rice cooked in coconut milk, a boiled [chicken] egg, and one cigarette. (Idem)

Although they released the octopus to the sea, the parents, brother and other close relatives actively sustained a relationship of care and acknowledgement with their sea-dwelling kin:

Since then, this [the same provisions] is what the family prepares for the octopus to feed him. We do this at least once a year. It doesn't really matter when exactly; the important thing is that we let him know that we haven't forgotten him. If we don't do this, he comes and asks for our attention. (Idem)

Years had passed since the birth of the octopus, and Hamma [Hamma Ali's father] had already passed away. Yet to Hamma Ali, his uncle was still an important part of the family:

He must be about a hundred years old now. He is not only my uncle, he is also our ancestor (*nenek moyang*). My father passed down his relationship with his brother to me. (Idem)

Kinship relations with sea-dwelling creatures was not my initial focus at the time, yet it triggered my interest while doing anthropological fieldwork in Masalima in 2013. As similar stories popped up in different situations, I started to take notes and follow these stories, out of curiosity. On the adjacent island Pamalikkan, I encountered a similar narrative of kinship with a sea-dwelling creature while chatting with a few Mandar women after lunch. Drinking tea, we informally exchanged stories of family and ancestry. Jumaira, an elderly woman who referred to herself as a descendent of the Mandar kingdom in Sulawesi, told me about her uncle, who happened to be a crocodile:

> Ambo Bisu was my grandfather, he was born with the crocodile. But the cro-
> codile baby came immediately after Ambo Bisu, so they are twins (*kembar*).
> As soon as the crocodile was born, the family prepared a basin filled with
> water for him so he could grow there. As a baby, the crocodile lived and grew
> in the basin. When he had outgrown the basin, he had matured enough to
> be brought to the sea. They gave him a silver bracelet on his right leg, and
> they prepared him provisions: Bananas, a raw chicken's egg, one cigarette,
> and a betel leaf, folded twice. He took it with him to the sea. (Jumaira, 22
> March 2013, Pamalikkan)

Like the octopus, Ambo Bisu's crocodile brother was also born and raised within
the intimacy of the household, yet ultimately, he headed seawards with ritual
provisions. From the sea, the sibling appeared again sometimes to reconnect
with his kin on land. In turn, Ambo Bisu regularly went to the sea, joining his
crocodile kin:

> After that, whenever Ambo Bisu went to the sea, his twin came along. He
> followed the boat, but usually he didn't show himself. He didn't need to,
> because they knew they were together. When Ambo Bisu called for help,
> his twin brother appeared. (Idem)

This all happened hundreds of years ago, Jumaira concluded. However, although
born with Ambo Bisu, the twinship had passed on to the rest of the family and
moved along with their migration overseas to Masalima:

> The twins were born on Gondengareng Island.[1] But we Mandar are seafaring
> people, we like to wander (*kuat merantau*), so part of the family moved here
> to Pamalikkan Island. But it doesn't matter where the grandchildren are. As
> soon as they are at sea, the crocodile is with them. (Idem)

In Masalima, twinships are common with a variety of sea-dwelling or amphibious beings, including also lizards and snakes. While kinship with lizards and
crocodiles is common among the Mandar population of Masalima, the Bajau

families I spoke with had octopus kin. The crocodile and octopus twinship caught my attention because it expresses a relation to a sea-dwelling agency that is both intimate and alien: part of the intimate 'us' of family and consanguinity, while simultaneously excessive to it as the twin is also part of another world. This kind of kinship challenges distinctions between human and non-human, land-based and sea-bound, without merging them into one.

Even more than kinship, the concept of twinship effectively problematises a clear distinction between self and other (Renne and Bastian 2001). What happens if this is extended to a twinship that involves marine or amphibious selves and others? What can twinship with sea-dwelling beings or agencies teach us about the figure of the human in relation to the sea? This is a question I address in this chapter. Prompted by narratives of twinship with sea-dwelling and amphibious kin in Masalima, I revisit the figures of the human and the sea in the context of how we think about their interrelation.

Such endeavour requires careful translation, while acknowledging that all ethnographic translation involves elements of distortion. Referring to the described twinship in post-humanist terms like 'human-non-human' or 'human-animal' involves a risk of reinstating a dichotomy that the twinship stories seem to undo. I will refer instead to 'amphibious twinship', in an attempt to stay with the movement in-between, keeping divisions of land/sea, human/non-human ambiguous. More than a curious ethnographic object of study, twinship with crocodile and octopus kin provides a situated or 'native' concept that prompts a rethinking of human-sea relations. It does so by intervening in the modern figure of the human as an 'us' in relation to the sea and its agencies as environmental Other.

Drawing from ethnographic accounts in Masalima, this chapter shows how both parts of the amphibious twinship are *manusia*, translated as 'humanity' or 'personhood', which indicates an ambiguity between sameness and difference, and between the twin siblings as humans and persons. As humans of different natures, from different worlds, they move together in twinship. Local narratives describe how in dreams and bodily visits the siblings partially merge, a process that confirms a co-existence in which the twins can move as one, while resisting a reduction to each other. What, then, may this amphibious twinship teach us about environmental alterity? Reflecting on how the twin sibling is an agency in the sea as well as an agency of the sea, I argue that the twinship expresses co-existence, but also environmental excess; a force or Other not contained in the figure of the twin sibling. Liquefying distinctions between thing and concept, figure and ground, amphibious twinship allows for thinking 'in-between' and stimulates consideration of what slips between the cracks of conceptualisation.

METHODOLOGICAL NOTE

The insights elaborated in this chapter are primarily based on the conversations I had with people in the Masalima Archipelago in March and April 2013, yet they are embedded in a long-term engagement with seafaring people in the wider region, including an 18-month fieldwork period (2011–2013) complemented by shorter visits to the region in 2008, 2017 and 2019. This anthropological study combined ethnographic research methods with a mobile methodology of follow-ing people, stories, vessels and things across the sea. Whereas the research was not focused on a particular site or ethnic group, the majority of people figuring in it identified themselves as of Bajau or Mandar descent, or a mix. Both Mandar and Bajau are known in maritime literature for their sea-oriented livelihoods and seafaring skills (Stacey 2003; Nolde 2009; Pauwelussen 2016; Zerner 2003).

The Masalima Archipelago is well known among seafaring people in the wider maritime region in central Indonesia and beyond as a fisheries and trade hub, and a stopover for people wandering, travelling or living at sea. Although the archipelago does not show on most maps, it can be considered a cosmopolitan place – an intersection of people, things and stories on the move. From a land-based perspective, the place is remote. Without regular transport, the easiest way to get there is a 24-hour ride on the occasional boat transporting supplies from the port of Makassar.

I came to Masalima with Masrif and Amir (pseudonyms). I travelled along with them from Berau in East Kalimantan to meet their overseas kin, while also following trajectories of the fish trade. Masrif had lived in Masalima for over 30 years before moving to Berau, and he was still a respected man in the archipelago's Mandar-speaking community. Amir was his adoptive son, born in the archipelago in a community of semi-nomadic Bajau people. While the two men could be rereferred to as 'key informants', to me they were (also) hosts, translators, teachers, travel companions, friends and – in the end – adoptive family. Their trust in me and my project has been vital to this chapter, as it brought about the necessary confidence and willingness among people to speak about what I call amphibious twinship. I have been open about my intention to publish these stories.

Interviews were held in Indonesian, sometimes mixed with the languages of Bajau and Mandar. My conversation partners generally spoke Indonesian quite well; however, their replies often mixed vernaculars, and Indonesian words sometimes carried meanings different from standard 'dictionary' Indonesian. Because my own understanding of Bajau and Mandar was basic, Amir and Masrif helped me out with the translation between Mandar, Bajau and Indonesian terminologies and meanings. Most of the conversations about twinship were recorded, with consent.

AMPHIBIOUS TWINSHIP IN SOUTHEAST ASIA

Twinship with crocodiles and other amphibians has been reported as a common phenomenon in several parts of Indonesia and neighbouring island states, particularly among coastal and maritime communities (Blackwood 1932; Boomgaard 2007; Fauvel and Koch 2009; Koch and Acciaioli 2007; Kunert 2017). Still, ethnographic coverage of the phenomenon is thin, save some accounts of kinship with spirit-animals in Southeast Asia.

In a paper titled 'animal children', Alexander Krappe (1944) has chronicled stories and myths of women giving birth to animals. In some cases, which he refers to as the 'werewolf type', the mother transforms into an animal and – as animal (shape and/or spirit) – gives birth to animal babies. In another variant, mothers give birth to what the author refers to as human-animal twins. In this context, he reports that in many Indonesian Islands, women are known to deliver a child and a crocodile at the same birth:

The midwife is believed to carry the crocodile twin carefully down to the river and to place it in the water. The family propitiate their amphibious relative by putting victuals in the river, and the human twin is bound for the rest of his life to do his duty by his crocodile brother or sister. Sickness and death would inevitably ensue, should he remiss in this obligation (Krappe 1944: 48).

James Fraser (1935, in Krappe 1944) describes the village of Simbang at the mouth of the Bubui River in New Guinea, where crocodiles are kinsfolk, and where an aged crocodile known as Old Butong, born of a 'human mother', was recognised as head of the family. Fauvel and Koch's more recent account of a twinship with a monitor lizard on the Indonesian island of Sulawesi recalls the mother saying that once grown up, the twin came back, 'looking for its twin sister and parents. When the family moved to kill the monitor, it 'raised its leg and started crying' in the most moving fashion, so the family came to believe it was really a human being with the appearance of a scaly monitor' (Fauvel and Koch 2009: 78).

Likewise, a 2010 documentary shot on Sulawesi follows a Buginese household with their varanid daughter Ali Douyung. Titled *The Twins of Lake Tempé* the documentary shows the creature being cherished, fed, washed and played with as a full family member (Corillion 2010). Here, kinship to the lizard is traced to the legend of a Bugis queen who gave birth to twins, one of them a lizard. At birth, the human infant died but the lizard survived. The lizard son was taken to the edge of the water, but the king told his son to reappear in a dream if he ever wanted to come back. In a similar way, Ali Douyung came to her family's home and appeared in the father's dreams. He then knew that Ali Douyung was his son's twin sister, and the family adopted their lizard kin.

Outside academic literature, stories of twinship and kinship with octopuses and crocodiles in Indonesia feature prominently on blogs and news sites. Online news portal VIVA published a story of how in 2015 fishers from Ambon Island killed an octopus more than a meter long and took it to their village. There, they discovered the octopus's head appeared human, its body covered with something shawl-like. A street vendor from Ambon city – Wa Rukia – was reported to have arrived in the village, crying. The octopus was his twin sister Ode Marjin, born 53 years ago from the same mother's womb. Wa Rukia recognised his sister by her shawl and blue eyes, he said to the news reporters. He then took the octopus's body to bury her like a human (VIVA 2015). Another news site reported a woman who gave birth to a human-crocodile twin (Putri 2013), showing pictures of the mother caressing a crocodile. More recently, the ButonPos news site ran a story of a grandmother's reunion with her twin sibling after decades apart. While also considered 'human', her beloved twin sibling was of a different nature: an octopus who had been living in the sea but was now in a bucket filled with water, surrounded by her family (ButonPos 2017, see also Karim 2017; Patty 2017 for recent examples).

Reports of twinship with marine spirit-animals in Southeast Asia show a tendency to document the phenomenon as merely a folkloristic curiosity. Yet native stories and concepts of environmental kinship can do more than this: they can be mobilised for conceptual reflection and inquiry and stimulate a critical rethinking of human-environment relations (Rose 2005). In this regard, narratives of twinship with crocodiles and octopuses in Masalima challenge established ways of thinking the figure of the human in relation to the marine environment. The next section shows how such 'amphibious twinship' destabilises the notion of humanity as restricted to a distinct 'human' category, instead emphasising a shared personhood with environmental others.

HUMANS OF DIFFERENT NATURES

After Jumaira told me about her crocodile uncle – the twin brother of her grandfather Ambo Bisu – I learned that new crocodile twins had been born more recently. Jumaira referred to them as the grandchildren of Ambo Bisu:

> Among his grandchildren the new crocodile twin was born. This crocodile is a different human/person (*manusia*), a different twin, but both [crocodiles] are of the same family. (Jumaira, 22 March 2013, Pamalikkan)

She also introduced me to the mother of these twins; Marsuki. Later, in her own home, Marsuki narrated:

> When I was pregnant, I didn't know I was pregnant with twins, until I gave birth. There was a lot of blood though, more than usual. I went to the seashore to wash away the blood. My son grew up to become a seaman. He went sailing. He often sailed to Mandar [West Sulawesi], and after a while he had a girlfriend over there. It was there in Mandar that my son met his twin sister for the first time. That was through the photo. He realised he was twins with the crocodile when she appeared in the photo on which he posed with his girlfriend. When they developed the photo, a crocodile stood next to him, instead of his girlfriend. (Marsuki 22, March 2013, Pamalikkan)

The twin came unexpectedly to Marsuki, though the excessive blood was probably a sign, she said. Different from Ambo Bisu's twin brother, this crocodile twin sister wasn't first cared for and brought to the sea by her mother. She appeared much later, to her brother first, and through a photograph. The miraculous appearance of the crocodile sister on a photograph was an event and story widely known and narrated in Masalima, and beyond. Later, the twin sister started visiting her twin brother on Pamalikkan, in a shape that moved between crocodile and human appearances:

> It was here in Pamalikkan that she first visited [my son], as partially woman and partially crocodile. She said: 'Bring me home'. He [her son] knew it was his twin sister and that she wanted to go back to the sea. My son prepared provisions for her: a blouse, a sarong, bananas, and sandals. These are the things a woman needs for a journey, he thought. He put the provisions in a bucket and gave them [placed it into the water]. But his sister didn't go home, she didn't leave. He then realised that something was missing: gold. As soon as he added gold to the basket, his sister went back to the sea. (Idem)

When describing the twin siblings, people in Masalima were not so much interested in the question of what these amphibious twins 'really are'. Their discussions and explications revolved around how the twin siblings 'appear' and how they relate to their kin. When describing her crocodile great-grandfather, Jumaira said:

> The crocodile twin visits in dreams. He mostly comes in the appearance of a crocodile. He then has four fingers instead of five. From that we know he is one of us (*orang kita* – literally 'our people'). He is our family. (Jumaira, 22 March 2013, Pamalikkan).

Similarly, Hamma Ali said about his octopus uncle:

> If the octopus appears, he does so as a person/human being (*manusia*), sometimes in front of our eyes, at other times in our dreams. His shape is not fixed. Sometimes he is like an octopus, at other times he has more of a shape like you and me. But then only the face is human, and it is vague. When he is more like an octopus, he can be distinguished from the regular octopuses we encounter in the sea because he is white and has five arms instead of eight. (Hamma Ali, 28 March 2013, Pamantauan)

Both Hamma Ali and Jumaira referred to the twin sibling as *manusia*. In standard Indonesian language, *manusia* translates as 'humanity'. However, in Bajau and Mandar language traditions, the term is commonly used to refer to a 'personhood' that is not restricted to a distinct human category clearly distinguishable from other animals and spirits. In Masalima the term *manusia* is used both as a reference to a more exclusive humanity (excluding other animals and spirits), and as a reference to an inclusive humanity that is probably more accurately translated as 'personhood' or 'familiarity'.

Jumaira said that the twins are both *manusia* but of a different kind. As a more inclusive form of 'we', *manusia* as personhood opens up the term to include amphibious siblings, as well as (ancestral) spirits in a more general sense (Bottignolo 1995). It may also include animals, which are part of the spectrum of spirits and agencies that make up the living world. For example, Bajau fishers commonly referred to dugongs and dolphins as being 'from their

own 'humankind' or 'personhood" (*dari manusia sendiri*), while Mandar fishers sometimes refer to fish as children (Zerner 2003, and own observations
2011–2013). Rather than saying that *manusia* includes animals and spirits in
a relational notion of 'humanity', it is perhaps more accurate to state that there
never really was a clear distinction between these three categories in the first
place.

Manusia expresses ambiguity regarding sameness and difference between
twin siblings as humans and persons. It may indicate an exclusive humanity,
but it is also used to indicate an open-ended familiarity relating a spectrum
of agencies into shared personhood. In this latter sense, the amphibious twin
siblings constitute each other in a shared *manusia* personhood traversing the
water surface. This ambiguity in the use of the *manusia* concept indicates how the
sea-dwelling twin sibling is both familiar and Other. In Masalima, amphibious
siblings are part of an inclusive *manusia* 'us' being born into Masalima families,
through birth together with a human baby, yet they are also excessive to it. They
ultimately head back to a different home underwater.

BETWEEN SELF AND OTHER

I am I,
I am not you.
I live apart.
Do you live, too,
With dreams and hopes
That are your own?
We will be two
When fully grown?

(Excerpt from 'Twindependent', Lewis and Yolen 2012: 47)

Twinship plays with the trope of a mirror between beings that are conceived
together, reflect one another but are in the end not the same. In popular culture,

anthropological theory and in indigenous philosophy the concept of twinship has problematised the figure of the individual, as it is associated with fluidity or ambiguity between being same and different, more than one and less than two separate entities (Dillan 2018; Evens 2012; Renne & Bastian 2001). Likewise, narratives of amphibious twinship in Masalima express a movement between difference and sameness that becomes particularly apparent when the twins temporarily merge into one. In these events, it is said that the amphibious twin appears 'in reality' (*dalam nyata*).

After the twin sibling is released to the sea (after birth), there are two common ways in which he or she reappears to the Masalima family: in dreams, and *dalam nyata*. A twin sibling appears 'in reality' as it becomes visible, hearable or otherwise perceptible. The sibling is seen as an animal walking along the coastline or swimming along with a boat. It may also be perceived as a shimmering shape, a light, a sound, a tingling sensation, or through the heavy blooding of its mother during birth. The twin sibling's reality as an appearing *dalam nyata* is best characterised as a relational effect; it is confirmed in its affective consequences.

The twin sibling also appears in reality when it visits and takes over the body of its sibling or a close relative, the two partially and temporarily merging into one. As a Bajau *orang pintar* ('smart person', someone who communicates with spirits), Umar, said: 'Particularly at sea, spiritual presences are strong. They usually make themselves known as they enter our body' (18 February 2013, Berau). Sometimes, the events were explained to me as spirit possession ('*dirasuki*'). However, the families of amphibious twins preferred the term *dikunjungi* ('being visited') as a gentler notion of temporarily sharing one body. Hamma Ali elaborated:

> Sometimes, the twin octopus visits. He visits us by occupying my body. He did that with his twin brother, and now with me. He then becomes part of me. When he visits, he wants to be dressed in a red sarong, a red blouse, and a *topi songkok* [a traditional Muslim cap] in Bone style. He asks for these clothes, and he puts them on. We used to be looking frantically for it whenever he visited us unexpectedly, but nowadays we always have these clothes prepared just in case he wishes to spend time with us. Usually, cold

shivers announce the visit of my uncle. When he visits, he is very emotional, he cries and cries. He misses his family; he wants to touch his grandchildren; he wants to see the new baby. The family comes together in the house when the octopus visits, to be with him while he crawls about the room. Only if he has seen and touched all his relatives does he feel better and go home. When I come to my senses again, I am surprised! All these people in the room!' (Hamma Ali, 28 March 2013, Pamantauan)

Whether one can call on the twin sibling for a visit depends on the relationship one sustains with him or her and is ultimately up to the twin sibling. He or she cannot be employed, as Amir (Hamma Ali's nephew) said:

My uncle [Hamma Ali] and his younger sister, they are able to feed (*kasih makan*) the octopus. For them, the octopus is willing to come. But with another, it may not work. All the children know how to feed the octopus, but it is always up to the octopus whom he visits. Until now, the octopus has only visited Hamma Ali and his sister. (Amir, 28 March 2013, Pamantauan)

Jumaira's husband explained what happens when his family is visited by their crocodile grandfather:

If he is not given attention, he will visit his grandchildren, he misses them. The spirit (*roh*) will pervade/possess (*merasuki*) them. He [the human and crocodile becoming together] then appears crawling like the crocodile. He will act and move as the crocodile. If this happens, if one of the grandchildren is visited, the following is to be done: we offer the crocodile [now in, or part of, the grandchild] a raw egg. He sucks and empties the egg without breaking the shell. As soon as he wants to go home and leave the visited kin, he crawls towards the sea. He wants to go back home. He does not need help to go to the sea, he knows his way. As soon as he is soaked, he leaves the human body. The visited now feels one again. (Jumaira's husband, 22 March 2013, Pamalikkan)

Note the similarity with how Marsuki's son is visited by his crocodile twin sister:

> Nowadays, he is very close to his sister, and he can call her now, asking her to visit him. Here, in this house, he will let her visit him. They then move together like a crocodile. (Marsuki, 22 March 2013, Pamalikkan)

Although twins from the sea cannot be called or employed by just anyone, they do appear sometimes to people who are not kin:

> It is possible we unexpectedly deal with a sea twin of another family. It's a matter of recognising them and dealing with them respectfully. For example, the other day I saw a snake coming out of the water. A snake with scales, of a kind I had never seen before. As soon as it left the water, it had legs. It crossed its legs and just stayed there quietly. I was there with an uncle, who said to me: 'Leave it, don't bother it, because I suspect that it is the twin sibling of someone else'. (Ibu Susy, 22 March 2013, Pamalikkan)

The crocodile and octopus twins are not just an abstract category of spiritual beings. As relatives, they have their own personality, mood swings and preferences. As family, they are treasured, and their visits welcome yet not always convenient. The personalities of the twin siblings – being people and part of *manusia* – shows in how they all have different wants and wishes when they visit their kin, while there are also differences in how often they want their family's attention, and when. Some wish to be remembered once a year, while others show up uninvited when they feel neglected. Jumaira's crocodile grandfather, for example, was known as a creature of habit, demanding on his visits what was given to him when he was released to the sea for the first time: a raw egg, a cigarette, a banana and betel leaf. 'Once a year we offer this to the crocodile. There is no fixed day to do this, but it is important that it is done'. (Jumaira, 22 March 2013, Pamalikkan). The narratives of visiting twin siblings express the obligations that the twinship entails. They also express the affection and longing that the twins have to be reunited, to become part of the other, albeit momentarily.

While the previous section showed how the twin sibling from the sea moves between human and animal shape, in the narratives above the 'human' sibling shifts between human and animal shapes too, moving like a crocodile or octopus. As family reunions, the visits reconfirm twinship by the temporary becoming-one of the siblings or their nearest kin. Again, the twinship expresses a productive ambiguity here of being similar and different. Both are humans of different kinds, with different homes, but through twinship they move together *dalam nyata* – in reality. In dreams and bodily visits, the twins temporarily and partially merge to acknowledge and vitalise their co-existence while resisting reduction to each other. They express a difference that is not pure 'otherness', but rather a becoming-with of sea-bound agencies not contained in themselves but neither yet safely Other (after Haraway 2016: 98). Amphibious twinship thus emerges here as a transformative force that challenges distinctions between human, animal and spirit, as well as between self and other.

Still, while amphibious twinship expresses a moral and affective linkage between different worlds, it also embodies a certain eeriness and capriciousness of the sea, which lies beyond human conception and control – an environmental excess channelled through the familiar/strange relationship between the twins. Although created together, born from the same womb, amphibious twins never completely map onto each other as they proceed to live different lives in different worlds that only partially flow into one another. What then does amphibious twinship in Masalima tell us about environmental otherness?

THE SEA AS INTIMATE AND OTHER

Stories of amphibious twinship are frequently accompanied by references to the sea as dangerous, intimately present, yet ultimately beyond what can be controlled or understood. The sea's mood and rhythm conditions almost every aspect of daily life on and off the islands and is subject to repeated discussion and ritualised practices. In Masalima, Mandar fishers engage in open sea fishing, braving dangerously stormy seas to search for the eggs of flying fish. Many of the Bajau fishers engage in risky work underwater, by hookah diving for sea cucumber and reef fishes (Pauwelussen, 2021). Situated in a convergence of strong sea currents, the Masalima Archipelago and adjacent waters are also known for their strong spirit presences, particularly during the monsoon season. As elaborated below, amphibious twinship involves relations with agencies *in* the sea, but the sea-dwelling twin may also be an extension *of* the sea – diffusing a division between figure and ground. The twinship thereby speaks to relationality and the limits thereof in human-sea relations.

As agencies *in* the sea, the crocodile and octopus twins are situated in a spectrum of agencies known to dwell and move in marine and intertidal spaces. Although the spirit worlds of the Bajau and Mandar do not neatly map onto each other, both are constituted by a plethora of spiritual, material and animal beings and forces that shift shape, scale, direction, intensity and perceptibility (Bottignolo 1995; Lowe 2006). Some are considered as an extension of the familiar – as 'allies' or 'kin', while others are feared as malevolent beings. Some can be manipulated to do good or harm. Others still are other-worldly and utterly unpredictable, up to the point that they are unknown, accepted absences in understanding and of relating.

As I have elaborated elsewhere (Pauwelussen 2017: 39–67), making and sustaining a living in this vibrant world requires a kind of cognitive and affective navigation that resembles dialogue between seafarers and the multiple and shifting moves, rhythms and agencies of and in the sea. In Masalima, amphibious twins are also discussed in relation to such affective engagement, in which the twinship relation mobilises practices and sentiments of mutual care and moral responsibility from both sides. Many of the stories of amphibious twinship that I documented express intimacy and caring relations. The mother-in law of an octopus twin said:

> At the beginning... we knew there would be twins because there was a lot of blood in the sarong. We were upset. Why is there so much blood? Maybe there are twins? But we saw only one baby; that was Rijal. After that, the mother who gave birth had a dream. In it, an octopus was clinging to her. It was her baby in the form of an octopus. A couple of years later, her husband Hajar [the father of the twins] went to the sea to fish. He caught an octopus

and he pulled the octopus to his canoe (*sampan*). The octopus didn't die, and he then realised that it was his son. He released his son back into the water. But the octopus didn't leave. Instead, he clung to the boat. He hugged and caressed the boat, and only after a while doing that did the octopus leave and go down. (Marlina, 29 March 2013, Pamantauan)

Among the Bajau families I consulted, twinship with an octopus involves a taboo against catching and eating it. It also involves a family obligation of care and remembering, feeding, releasing and protecting. This relation of obligation and care goes in both directions. Just as the human family extends its care to the octopus beyond the individual twin sibling, the octopus also extends its affection and care beyond its twin sibling to the wider family. The octopus's father (who first identified his son at sea) was particularly explicit in how his [octopus] son, now 15 years old, just like his other son, helps him at sea:

I am often at sea alone, but with my son. I have had accidents, but I have been lucky every time. Once, when my boat capsized, he helped me. The boat was upside down. Normally, it is impossible to turn back the boat, but I managed to do it, so I surely received help with that. Another time, I went fishing, but my boat capsized again. I was drifting for one day and one night. People here were worried, they went looking for me. I tried to swim, but I was tired, hungry. I held on to the boat, but I almost collapsed. That's when I saw the dolphins swimming around me, checking in on me. They stayed with me, they kept me company. Finally, my people from here found me. They pulled me onto their boat. Just when they did that, the two dolphins appeared from the water, they put their heads on the boat too, they splashed around a bit and then they left, back to the sea. The octopus, he helped by calling the dolphins. (29 March 2013, Pamantauan)

Similarly, Hamma Ali's octopus uncle helped him when Hamma experienced misfortune at sea:

> Years can go by without him [his octopus uncle] visiting us. But in some years, he comes several times. This is when we need each other. Once, a couple of years ago, I was stung by a big stingray. It was a dangerous situation, I was very ill, and I probably wouldn't have made it without the strength of the octopus. He also helped me when I once sailed from Pamantauan to the West coast of Sulawesi. The weather was bad, the waves dangerously high. At night, I saw the octopus below in the sea. His white shape spread light below the water surface. I knew it was my uncle. His shape had five arms. He stayed close to the boat until I had reached safe waters. (Hamma Ali, 28 March 2013, Pamantauan)

Hamma Ali said he was a dive-fisher, collecting sea cucumbers from the sea floor. He explained that although his uncle doesn't usually show himself, he is always present during dives, ready to support his nephew. Once, Hamma Ali's engine broke down, leaving him at the mercy of the strong currents of the Makassar Strait. His uncle pulled his boat to the land: 'My engine didn't work anymore, and still my boat moved in the right direction. I know it was the octopus'.

Still, it's not only in times of trouble that the octopus accompanies his kin. As Hamma Ali said:

> Sometimes, he just comes to keep his nephew company. Sometimes, he comes up to the boat and sits on my lap. Here, here he sits [Hamma Ali slaps his right knee]. He asks for a cigarette. I give him one, and usually he leaves right after receiving it [the cigarette]. He goes back to the sea. At other moments, the octopus appears – not visible to the eyes – by obstructing those who try to hurt me. Should people intend to do me harm, it is in the power of the octopus to pull their boat [in]to the sea. (Idem)

Jumaira and Marsuki narrated similar stories of their crocodile kin. Jumaira mentioned how her crocodile great grandfather warns her in her dreams when relatives are in trouble at sea. Marsuki, the mother of the crocodile that first appeared on a photo, likewise explained how the crocodile twinship informs her son:

My son is in Kalukuan Island now, he builds boats there. He connects with her, and distance disappears. He feels what happens at other places, even those that are many nights sailing from here. If his father is ill, he knows over there in Kalukuang. He comes home, even before anyone has had the opportunity to bring him the news. [A sister adds]: 'That's his twin sister telling him'. (Marsuki, 22 March 2013, Pamalikkan)

While the twin sibling is often personified in narratives, by extension it figures as an agency *of* the sea just as it is one *in* it. This bears resemblance to the way Indonesian legends and stories have portrayed seas, oceans and major currents as kingdoms and forces personified in queens and prophets (Schlehe 1998).[2] While the sea may be an agency and a multiplicity thereof (see Pauwelussen and Verschoor 2017), in conversations people were not so much concerned with what the sea 'really is', but rather how best to relate to, and live with it, in which the 'it' never acquires a uniform nature. In this ethics of relational co-existence, the twin sibling *is* the sea as much as it is *part of* it, and the sea is therefore in the human just as the human is also in the sea, diffusing a division between figure and ground and rendering both sides of the twin-mirror ultimately amphibious, moving in-between. They were never separated, and they may constitute one another without merging into one, as one does not capture the other either as a body or a concept.

As the ethnographic excerpts above illustrate, amphibious twinship expresses an ethics of care that may involve helping each other, not eating one another, or exchanging (ritual) food and messages. The twins appear to share a moral domain of co-existence, although at the same time, as an agency of the sea, the octopus or crocodile sibling belongs to a different *dunia*, which translates into 'world', 'realm' or 'order'. When dealing with a twin sibling, one is also dealing with a force that is not contained in the figure of the twin. Perhaps this is also what Kunert's documentary *O Brother Octopus*, shot in Sabah (Malaysia) about 1200 km to the north of Masalima refers to when citing a Bajau elder:

The mother gives birth to a child, and to the child's twin, born in the form of an octopus. It becomes our lifelong companion. We cannot eat or kill any octopus. If we break this rule, we need to seek forgiveness or a giant octopus will rise from the water, bringing us misfortune. (Kunert 2017)

In amphibious twinship, the Bajau and Mandar relate to the sea environment both as an intimate presence and an 'order of the Other' (after Helmreich 2009: 15). It is Other because it exceeds colonisation and eludes attempts to capture it as a body or a concept. The Bajau and Mandar 'theory of twinship' acknowledges a limitation of relationality, as one never really knows what the twin sibling – as a force in and of the sea – can do. It might rise from the water as a giant octopus.

TWINSHIP THEORY

Prompted by narratives from the Masalima Archipelago, I have discussed twinship between human and sea-dwelling kin as both a phenomenon and a concept. As a phenomenon, amphibious twinship is sustained in affective performance – whether dream, being 'visited', or the caring for a 'flesh and blood' animal in a backyard basin. As a native concept, it expresses thinking and doing human-sea relations in Masalima, while its logics may also intervene in current debates in anthropology and science and technology studies on environmental alterity.

This final section reflects on twinship with crocodiles and octopuses in Masalima as a theory or ethics of co-existence and alterity in human-sea relations. As argued, twinship speaks to ambiguity between being same and different. It plays with the trope of mirroring beings that are intimately familiar, but also of a different nature. In amphibious twinship, this ambiguity extends to the human-sea relationship. As twinship diffuses distinctions between self and other, engaging with amphibious twinship stimulates a rethinking of a human 'us' relating to a sea 'Other'. I have shown how in Masalima, both sides of this twinship are human or person (*manusia*), yet of different natures. They share a moral universe but belong to different worlds. In correspondence with Viveiros de Castro's (1998) discussion of multinaturalism in a South American context, this problematises the modern notion of 'human' as distinct from a 'non-human' Other.

The twin sibling Other is both part of the intimate 'us' of kinship and *manusia* as an extensive humanity, while also part of another order – a world considered excessive to control and comprehension. Although of different natures, the twins are born from the same womb, and share an ethical disposition of co-existence that is revitalised through mutual obligations of care and attention, affective relations and moving together as one during reuniting visits. Still, despite the re-enacted intimacy, the twins' reunion does not last. The Other remains partly elusive – one doesn't know what it can do and how it will appear.

How does amphibious twinship relate to academic discussions of environmental otherness, and particularly the sea as a familiar Other? In literature and academic scholarship, the sea has often figured as the order of the Other – a zone beyond a steady and grounded self (Helmreich 2009: 15). It allows for immersion, while precluding extended human presence in it (Anderson 2012). Creatures and spirits of the sea (whales, dolphins) figured prominently in early modern literature (e.g. Shakespeare) as an expression of the uncertainty and alterity of the sea, while also articulating a 'strange kinship' to land-dwelling people – a disconcerting mirror of ourselves (Brayton 2012). While amphibious twinship shows resonances with the trope of mirroring through kinship, it decentralises and problematises the latent assumption of a distinct human category that is reflected in a water surface. Moreover, amphibious twinship involves a figure/ground collapse that destabilises the very idea of the sea as a reflection of, or background for, human action.

Here, amphibious twinship as theory relates to critical scholarship that considers the sea as inherently relational and enacted, while it also intervenes in it. This 'relational turn' has challenged the modern rendering of 'nature' and 'environment' as taken-for granted domains situated at either end of a nature/culture dichotomy (Descola and Pálsson 1996; Howitt and Suchet-Pearson 2003). Instead of a background for human action, 'environment' becomes performative and affective: an ongoing interweaving of relations between agents and elements that defy clear categories of nature or culture, human or non-human (see for example Archambault 2016; Hayward 2010; Ingold 2010; Whatmore 2002).

What we are accustomed to calling the 'sea' or 'marine environment' can – in this line of thinking – be envisaged as such an interweaving of relations and material resonances. Indeed, Lambert et al. write that to understand the sea requires acknowledging its inherent relationality, and the way sea worlds are produced through the entanglement of diverse elements, such as wind, currents, water, salt, plastics, technologies, microbes and animals (Lambert et al. 2006). As such, this relational turn has also been linked to 'oceanic thinking' in which the flow and lively materiality of the sea stimulates thinking about the world as enacted, assembled – a dynamic meshwork that's always on the move (Anderson 2012; Bear 2012; Steinberg 2013; Steinberg and Peters 2015). A turn to the moves and substance of the sea may, however, conjure new reifications. Helmreich cautions that oceanic fluidity and the lively materiality of the sea may have no meaning outside human conceptions of it (Helmreich 2011: 133). Is the conceptual the end point then, or does something still escape?

Envisaging the sea as a dynamic meshwork of heterogeneous relations shows similarity to how my Bajau and Mandar interlocutors narrated the sea and their relation to it in twinship. Indeed, twinship with crocodiles and octopuses speaks to such relationality too. Yet there is also something in how people in Masalima relate to the sea that defies the idea of an ever-expanding meshwork of human-environment relationality. This is the understanding that the sea as a concept, an agency or multiplicity thereof cannot be captured. That is: relationality may be assumed, but it is not necessarily human-centred, as the sea is excessive to human modes of relating to it in kinship, as well as in conceptualisation. Through twinship, the sea dips into dreams, senses and bodies in a way that is mostly uncertain. One never knows what the sea – both agent and a multiple thereof – can and will do.

Amphibious twinship thus renders the sea an environmental otherness that partly escapes practices of enacting it. It does so by expressing a liquification of figure and ground, and concept and thing. Narratives of twinship with agencies of and in the sea allow for a figure-ground reversal (or even collapse) between humanity and the sea; *manusia* as humanity or personhood may be an environment for the sea's agency as much as the sea is an environment for *manusia*. The very juxtaposition of figure and ground is diffused as both human and sea are already part of each other. While the sea enters human dreams, emotions and bodies, humanity is also in the sea, through twin siblings born from a human mother. As an effect, it may express an ethics in which 'human' responsibility is a response to the sea (dwelling twin) instead of a planned mastery of its behaviour, as common in environmental conservation (Pauwelussen and Verschoor 2017; also see Rose 2005 for a similar argument in a terrestrial context). We are presented here with a question of figure and ground in which the 'ground' becomes fluid, problematising any neat division between the two (see also Helmreich 2009: 169).

Moreover, amphibious twinship collapses the distinction between a material world 'out there' and conceptualisations thereof, leaving room for ambiguity and excess. At first sight, the twin Other can be seen as a conceptualisation of the sea, with the twinship narrative as a native theory of human-marine interrelation. However, in amphibious twinship, the twin sibling *is* the sea as much as it is part *of* the sea. And as it becomes real in dreams, memories and embodied encounters, it destabilises a distinction between the sea as a fluent material reality and conceptualisations thereof. At the same time, this very conceptualisation is seen to be partial, in the sense that twin and sea resist full capture. The twinship expresses a force or Other not entirely contained in the figure of the twin sibling. Without retreating to a new fluid materialism that renders the sea as a vital materiality, amphibious twinship nevertheless stimulates thought about what slips between the cracks of conceptualisation. Liquefying distinctions between thing and concept, figure and ground, amphibious twinship allows for thinking along the movement in-between.

NOTES

1 Presently, Gondengaring island is part of the village (*desa*) Ujung Tanah, part of the Makassar municipality in Southwest Sulawesi.

2 Famous in this respect is the goddess *Nyai Roro Kidul* in Javanese tradition, notorious far beyond Java as the *Ratu Laut Selatan*, literally 'queen of the South Sea' (Schlehe 1998).

REFERENCES

Anderson, J., 'Relational Places: The Surfed Wave as Assemblage and Convergence', *Environment and Planning D: Society and Space*, 30 (2012): 570–587.

Archambault, J., 'Taking Love Seriously in Human-Plant Relations in Mozambique: Towards an Anthropology of Affective Encounters', *Cultural Anthropology*, 31.2 (2016): 244–271.

Bear, C., 'Assembling the Sea: Materiality, Movement and Regulatory Practices in the Cardigan Bay Scallop Fishery', *Cultural Geographies*, 20.1 (2012): 21–41.

Blackwood, B., 'Folk Stories from the Northern Solomons', *Folklore*, 43 (1932): 61–96.

Boomgaard, P., 'Crocodiles and Humans in Southeast Asia: Four Centuries of Co-existence and Confrontation' [Keynote address for the symposium 'Environmental Challenges Across Asia' at the Centre for International Studies, University of Chicago, 2 March 2007].

Bottignolo, B., *Celebrations with the Sun: An Overview of Religious Phenomena among the Bajaos* (Manila: Ateneo de Manila University Press, 1995).

Brayton, D., *Shakespeare's Ocean: An Ecocritical Exploration* (Charlottesville, VA: The University of Virginia Press, 2012).

ButonPos, 'Kisah Saudara Kembar Beralam Beda Bertemu Kembali Setelah Terpisah Puluhan Tahun, *ButonPos*, 14 December 2017, <http://butonpos.fajar.co.id/kisah-saudara-kembar-beda-alam-bertemu-kembali-setelah-terpisah-puluhan-tahun/> [accessed 16 March 2019].

Corillion, J. M. (director), *The Twins of Lake Tempé* [Documentary 'Land of Legends series', ZED/La Cinquieme/AB Productions, France, 2010].

Descola, P., and G. Pálsson, eds., *Nature and Society: Anthropological Perspectives* (London: Routledge, 1996).

Dillan, K., *The Spectacle of Twins in American Literature and Popular Culture* (Jefferson: McFarland, 2018).

Evens, T. M. S., 'Twins are Birds and a Whale is a Fish, a Mammal, a Submarine', *Social Analysis*, 46.3 (2012): 1–11.

Fauvel, J. B., and A. Koch, 'Zoo-Ethnological Observations in Southwest Sulawesi, Indonesia: A Case Study of Kembar Buaya (Monitor Twins)', *Biawak*, 3.3 (2009): 77–80.

Haraway, D. J., *Staying with the Trouble: Making Kin in the Chthulucene* (Durham and London: Duke University Press, 2016).

Hayward, E., 'FINGEREYES: Impressions of Cup Corals', *Cultural Anthropology*, 25.4 (2010): 577–599.

Helmreich, S., *Alien Ocean: Anthropological Voyages in Microbial Seas* (Berkeley: University of California Press, 2009).

——, 'Nature/Culture/Seawater', *American Anthropologist*, 113.1 (2011): 132–144.

Howitt, R., and S. Suchet-Pearson, 'Ontological Pluralism in Contested Cultural

Landscapes', in K. Anderson and others, eds., *Handbook of Cultural Geography* (London: Sage, 2003), pp. 557–569.

Ingold, T., *Being Alive: Essays on Movement, Knowledge and Description* (London: Routledge, 2011).

Kalim, A., 'Cerita Mistis Gurita Berselendang Batik' *Liputan6*, 16 November 2017, <https://www.liputan6.com/regional/read/3163965/cerita-mistis-gurita-berselendang-batik> [accessed 13 March 2019].

Koch, A., and G. Acciaioli, 'The Monitor Twins: A Bugis and Makassarese Tradition from SW Sulawesi, Indonesia', *Biawak*, 1.2 (2007): 77–82.

Krappe, A. H., 'Animal Children', *California Folklore Quarterly*, 3.1 (1944): 45–52.

Kunert, F. (director), *Oh Brother Octopus* [Documentary, Cologne: Kunsthochschule für Medien, Germany, 2017].

Lambert, D., L. Martins, and M. Ogborn, 'Currents, Visions and Voyages: Historical Geographies of the Sea', *Journal of Historical Geography*, 32 (2006): 479–493.

Latour, B., *We Have Never Been Modern* (Cambridge, MA: Harvard University Press, 1993).

Lewis, J. P., and J. Yolen, *Take Two! A Celebration of Twins* (Sommerville, MA: Candlewick Press, 2012).

Lowe, C., *Wild Profusion: Biodiversity Conservation in an Indonesian Archipelago* (Princeton: Princeton University Press, 2006).

Nolde, L., '"Great is our Relationship with the Sea" Charting the Maritime Realm of the Sama of Southeast Sulawesi, Indonesia', *Explorations*, 9 (2009): 15–33.

Patty, R. R., 'Gurita Berkepala Mirip Wajah Manusia Ditemukan Warga di Pulau Seram', *Kompas*, 25 October 2017, <https://regional.kompas.com/read/2017/10/25/16114561/gurita-berkepala-mirip-wajah-manusia-ditemukan-warga-di-pulau-seram> [accessed 16 March 2019].

Pauwelussen, A. P., 'Community as Network: Exploring a Relational Approach to Social Resilience in Coastal Indonesia', *Maritime Studies*, 15.2 (2016).

—, 'Amphibious Anthropology: Engaging with Maritime Worlds in Indonesia' (PhD Thesis, Wageningen University, 2017).

—, 'Leaky Bodies: Masculinity and Risk in the Practice of Cyanide Fishing', *Gender, Place and Culture* (2021): 1–21.

Pauwelussen, A. P., and G. M Verschoor, 'Amphibious Encounters: Coral and People in Conservation Outreach in Indonesia', *Engaging Science, Technology and Society*, 3 (2017): 292–314.

Putri, R., 'Ibu Lahirkan Bayi Buaya Hebohkan Warga Sinjai', *Kompas*, 24 February 2013, <https://regional.kompas.com/read/2013/02/24/11535638/Ibu.Lahirkan.Bayi.Buaya.Hebohkan.Warga.Sinjai> [accessed 16 March 2019].

Renne, E. P., and M. L. Bastian, 'Reviewing Twinship in Africa', *Ethnology*, 40.1 (2001): 1–11.

Rose, D., 'An Indigenous Ecological Philosophy: Situating the Human', *The Australian Journal of Anthropology*, 16.3 (2005): 294–305.

Schlehe, J., *Die Meereskönigin des Südens, Ratu Kidul. Geisterpolitik im Javanischen Alltag* (Berlin: Dietrich Reimer Verlag, 1998).

Stacey, N., *Boats to Burn: Bajo Fishing Activity in the Australian Fishing Zone* (Canberra: ANU E-Press, 2007).

Steinberg, P., 'Of Other Seas: Metaphors and Materialities in Maritime Regions', *Atlantic Studies*, 10.2 (2013): 156–169.

Steinberg, P., and K. Peters, 'Wet Ontologies, Fluid Spaces: Giving Depth to Volume through Oceanic Thinking', *Environment and Planning D: Society and Space*, 33 (2015): 247–264.

VIVA, 'Gurita Berkepala Manusia Gegerkan Warga Ambon', *VIVA.co.id national news*, 5 September 2015, <https://www.viva.co.id/berita/nasional/670004-gurita-berkepala-manusia-gegerkan-warga-ambon> [accessed 16 March 2019].

Viveiros De Castro, E., 'Cosmological Deixis and Amerindian Perspectivism', *The Journal of the Royal Anthropological Institute*, 4.3 (1998): 469–488.

Whatmore, S., *Hybrid Geographies: Natures, Cultures, Spaces* (London: Sage, 2002).

Zerner, C., 'Sounding the Makassar Strait: The Poetics and Politics of an Indonesian Marine Environment', in C, Zerner, ed., *Culture and the Question of Rights: Forests, Coasts, and Seas in Southeast Asia* (Durham: Duke University Press, 2003), pp. 56–108.

ENVIRONMENTAL INFRASTRUCTURAL ALTERITIES AND COMMUNICATIVE POSSIBILITIES

A conversation between Penny Harvey and Stefan Helmreich

As a way to generate further reflections on the ideas proposed in Course's and Pauwelussen's chapters, but also seeking to avoid formats that might summarise or resolve the questions the chapters pose, we invited Penny Harvey and Stefan Helmreich to have an open conversation about the chapters, in relation to the introduction to the book. We recorded the conversation and then transcribed it verbatim. Afterwards we asked each scholar to edit the conversations, and only then did we lightly edit them ourselves – this in order to try to keep the stylistic effect of a conversational format, an exchange of ideas and a non-linear narrative. In so doing, rather than an ending, we hoped to provide readers with further open directions in which to think.

BY CONSIDERING THE SEA AS A DOMAIN THAT EXCEEDS HUMAN ENGAGE-ments, in what follows Harvey and Helmreich consider to what extent the sea portrayed in the previous chapters is a 'domestic sea', very close to land and the human engagements this vicinity affords; a sea that is thought and enacted through idioms of kinship and certain kind of reciprocity between humans and the environment. Moreover, and by critically thinking about the limits and possibilities the idiom of figure-ground affords as an analytical solution for engagements between humans and non-humans, Harvey and Helmreich explore how the concept of environmental alterities, (and the question of what comes after after-nature), can do interesting work if we put it in conversation with environmental infrastructures, or infra-natures. This move complements the domesticity of the sea discussed in the chapters and brings to the fore the political relevance of thinking about the plastic sea, radioactive oceans or our nuclear environments as historical outcomes producing unforeseen alterities that exceed and will survive human relationalities.

STEFAN: I am interested in the question posed in this book's introduction: 'what comes after *after-nature*?' It seems to me that there are at least two versions of 'after-nature' we would want to consider in pondering the question. Both are genres that Marilyn Strathern alerted us to back in 1992, in her book, *After Nature*. First is nature as a kind of aspirational form, something to *take after*. Another is a version that poses nature as something to be superseded or gone beyond. What comes after those after-natures? Well, *not* following nature as a model. But/and also *not* accepting that there are easy ways out of the cosmological histories we (or some of us, with the folk category 'nature') inherit.

It might be useful to try an additional angle into the question, to consider a classical (and ordinal) approach to genres of nature – to ask after first nature, second nature and third nature. What might it mean to be 'after' those – and then to be after those thoses?

First nature was and is that mythic nature understood as unmediated by human knowledge projects. Second nature – theorised by Cicero, Marx, Lukács, Adorno and any number of others – is cultural production that is reified as *taking after* nature or as human enterprise built upon nature. Culture as second nature. In *After Nature*, Strathern was pointing in part to the way nature has been taken as a foundation for warranting, or legitimising, or rationalising, human enterprise. But she was also pointing to the fact that recognising that function actually makes the very idea of 'nature' as a cultural category explicit. After *that*, it's hard to have any sense of nature as outside history or as simply the frame that makes *culture* the natural condition proper to humanity. What comes after after-nature? Perhaps a *politics* of nature. Or maybe a jumping ship to the word environment?

But to keep counting: there's also the idea of third nature. David McDermott Hughes published a piece in *Cultural Anthropology* several years ago called 'Third nature: Making space and time in the Great Limpopo Conservation Area' ; for him, third nature named bureaucratic articulations of nature as potential, specu-lative, conditional biodiversity. In the recent work of Anna Tsing, third nature has come rather to name contaminated diversity, to point to the organic and material substances that now appear as and in the ruins of capitalism. Jedediah Purdy's 2015 book, *After Nature,* is pointing to that third nature, though coming, I think from a different place than Tsing or Hughes, much less ethnographically particular, more willing to ratchet the story up to a big Anthropocene.

So, I think the 'environmental alterities' frame and phrase, and the query that animates it – namely what comes after after-nature – asks us to go back and name the histories that have given us 'natures' in the first place …

PENNY: That's great because I came to the same kind of space but from a slightly different angle: I also thought that the question of 'what comes after after-nature?' was key, and the thing that the two chapters we were asked to comment on were explicitly picking up on as their challenge. It's a great question, and it made for a really interesting introductory essay that unravelled some very complex arguments, and then put them together again. I'm interested in how things get put together again. So, following the way the introduction is structured around the dynamic relationship between limits and heterogeneities, I found myself thinking about the different kinds of limits. One limit appears as the autonomous outside, all that is just simply there beyond our means of knowing – ('our' being a moot point but referring in some vague way to the reach of Western science), but also – which I think is different – beyond the possibility of human relationality, and thus beyond any kind of mutual experience. I'm particularly interested in the one-sided quest for knowledge of all that is beyond our current capacities of apprehension. 'We' might be out there prospecting and looking for all kinds of ways to extract value, even from the deepest parts of the ocean, but that doesn't mean that the ocean is looking for us; so that notion of a reciprocal understanding is absolutely not there. That's a limit. In the introduction there is a nice phrase about the limit being 'beyond our ground', independent of us, which could be another way of thinking about this lack of reciprocal interest. And then there's also the question of the limits of sensory perception. Those limits connect to some things I wanted to talk about with regards to the chapters by Course and Pauwelussen, both of which draw on narrative and myth as a particular way into these otherwise inaccessible spaces.

So, that was my initial response to the idea of limits, but then the simultaneous presence of heterogenia produces a contrasting sense of expansive relationality that constantly multiplies itself, and it is in these contrasting ways of making difference that we might find new possibilities for thinking about the politics of coexistence, the possibility of articulating different terms of coexistence, the 'making with' idea. This idea is recognisable in the contemporary focus on relationality or the current preoccupation with thinking about what exists in the world and how it comes into being. These are preoccupations with a long history of anthropological concern. And I think that, in some sense, Strathern's position grows out of that kind of space. I really liked the move in the introduction to think about 'heterogeneous limits', but the more I thought about it, the more I wondered: I completely get the figure/ground reversal and I think that the dynamic relationship between figure and ground offers an interesting starting point for analysing this relationship between limits and heterogenia – it's an idea that Kregg Hetherington explores in his work on infrastructure which I have found very useful; but of course in a sense the possibility of figure/ground reversal also hinges on the possibility of relationality, a point that Strathern has explored in very creative ways. So I began to wonder about whether the notion of 'heterogeneous limits' requires an interdependence of some kind, and if that interdependence gets posited from the human point of view, do we then find that we have somehow erased the limits of the autonomous outside? And that got me thinking about the limits of this 'heterogeneous limit' – which starts to get very abstract and confusing, but which might perhaps be more interesting when we look at specific cases. When thinking about how limits and heterogeneities coexist, is it enough to talk through the idiom of figure/ground? Or is it possible that there might also be a politics of erasure in play? I think this possibility comes to the fore when we introduce the Anthropocene as a space of extinction as well as of new possibility.

So, I'm not sure – the concept or image of figure/ground maybe provides us with an analytical solution to how to think about or describe the relationship between limits and heterogenia, but I'm not sure how far it goes in offering the basis for an alternative practice with respect to how human beings engage the wider non-human environment. I was just listening to a really scary report on the radio about the 'resources' of the deep ocean – which I'm sure Stefan knows all about: apparently there are five times more precious metals in the deep ocean than under the existing land mass, and a huge number of species, including bacteria, living in the vents of the deep-sea volcanoes, that could be used to cure all human illnesses. Two huge companies already have prospecting licenses to exploit this potential source of value. Faced with this kind of scenario I feel less sure about whether the figure/ground analytic is going to be powerful enough to provoke delay, or indeed where the politics of this approach might lie. But maybe it's better to discuss this kind of thing through the examples.

s: Are you thinking about the figure/ground story as necessarily always implicating a human interpreter?

p: I suppose so, yes. I feel that this relationship between limits and heterogenia does posit a human interlocutor. The limits are the limits of the human, and the heterogenia are the various ways in which the human might fold into all kinds of diverse relationalities which extend well beyond the human. So, I suppose I do read it like that, I don't know if that was the intention.

s: I think I read it like that too. I do struggle with attempts to get beyond human relationality in ethnographic representation. I like Timothy Morton's notion of hyperobjects – those objects or processes too big to get our heads around, like plutonium and its long, long life – but there's still a part of me that wants to say, 'well, understanding such things inevitably gets us back to questions of how we represent them!' There's that really interesting conversation in the 'limits' section of the book's introduction about the differences and similarities between what Nigel Clark and Kathryn Yusoff are up to. Clark is trying to consider some kind of beyond-human-relationality and (but?) finds that scientific language is a satisfactory tool for articulating that consideration. As somebody who thinks in STS and history of science ways, I'm sceptical of taking on scientific terminology without qualifying or historicising it. For the same reasons, I'm also unconvinced by new materialisms when they are articulated – as in Diana Coole and Samantha Frost's framing in *New Materialisms* – in terms that sound like they come from nineteenth-century thermodynamics, that take that historical formation in the discipline of physics as disclosing the ontology of the world. I like Yusoff's call to not settle the question.

P: I work on the nuclear at the moment, so I'm quite happy with the hyper-object, and the idea of something absolutely beyond the human capacity to address, and yet we have no option but to address it. So, there is an absolute limit and at the same time a need to address that limit in ways that might bring to the fore, or figure, notions of relational possibility. But then we might want to draw on the notion of environmental alterities to posit other imaginings. I like the idea that came up in the chapters, that we might use environmental alterities as theoretical devices or as conceptual or theoretical machines. I still feel this space of the inaccessible has to be kept in mind (which as you say requires some form of representational practice), and thus to some extent frames the struggle to act in meaningful ways. As I watch the nuclear industry I'm always intrigued by how quite uncontroversial, established nuclear science is often sidelined in debates about the politics of nuclear power, to the extent that 'science' doesn't figure in conversations. I felt the spirit of the introduction was that you could actually hold the Nigel Clark-type position at the same time as acknowledging that that wasn't going to be the only or even the most relevant possibility.

S: There's also the question of the *affective charge* of the hyperobject, and how much of the notion of the hyperobject is bound up with it being *scary*.

P: Yes...

S: Is the hyperobject a genre of the sublime? If *that's* the case, then there's this affective charge to it is still *very much* about human relationality – even if it's about the impossibility or difficulty of representation.

P: Yes, I really agree with that. I think that's exactly it: the space is produced by the human. I'm always fascinated by how the nuclear rushes to the top of the chart table of scariness while there are many other things that are equally destructive. The environmental effects of mining, for example, don't seem to produce the same affective force as the spectre of nuclear accidents – despite the tangible and ongoing damage produced by routine, non-accidental opera-tions! So yes, in that sense I totally agree that the affective charge is historically and culturally specific. And yet, we could all drop dead tomorrow, and these material forces would still exist, so the notion of a beyond or an autonomous outside remains important even as we recognise that awareness of the relevance of such forces can only be produced through human concern, fear or even excitement. And this raises another question about what provokes concern, fear or excitement. I'm living now in a community right on the edge of a nuclear site, and on the whole people show very little concern and no fear of the nuclear materials on their doorsteps. When then, are concerns provoked, how do they come to appear and disappear? The answers to these questions of course always register both contingency and specificity – and that's where an ethnographic (and historical) mode of enquiry becomes so important to see when and how things get configured as problems, and to follow the kinds of things that appear and disappear over time and in different contexts. So, I guess I don't have that much trouble in holding the limit and the heterogeneity together at the same time – the challenge is not to collapse them.

s: That's interesting about the alterity that continues to exist, because it seems – well, it's different than the sort of alterity that Michael Taussig wrote about in *Mimesis and Alterity* where it's always about a kind of cultural...

p: Projection...

s: A projection, yes. And a relationality within structures of social inequality – hierarchies, for example, between self and Other. The Other becomes the surrogate self. The subaltern speaks, but only in the language of the orienting self. It occurs to me that the word 'alterities' should never leave out those questions of inequality. I also think of Michelle Murphy's recent work on what she calls 'alter life', – life in the wake of toxic dosage, poisoned land, poisoned bodies. 'Alter life' might suggest that we think, too, about *alter nature*. I wonder: is environmental alterity a synonym for Murphy's 'alter life'?

p: I read 'environmental' as a medium of life, in the way that John Durham Peters talks about elemental media. 'Nature' does carry all these ideas; as you were laying out before, there are at least three dominant 'nature' concepts in circulation. When you were talking about the idea of alter life, I began to wonder about toxic thrivings as being not only after nature, but also as pre-human – if we think about environmental histories and all the ecological happenings that shaped the planet before human life took over.

s: Right.

p: The wipe-outs and things that happened before humans ever even appeared on the scene. The deathly antagonisms, if you like, of which the story of evolution is also an example. I always think 'well, ok we blow ourselves out with a nuclear bomb, it's not necessarily the end of the planet'. There are many possible and plausible after-human thrivings – some of which come into view in the wake of human destruction. And so, in that sense, I think all these scenarios are quite thinkable without the human, except obviously we wouldn't think them because...Why would we?

s: Right. At the same time that it's interesting to think about the historical production of those different kinds of worlds without humans (which would also be worlds without some other species, like variously domesticated organisms and other entities that have adapted or exapted around hominin being). I'm now thinking back to what Donna Haraway says in *Modest Witness*, about the transuranic elements and the production of the Periodic Table, which offered up these empty spaces that later got filled with things like plutonium – which was posited as possible prior to it being wizarded up by human enterprise. And so, the world after humans – which will come – has plutonium in it in a way that the world *without* humans, before humans, didn't. And so, there's this interesting question of how to think about the world after humanity as still inheriting, for example, nuclear humanity's history.

p: Yes, I think it is really important.

s: And so, thinking too about limits as limits that unfold within history ... The limits during the Jurassic are not the same as the limits during the Holocene...

p: Yeah, and I guess that's part of the work that Anthropocene tries to do...

s: Right! Exactly.

p: To suggest that we produce new limits now.

s: Right.

p: And I suppose one of those limits is this one very specific form of 'after nature' that is nature destroyed, and the lack of possibility of a thriving biodiverse world that the humans are destroying.

s: Yeah, and that's where it may be generative to bring together *heterogeneity* and *limits*. Because that section of the introduction about heterogeneity points to all of those historically produced, historically various arrivals at limits, from Donna Haraway's Chthulucene to Marisol de la Cadena's Anthropo-not-seen. And now I'm thinking of a piece I just read by Karen Barad about nuclear waste in the Marshall Islands and the idea that the end of the world has already happened in many different ways for many different people, at different speeds. I think that the notion of *heterogeneous limits* is a compelling way of actually *pointing* to history, to how various limits have already been arrived at. 1945 is one marker…

P: Yeah. So, I guess that in a way what you are saying connects to my starting point, which was to think about how this heterogeneous limit does depend on the possibility of relations, so that kinds of stands against...

S: Right.

P: ...the kind of thing that Karen Barad is talking about, in that sense.

S: Yeah.

P: Yeah, that kind of fits nicely.

S: I'm thinking too of various Indigenous articulations of environment and land that offer very heterogeneous apprehensions of *when* things happen, when the world ended, when the world might yet begin again. I'm thinking of the marine ecologist Max Liboiron and her lab in Canada working with plastic pollutants in First Nations and Indigenous ecologies. Liboiron, who locates herself as Michif (Métis)-settler, argues that *pollution is colonialism*. Colonial enterprise *produces* the idea that there are available sacrificial landscapes into which trash can be placed, thrown 'away'. That then means that the experience of things like toxic leakage from plastics in the sea is totally part of a history of settler colonial dispossession. I think of that as one example of the kind of heterogeneity in environmental politics to which Antonia and Cristóbal are pointing.

P: I think that's a good point… and we should talk about the sea.

S: Oh, yes, right.

P: You mention landscapes, but I was quite struck that Antonia and Cristóbal asked us to talk about the sea as a particular kind of environment and as a specific domain of coexistence. And given that I don't work on the sea – although I do have one good story about the sea – I was struck by a sense that the sea, as it appears in the chapters by Course and by Pauwelussen is very domestic and close to land. It wasn't like your sea [Stefan], and it wasn't like the kind of sea that I worry about, the water that is dragged in and out of the cooling systems of coastal nuclear power stations, 'sea' that is close to land but where the speed and height of the tides and the relationships between marine life and toxicity produce the sea as both a limit and a relation. I was thinking particularly about plastic – and the notion of the limits posed by things that are inaccessible to the senses – stuff like microplastics or isotopes. I don't know what you felt, but I found the sea in their chapters was quite domestic?

s: Yeah.

p: But there was also danger, and there were certainly important forms of life beyond the human and in many ways beyond human control – that was all perfectly clear. But the sea still felt very close to land, it felt like the sea of 'land people', despite the fact that they were fishermen. It wasn't the sea of the deep-sea diver, it wasn't the alien ocean, or sacrificial spaces which are sometimes deemed to be nowhere, when of course they are never nowhere.

s: I agree with that. The seas in both Course's and Pauwelussen's chapters are very domesticated. Each chapter is about a coastal place, a meeting place between land and sea, a site of encounter that is also a zone, for some, of homemaking. The ocean in these pieces is not simply a mirror – not simply a medium – that reflects landed social relations. It animates them. Given the kind of cross-species and cross-medium relations under discussion in both Course and Pauwelussen, I kept thinking of kinship diagrams. These sorts of mappings are usually rendered as rectilinear lines that tie together kin groups 'across' and 'down' generations. Reading Course and Pauwelussen, I kept imagining kinship diagrams taking the form of rectilinear lines that become *refracted* as they cross the water's surface, as they move into that mirror space where they become angled and tangled – like seaweed. I was interested in Course's reporting on Gaelic stories about family members entangled in seaweed, and in Pauwelussen's recounting of crocodile and octopus kin stories in Indonesia. Crocodile-octopus twinship is both intimate and alien. It's about family and consanguinity while simultaneously excessive to it. I agree that the ocean is quite domesticated in the cases treated in Course and Pauwelussen; it's also interesting that one of the ways that happens is through the kinship imaginaries, the kinship practices, that organise this crossing over the surface.

p: Yes, and I was struck how in the two chapters, it happened in quite different ways in terms of this notion of what, or who captures whom? The seals get captured by humans and that sets off a fascinating account of the relationship between form and recognition. This connects back to the discussion of limits and heterogeneities, and the notion of alterity as a form of life that's different from one's own, and yet it is recognisable as such, and a relationship can be made on the basis of that recognition. But some life forms are not recognised as beings with whom one would or could have a relationship, let's say, of care. And then in the case of the seals there is a narrative of capture, a sense of colonisation which dominates those narratives, in the way that the humans keep the clothes of the seals, and thereby prevent them from re-assuming the form in which they can thrive, or even take control. The relationship rests on that sense of capture, which might nevertheless linger on and make other associations, so relations can form, but capture is somehow at the heart of it. Although, I like the fact that there's also the curiosity. I'm very intrigued by the fact that these seals are interested in humans. So, they're popping up, having a look, and laying themselves open to capture. While with the octopus and the crocodile, it is the other way around, it seems to me: that they impose themselves more literally upon the body of the human and in various ways, when they turn up and repossess the – their – human body.

So, I quite like that play between the two case studies. There is kinship in the twinning and definitely a kind of mutual interest, but what I think is really interesting to think about is whether the mutual recognition is primarily about a communicative possibility or whether it's about the right to life. Pauwelussen's chapter seems to be built around this sense of communicative possibility, but the question of who dictates the terms of that communication is quite different from Course's discussion of the human/seal interactions. Environmental politics is often not particularly concerned with communicative possibility, it's about the kind of recognition that underpins a sense of the right to life. I was trying to think of it in terms of the difference between an acknowledgment of interdependence, or its denial, and the sense that human thriving relies on an acknowledgment of interdependence, and the fear that denial is going to catapult us into the worst extremes of the Anthropocene. But then there is also this recognition of communicative possibility, which is what is often most fascinating to people. What kind of communication is possible between species and across alterity? And that seems to be quite a different kind of thing – and kinship idioms play on that question, I think – somehow it's not just about the right to life, it's about communicative possibility.

s: Yeah, that makes a lot of sense. I wonder then if the concept of humble anthropocentrism that Course proposes, kind of actually answers that. I wasn't fully convinced that the anthropocentrism was scaled down or innocent...

p: No. I feel that could only work if you assumed an environment of mutual interest, which isn't usually assumed. So, the fishermen can assume it to a certain point, because they don't want their fish stock to disappear, and they realise they have a vulnerability to the sea. The Indonesian case felt different: there the mutual interest was on terms that the humans couldn't necessarily understand.

s: Right.

p: And these twins turn up in your body.

s: Right, right.

p: It's initiated by the non-human twin, that's what I thought was really different between the two examples; it was quite fascinating actually, and it seemed what was being suggested was a different theory of how humans might consider their place in the world, and what it meant to be human.

s: Right.

p: And how do they then mobilise that possibility? It goes back to my original question of what you actually do with that awareness, in relation to the kind of threat that gets posed by the other models...

s: The threat posed by the other models?

p: Well, the threat posed by this idea that you may or may not recognise interdependence. Because the Indonesians do posit this idea that connects to Viveiros de Castro's discussion of Amerindian commitment to the possibility of a common humanity; there's some sense that things are connected in that way through ideas of something which humans call human, but which would fit with what Course was talking about, as a kind of condition of moral possibilities, set against this idea of whether you recognise the interdependence of things that don't necessarily appear to have that connection at all. I think that the analytical separation of limits and of heterogenia in the introduction helps to think about that kind of complication, and the two chapters demonstrate that limits and heterogenia can come together in quite different ways.

s: Yes. It's useful to multiply the kinds of kinship being imagined here, now having brought in the Viveiros de Castro story. In the Gaelic case, the kinship is very much about lineage and genealogy, whereas, with the Indonesian case, it's much more about incorporation and feeding and those kinds of lateral productions of relationality that aren't only about the heteronormative, patriarchal, patrilineal family.

p: Exactly.

s: Which so much of the selkie story is...

p: Yes, definitely.

s: I just read a science-fiction book by someone called Becky Chambers. It's a book called *To Be Taught, If Fortunate* and it's about exobiologists travelling to other planets, who, in order to accommodate themselves to these other worlds, engage in a practice that they call 'somaforming'. Rather than terraforming and making the environments like Earth, they undergo treatments in which their bodies are transformed to fit within the ecologies that they're going to be examining. I think Chambers means to create a frame for humble anthropocentrism in the way that Course writes about. And it is all about what you're talking about, Penny, this communicative possibility that permits going elsewhere but that also always needs to somaform. And I kept thinking of the cases in these two chapters as kinds of *amphibious multispecies somaforming*. But then I also do wonder to what extent such somaforming is still on *some* people's terms rather than *others*. I fall back into the old Taussig mimesis and alterity question, thinking that the *kind* of alterity that seems to be at stake here is one in which mimicry ultimately secures the centring of the person doing the mimicking.

p: Yes, but it makes me think of your deep-sea scientists actually. They kind of somaform themselves through their technology, they produce environments, their bodies, they become part of these things that can then do something that nobody can do without their casings...

s: Right.

p: So, in that sense it feels like a colonial move to get right down there to the deep ocean and find out what's there so you can take it away. Whereas the octopus is different, in the way they move into the body of another who is also not other, this suggests a different form of somaforming, because the twins are a part and parcel of each other, and they have to find ways to mutate that are not predatory. Maybe that is what is surprising to me, coming from an Andeanist background where beings constantly shape-shift and you can't trust the external form of anything or anybody, because that's the least trustworthy thing. But the transformations are always predatory, so it's always about stealing and killing and getting life force out of another body, as something for your own end. While in this Indonesian case, there's a kind of mutuality to it that's not under control of the humans, which makes it quite interesting – it happens *to* people. Yet at the same time it doesn't seem to damage them unless they make the mistake of not attending to what's going on.

s: Right. I mean, the language that Pauwelussen uses – but I guess is also in circulation among the people she's talking to – is the language of twinning and twinship. So, going back to your observation about domestication, does twinship keep that alterity legible?

p: I suppose there was that sense that you never quite know your twin.

s: Right! Wow.

p: So that the twin is you, but not you, it has that kind of 'but not only' you, in Marisol's terms. It kind of is you, but isn't.

s: Right.

p: Because there's also a sense that if you don't acknowledge your twin, then that could destroy you in some way or other. In both of the chapters there's a sudden moment where the absolute force of the sea as complete limit in terms of this autonomous outside does appear; it's kind of lurking in the background, and so the focus ethnographically is on the relations, but the limit on the relation also exists as a threat, I feel, in both of these pieces.

s: That's interesting to put back into dialogue with limits and heterogeneity: twin and then this kind of outside...

p: This twin that isn't you, so it's not under your control – that's how I was reading it – so that you can kind of seduce it – but I could be just laying the Andean stuff on top of this because this is how they deal with these kinds of issues there – you can treat other kinds of being well, but you can never be sure that you actually really have treated them well. If you do your utmost then things should work out ok, but when you don't – or worse, should you deliberately disrespect – then you've had it, you know, because there's this whole other force that's not you, and could never be you because then you become simply human and this other stuff isn't – so I wonder whether this kind of partial twinning or...

s: Is that a tarrying with limits then? I guess?

p: Yeah, I'm wondering, there is a limit to what twinship is, the limit to the humanity of twinship, let's say. Because the human doesn't become octopus or crocodile, they're quite uneven relationships, I think in both cases. That's why I started, I didn't say so clearly, but I feel the seals are at a bit of a disadvantage... but somehow in Indonesia, the humans seem to be at a disadvantage, in terms of where the power lies. And in the Andes, it's definitely the case that, in this very sentient environment that requires a lot of care, humans can definitely damage the other-than-human beings, but at the same time humans are ultimately more vulnerable, more likely to be wiped out, this kind of apocalyptic thought is very strong there.

ANTONIA: One of the things that we did want to get around to talking about, if possible, was something, Penny, that you started with, which was the extent to which this kind of thinking does or doesn't have a political element to it, and the extent to which this kind of slow thought and slow thinking that we're proposing here, that kind of figure/ground conceptual choreography, is up to the task. And the question that that begs is, what is the task? We're proposing this in a highly charged context of environmental politics that has only accelerated since the time that we first started writing this. So, we're interested in people's reflections on the extent to which this kind of conceptual work is or isn't political, and in what sense it is political, and what kind of politics it might speak of or speak to. Getting together a whole lot of people to talk about the everyday alterity of the environment in a time of urgent crisis, you know... and this is a broader question for academics, I think.

s: Right. Well, I think there's the calling attention to a moment of crisis but also the recognition that there have been many moments of crisis. This is maybe where the analytic of heterogeneity seems super useful – calling attention to the ways in which the world has already ended, as a way of attuning to environmental politics. So that it's not that suddenly there's THE Anthropocene and everything has changed, but rather that there are longer histories of dispossession, of radioactive colonialism, of the Plantationocene, of all of this – and all of these stories that need to constantly be kept visible and constantly remembered.

P: I think something else on that question I wanted to pick up on was this: we've kind of talked about it, but instead of talking about the sea as being domestic, I was also thinking about how the sea is home, the 'sea home' to the seals and the octopuses, but also to the fisherman in a kind of a way, and I was thinking about this relationship between home and displacement because that seems to be a massive human crisis, which is part of the problem with the Anthropocene. There is a massive displacement of humans, the millions of people on the planet who have no home, so the whole notion of the home, and what happens when the home is taken away or destroyed. And there's also this notion of human invasion and colonisation, all these histories of how the colonising impulse places the limits on who has a home and what kind of home gets attended to.

All these questions that we've already discussed, of who or what will thrive, the sort of thrivings of non-humans versus thrivings of humans – most of our concerns are about human thriving. But in fact, our concerns have become about a very limited number of humans busy thriving away, while most humans are displaced. So, I think there is a way in which these questions do raise this as something to think about… I can quickly give you my one example of thinking with the sea, that is really to do with this relationship between species or populations and living beings. The nuclear industry is very sensitive to issues of environmental impact, as are its critics. The particular case I'm referring to arose with respect to the humongous amount of water that is sucked out of the sea, every single hour of the day. These water-cooling systems kill tons of fish. I recently began to follow the case of an energy company that had promised to install acoustic fish deterrents, a specific infrastructure of environmental protection designed to scare fish away from the inlet tunnels. What I found interesting in the light of our current discussion was that these infrastructures could be seen as a kind of place-making technology – enabling fish to remain at home in an environment that was otherwise being made deeply alien to them.

But in the move from the design to the construction process, the company decided that maybe these deterrents were not going to work after all. To drop the idea they had to consult with the public, and demonstrate why they had changed their minds. All kinds of things then came into view. The complexity of this specific estuary – the strengths of the tides, the dangers to those who would have to install and maintain the systems, the complexity of the ecosystems, the many different kinds of fish – fish that can hear, fish that can't hear, big fish, little fish, fish that would never get sucked in anyway, and fish that would get sucked in even if the deterrent was installed. In the end the argument rested on the claim that the fish in question are not in danger, there is no need for these measures because the affected fish are not of 'endangered' species. They're only in danger as individuals and, do we care about individuals? I am fascinated by the concerns that start to appear when the company start messing with the proposed infrastructures of protection. And I began to think about this, about what these human interventions actually mean in relation to whether you are trying to design an environment that in some way is going to maximise a particular possibility, and how at the same time every design is also an improvisation, so everything is both designed and improvised. It's experimental in the one sense of being very controlled, and in the other sense of being experimental in the sense of 'well it's a bit open ended, we'll see where it goes'.

So, I was thinking about the relations that come to the fore when you apply this frame of heterogeneous limits. What limits are in play? What are the limits between species? And between lived lives, whether of fish, or of fishermen, or of nuclear industrialists or whoever? And then also what multiplies in that space? When you start to think about that, you get this massive multiplication which does, I think, pose serious political questions about which fish, or which thrivings we care about, and how we balance energy production against the life of specific fish, or the lives of particular fish species versus our own species. And as the engineers try to work out if there is an optimal way to combine sound and light to scare away particular fish, we find ourselves at the limits of the sensible, with fish that cannot hear, and with humans who cannot know what else they are affecting as they set out to protect fish, either as species or as living beings. Might you kill some other species that you haven't even bothered to think about by interfering with the ecologies of predators and prey, for example? So that kind of multiplication of the field of intervention then brings up all this stuff about the logics of what kind of care is actually being posited here and *how* you limit the intervention. Does the political require you to actually limit something in order to know what are you being political about?

I think the example does actually raise loads of interesting questions, but I don't think it gives an easy answer, but maybe that doesn't matter – maybe it's opening new fields of enquiry that people should stay attentive to. I'm constantly trying to think about this relationship between the engineered solution, the conscious intervention, and the unconscious effect or the kind of fortuitous outcome that you may or may not be attentive to.

s: And the openings and closings that infrastructures are *for*, because while they do offer certain kinds of openings, they also offer closings. So now I'm thinking back to a piece that Corsín-Jiménez and Willerslev wrote about limits. I pulled out a quotation from them, about limits: 'at the moment of their conceptual limitation, concepts capture their own shadow and become something other than what they are'. They're talking about different modes of subsistence, and the concept of a particular kind of hunting, or a particular kind of gathering – when it's pushed to its limit it becomes something other than what it is. Which is what I'm hearing you say, Penny, with respect to these kinds of acoustic infrastructures: when they're pushed to their limit, they start to become something other and open up these different possibilities. But then I'm also interested in the ways that they close them down as well, or they ossify certain social relations and install those as environmental infrastructures. And I've been feeling that the conversation about *environmental infrastructures* and the conversation about *environmental alterities* will be interesting to put together... environmental infrastructural alterities and their discontents. Who are the infrastructures for?

p: It's also how the infrastructures become environments, you know?

s: Exactly.

p: I'm interested in that as well because I think that opens another set of questions about what the *sea* is, again, because the sea in these chapters is very stable. It's not full of previous interventions that are still just there, but not recognised, you know? That's what takes me back to the very beginning, that made me think about the existence of isotopes and microplastics, and things that are just what the sea is made of, let alone how the currents are moving or the sea itself as a temporal environment, which has all kinds of infrastructural histories. I suppose we're both saying in the end that these historical questions are incredibly important to thinking the politics of how we got to be where we are, and where things may go next, I guess.

S: Yeah, and trying to surface what those histories are, because thinking with notions of *after nature* and infrastructure together, I think of the possibility of theorising something like *infra-nature*, like the nature that has become so worked upon that it is taken to *be* nature itself. So, the plastic ocean is the infra-nature that we live with now. And that's a historical arrival and it's useful to constantly push that notion of infrastructure as a *query* into what counts as the environment. How does infrastructure or infra-nature produce kinds of alterities, or certain kinds of environmental alterities? The environmental alterity that we live in now of a radioactive ocean that's acidifying, that is rising – those are all kinds of *alters*, these are *alter natures* to what the ocean was prior to 1920.

P: Definitely. And I guess infrastructures do produce moral architectures, in the sense of opening a space to think about this relationship between human and other species as an issue of moral and ethical recognition… Maybe that's something that connects.

S: Yes.

P: Yes, that's a cool place to end.

REFERENCES

Barad, K., 'After the End of the World: Entangled Nuclear Colonialisms, Matters of Force, and the Material Force of Justice', *Theory & Event* 22.3 (2019): 524–550.

Chambers, B., *To be Taught, If Fortunate* (London: Hodder & Stoughton, 2019).

Coole, D., and S. Frost, *New Materialisms: Ontology, Agency, and Politics* (Durham, NC: Duke University Press, 2010).

Corsín Jiménez, A., and Willerslev, R., 'An Anthropological Concept of the Concept': Reversibility among the Siberian Yukaghirs', *JRAI* n.s., 13 (2007): 527–544.

Liboiron, M., *Pollution is Colonialism* (Durham, NC: Duke University Press, 2021).

Haraway, D., *Modest Witness@Second Millennium FemaleMan Meets OncoMouseTM: Feminism and Technoscience* (New York: Routledge, 1997).

Helmreich, S., *Alien Ocean: Anthropological Voyages in Microbial Seas* (Berkeley, CA: University of California Press, 2009).

Hetherington, K., 'Introduction. Keywords of the Anthropocene'. In K. Hetherington, ed., *Infrastructure, Environment and Life in the Anthropocene* (Durham, NC: Duke University Press, 2019).

McDermott Hughes, D., 'Third Nature: Making Space and Time in the Great Limpopo Conservation Area'. *Cultural Anthropology*, 20.2 (2005), 157–184.

Murphy, M., 'Alterlife and Decolonial Chemical Relations', *Cultural Anthropology*, 32.4 (2017): 494–503.

Peters, J. D., *The Marvelous Clouds: Toward a Philosophy of Elemental Media* (Chicago, IL: University of Chicago Press, 2015).

Purdy, J., *After Nature: A Politics for the Anthropocene* (Cambridge, MA: Harvard University Press, 2015).

Strathern, M., *After Nature: English Kinship in the Late Twentieth Century* (Cambridge: Cambridge University Press, 1992).

——, 'Cutting the Network', *JRAI*, 2.3 (1996): 517–535.

——, *The Relation: Issues in Complexity and Scale* (Chicago, IL: Prickly Pear Press, 2019)

Taussig, M., *Mimesis and Alterity: A Particular History of the Senses* (New York and London: Routledge, 1993).

Tsing, A., *The Mushroom at the End of the World: On the Possibility of Life in Capitalist Ruins* (Princeton, NJ: Princeton University Press, 2015).

Viveiros de Castro, E., 'Cosmological Deixis and Amerindian Perspectivism', *JRAI*, 4.3 (1998): 469–488.

SECTION 2

FORESTS

THE NON-RELATIONAL FOREST

TREES, OIL PALMS AND THE LIMITS TO RELATIONAL ONTOLOGY IN LOWLAND ECUADOR

Stine Krøijer

'I am unsure if I will ever be able to get to know them', Delfín said, as we were sitting in the late afternoon on the porch outside his house overlooking the Aguarico river. The same morning, we had visited a new plantation of African oil palms, which had profoundly transformed the forested territory of the Sieko-pai. Delfín, an elderly *inti-ba-ikë* (shaman-leader) of the community, was concerned, and spoke of the alteration of the landscape as an invasion of other beings that it would be difficult for him to know and relate to.

My interest in this particular plantation and its story was sparked by the news coverage about how an Indigenous people in lowland Ecuador, the Sieko-pai, had clear-cut part of their forest to engage in commercial palm oil production as subcontractors to a neighbouring plantation company (El Universo 2011). I had previously conducted fieldwork among the Sieko-pai – on their actual and virtual strategies to govern oil exploitation within their territory (Krøijer 2003, 2017, 2018) – but the news stories compelled me to explore 'the political life of trees'; that is, how people relate to trees, and the forms of politics that this might engender. The history of the plantation was surprising not only because the Sieko-pai had decided to fell their own forest, but also because the Ecuadorian Ministry of Environment accused them of violating 'the rights of nature'. A few years earlier, the indigenous movement in Ecuador had pressed for nature rights, which were integrated into the Ecuadorian Constitution in 2008, but with the felling of the forest the same set of rights was turned against part of the population who had first pressed for them. In public, the Sieko-pai's new plantation landscape constituted a break with the picture painted of indigenous peoples as 'natural' stewards of the tropical forest, but it also offered an entry point into understanding the role of trees in Amerindian cosmology.

Over the past decade, several works have been written about plantation economies, among others Greg Grandin's book on the rise and fall of automobile magnate Henry Ford's utopian fantasy of a 'Fordlandia' modelled on small town monoculture production in the American Midwest. In 1927, Henry Ford bought land in the Brazilian Amazon to grow rubber, extract raw materials for the production of cars and impose scientific management on both nature and local workers. By 1945, this project of taming, ordering and subjecting nature to capital was abandoned, after both plants and people had been devastated by plagues and illnesses, waste and violence (Grandin 2009). Donna Haraway and Anna Tsing, among others, have used the term 'Plantationocene' to describe such imperialist schemes of monocrop agribusiness that are characterised by land enclosure and alienated forms of production, and which involve processes of domestication, slavery and corporate control over human and non-human beings alike (Tsing 2012; Haraway 2015; Haraway et al. 2016). These authors show how new forms of human mastery and control mark the monocultural landscape of the plantation, even though the same studies also point to how other relations and world-making projects thrive at its margins.

This chapter follows a somewhat different path by describing the forms of alterity that emerge under the shadow of the substitution of a forested agro-ecosystem for a commercial agro-industrial one. By zooming in on Delfín's relationship to the large *ceiba* (kapok) tree, which still grows in a few places in the forest around the village of San Pablo Katëtsiaya where he lives, and the African oil palms of the plantation, I come to describe two figures of alterity: First, the spirit of the *ceiba*, the *yëi-watí*, which is an incorporated 'other' and subject to both control and care. And second, the oil palm plantation that is experienced as *po'say'yo* (empty), characterised by beings that escape human attempts at relating to, knowing and 'owning' them (see Fausto 2008; Brightman, Fausto and Grotti 2016). The tropical forest where the *ceiba* towers is not an external and stable 'nature' – in accordance with a 'Western' distinction between nature and culture – but is seen as 'culture' and full of relations between various forms of persons (see Rival 1993, 2016). The oil palm plantation, on the contrary, becomes a space of environmental alterity, at best inhabited by 'potential affines' (Viveiros de Castro 2001: 24).

Analytically, this work thus investigates the limits of a relational ontology that has underpinned most studies of the entanglements of nature and culture and multi-species relations over the past decade (see for example Blaser 2009; de la Cadena 2010, 2015; Tsing 2015). In only elucidating the relational fabric of the forest, or attending exclusively to multispecies relations, for example, this work could easily have overlooked non-relations, namely how capitalist relations of exploitation reconfigure not only what a tree is, but also what a nature could be. When using the term 'nature' in this sense, I am referring to new environmental alterities, or the realm of dangerous beings and potential affines that are not (yet) susceptible to encompassment and incorporation. Delfín's concern over the new beings of the oil palm plantation is a case in point.

In this article, I take my point of departure in conversations between 2014 and 2016 with the shaman-leader Delfín, his grandson Hernán, who studied forest management at the university in Quito, and other members of the village of San Pablo Katëtsiaya, including Esaias, who was the main person in the community promoting oil palm cultivation. I contrast their thoughts about large slow-growing trees with their concerns and experiences regarding the new plantation landscape. Among the Sieko-pai, large slow-growing trees such as the *ceiba* are seen as 'persons' holding 'capabilities' of their own – capacities which can be controlled by an able shaman. The new oil palm trees growing on the plantation are unknown 'others', a non-immanent forest, which (might) have other owners. Following this line of thought, the plantation is not the 'mono-culture' conventionally depicted in the literature (see Tsing 2012), but an environmental alterity or indeed nature, in the modern sense of the term, that is, a wild and uncontrolled realm that escapes human attempts at knowing and owning it, in the way that shamans usually relate to their auxiliary spirits.

In developing this point, I build on Viveiros de Castro's theorisation of Amerindian cosmology (1998) and on work on affinity and alterity, adoptive filiation and ownership in Amazonia (Viveiros de Castro 2001, Fausto 2007, 2008; Brightman, Fausto, and Grotti 2016). While the body of scholarship on

Amazonia has mainly focused on jaguars and pets, orphans and marriage alliances, the roles of plants and trees in a transformational cosmos have received significantly less attention. With this work, I will begin to make up for this omission while retaining the overall approach with its potential for understanding contemporary environmental conflicts. In the following, I first explain in further detail how the Sieko-pai became palm oil cultivators and outline the controversy it produced, before delving further into the cosmology of trees in this new context. This is my point of departure for unfolding a new form of environmental alterity, at stake in an epoch often referred to as the Anthropocene.

COMING TO AN END

The Sieko-pai belong to the Western Tucano linguistic group, historically dwelling between the Napo and Putumayo Rivers in what is today the Amazonian border zone between Ecuador, Peru and Colombia. The Ecuadorian Secoya – or Sieko-pai, as they have auto-denominated themselves for the past ten years – have been described in the ethnographic literature as able horticulturalists and as a group having 'a flexible adaptation strategy' to their forested environment (Vickers 1981, 1989a; Krøijer 2017). Today they live in four communities along the Aguarico river, in an area that since the early 1970s has been marked by the expansion of the extractive frontier. Oil extraction was not the only economic activity launched at this time to develop and modernise this supposedly unproductive part of the country: in 1978 the company *Palmeras del Ecuador* was given a 9,850-ha title on land that the Sieko-pai considered to be their community hunting grounds.

The Sieko-pai first came to live on the Aguarico river by escaping brute enslavement during the rubber boom south of the Putumayo, after which they settled far up blackwater tributaries of the Putumayo and Napo Rivers, with only footpaths connecting the distant settlements. Conditions of continued debt peonage under an abusive patron on the Huajoya River led two families, their children and a few young people including Delfín, to flee the area in 1942. The Sieko-pai settled on the Cuyabeno River and at Sokorá on the Aguarico

River, intermarrying with Siona families (Vickers 1989a). While dwelling here, the Siona and Secoya were 'contacted' in the 1950s by the Summer Institute of Linguistics (SIL), who were sent on a civilising mission by the Ecuadorian state. Around the same time, the state launched its comprehensive colonisation policy of *tierras baldias* (empty lands), which urged poor peasant families, including indigenous people from the highlands, to take up life in these supposedly backward and unproductive parts of the country (Wasserstrom and Southgate 2013). This colonisation process also entailed a deliberate strategy of racial mestizaje, blending 'white civilisation' and 'Indian savagery' (Whitten 1981),[1] if not brushing aside the presence of people living there altogether. The missionaries convinced the Sieko-pai to move up the Aguarico River in 1973, to San Pablo Katëtsiaya, where, as Delfín and other elders later explained, the territory at first seemed not only abundant, but also endless.

During the first years in San Pablo, few were interested in working for money. In the 1970s some found temporary work within the booming oil sector, but even many years later work for the plantation company was considered too demanding and unrewarding. But *colonos* (settlers) also followed the oil, which caused struggles over territorial control. After a lengthy process to obtain territorial rights, which also fostered a stronger attachment to the growing indigenous movement, the Secoya gained the right to 42,614 ha on the Aguarico River in 1990 (NASIEPAI 2014). By then they were already surrounded by the *Palmeras del Ecuador* to the west, oil wells and *colono* communities to the north and west, and other indigenous groups to the south. Contamination depleted the fish resources, and illegal colonisation, overhunting and steep population growth all contributed to a new sense of enclosure and land scarcity. The Sieko-pai's decision to clear-cut part of their forested territory to engage in commercial palm oil production should be understood in the context of these historical antecedents, though they do not fully explain all the ways in which the territory became a matter of concern after the forest was felled.

Former president of the Secoya organisation, Esaias, who had headed the territorial claim since the 1970s, was now one of the people taking the lead in the new palm oil venture. When I visited him again, in 2014, he appeared from behind a palm tree holding a string trimmer, which, he explained, he used for weeding in the plantation. He agreed to sit down in the shadow below his house to tell me about the political controversy that arose after the felling of the forest: 'I called for a meeting to discuss the cultivation of oil palms', he began; 'I said, "We need to have something to live from when there are no more trees. The forest will come to an end."' Even though views had been divided among the families, he had managed to convince everybody that 20 families should be allowed to cultivate oil palms on part of the collectively owned land.

Esaias was a well-rounded man around the age of fifty-five, clad in one of his many bright coloured tunics that have given the Sieko-pai their name as 'the people of multiple colours' (*sieko-pai*). I had first met him in 2000, when I was conducting fieldwork in San Pablo Katëtsiaya, and he was the president of the Secoya Organisation *Organisación Indigena Secoya del Ecuador* (OISE), struggling to defend the land from a new round of exploration for oil (Krøijer 2003, 2018). Esaias and his brother were educated at SIL's Pentecostal mission-ary school, but also co-founded the first Siona-Secoya organisation to secure collective territorial rights in the face of rapid colonisation of their land.[2] Now, almost 40 years later, Esaias stated that his main concern is with 'the economy'. He had developed 'friendly relations' with the *gerente* (CEO) of the plantation company, and with his assistance the 20 families managed to get a loan from the public lending institution *Corporación Nacional Financiera*, in order to clear the land and purchase African oil palm seedlings, machinery and pesticides. With the clear-cutting of the land to plant oil palms, Esaias's own prediction of the forest 'coming to an end' became a self-fulfilling prophecy.

The Sieko-pai's decision to plant oil palms on their territory went against policies in Ecuador and beyond that seek to incentivise forest conservation, and constitutional provisions ascribing ecosystem rights to forests. The Ecuadorian Ministry of the Environment did not, therefore, take the felling of primary forest lightly, and in 2011, the 20 families were fined US $375,000 'for destructive action in highly vulnerable ecosystems'. This fine for an indigenous group alleg-edly violating 'the rights of nature' – a set of rights pressed for and won by the indigenous movement in the 2008 constitutional reform process under the newly elected President Rafael Correa (Acosta 2010; Gudynas 2015) – made national news. According to the constitution, nature rights entail that, ecosystems, such as primary forests, hold the right to exist and flourish (art. 10: 71–74).[3] These new rights were interpreted as a legal continuity of Amerindian cosmology and a reaction against a modern dichotomisation of nature and culture (see for example de la Cadena 2015).

In the media, the Sieko-pai's actions were represented as highly surprising, and in an interview, members of Ecuadorian NGO Acción Ecológica described the Sieko-pai's oil palm venture as yet another sad example of an indigenous group giving in to capitalism and abandoning their noble role as custodians of the tropical forest. Even though the wider implications of the new legislation are still unclear – including how the state will administer its duty to prevent harm, enforce the law and restore damaged ecosystems – the case shows how the forestry law and the 'rights of nature' were turned against a local community. At the same time, the plantation company's involvement in the felling of the forest and securing the bank loan went unnoticed. The public debate demonstrated that the Sieko-pai – somewhat contrary to their own view on the matter – were represented by the state and NGOs alike as external to the ecological system holding rights, and they were even described as standing against it.

The Sieko-pai publicly refused to pay the fine, a sum that was equivalent to the cost of regenerating the forest cleared from their land, but they did participate in a meeting with the Ministry. Esaias explained: 'We told them that we have tried to be flexible, but that we refuse to pay the fine, because we also need something to live from'. In the face of their refusal, he continued, the Ministry tried to compel them to adopt one of two courses of action to raise the necessary funds: they could either join the *Socio Bosque* programme with forests still standing on their land, and pay the fine from the incentive income, or they could use any future compensation from oil companies operating on their land to pay the penalty. The Sieko-pai rejected both options in an assembly of their organisation, arguing that either path would fundamentally undermine their sense of self-determination. Instead of fighting the Ministry directly, however, they opted to bide their time, avoiding open confrontation, and soon learned that the environmental authorities were not taking any further action on the matter. Through this flexible and somewhat evasive strategy, which involved avoiding state interpellation, the Sieko-pai were able to retain a sense of autonomy (Krøijer 2017).[4]

The problematic relationship to the Ecuadorian state did not hinder Esaias's ongoing friendship with the *gerente* of the plantation company – who helped with money (putting up collateral for the bank loan) and technical advice, and who acted as a reliable buyer of their new palm oil produce. In Amazonia, friendship is a form of relationship, often maintained with non-relatives for matters of lending, trading and work, guided by notions of mutual trust (Santos-Granero 2007; Killick 2008; Penfield 2016). 'For the time being we are living peacefully', Esaias concluded, pointing to the relatively stable income he and a few other families managed to gain from selling palm oil to their new powerful ally. After several failed business attempts in the past – involving different cash crops, transportation and cattle – the palm oil plantation, Esaias felt, had taken his business ventures to a new level. Today he was able to hire *colono* laborers to help out in the plantation, particularly with the strenuous weeding among the trees.

'For now, I am only at war with the grass', he ended our conversation with a smile, which in the situation seemed to indicate that after finishing the fresh juices brought to us by his wife, he would need to get the string trimmer and his workers back up to speed. I only later understood how this comment could also be interpreted as a hint at the unwanted agency of slow-growing trees and at the form of 'care' and ownership elicited by a plantation landscape (see Brightman, Fausto, and Grotti 2016).

TREE BEINGS

Not everybody was equally at peace. My hosts, Delfín and his extended family, were among the stern opponents of the palm oil venture. Delfín and his grandson Hernán, who accompanied me during the conversation with Esaias that day, had remained silent and uncommunicative throughout the tour of the plantation and the conversation about it. Even though they were cousins, Esaias and Delfín had chosen two different paths in life, the first being a stern pentecostalist, whereas the second descended from a renowned line of shaman-leaders in the Ecuadorian Amazon. As we were canoeing back home after the visit, Delfín suggested making a stop in a piece of intact forest behind his own house where we could visit one of the last large *ceiba* trees in this part of the territory. After walking around it, he explained:

> The spirit (watí) of the large ceiba tree is called yëi-watí. If you are near the tree in the early morning or at dusk, you can probably hear some noise: that is the sound of the spirits opening or closing the doors to their home. There are different spirits but they all like to live in the large slow-growing trees such as ceiba or cedro. They live their life much like we do. They are human beings (pai); the shamans can see them through their ceremonies. The shaman goes to visit their home and live with them for extended periods of time. The spirits of the ceiba resemble white people; they wear hats like the Kichwa. When they leave their home, they float through the forest and glide over the mirror of the water surface. They are carrying their babies. Sometimes you can hear them crying. They live like us in their daily activities, but they do not eat like us: they only consume worms, grubs and fungi.

As the quote illustrates, the *yëi-watí* are persons who, from their bodily point of view, lead human lives. This suggests that at least some trees are part of the same perspectival logic found across lowland Amazonia (see Viveiros de Castro 1998). The forest is full of different beings that all descend from a common condition of humanity – they are all *pai* (persons) – and the skilled shaman arrives at their spirit houses, lives with them and eats like they do. In this way, and aided by the drinking of *yagé* (the plant-based hallucinogenic also known as ayahuasca), the shaman comes to know the different beings of the forest. It is a process of knowing that relies on bodily metamorphosis; the shaman first 'gets to know' the beings, learns to receive their guidance and master their capabilities.

The beings of the forest are referred to as *watí* in *pai-koka*, which, due to the influence of missionaries, has been translated into *espiritus* (spirits). In the new spirit of evangelism in the 1970s, a time when missionaries from SIL moved into San Pablo, most Sieko-pai converted to Pentecostalism, and the drinking of *yagé* was prohibited (Payaguaje 1994). In the prolonged repression of 'pagan beliefs',

FIG. 2.1   Delfín Payaguaje and Ceiba Tree (Photograph by © Mike Kollöffel)

the *watí* were for years mostly talked about as 'malicious' spirits or beings, a view that has been reproduced in the scarce anthropological literature on Sieko-pai shamanism (Vickers 1989b).

According to Delfín, this rendering of the *watí* as inherently malicious was not entirely correct. Within the last ten years, he has resumed the drinking of yagé and the transiting of bodily perspectives that his father was so famous for, at the request of middle-class Ecuadorians and international travellers, who use the hallucinogenic brew in their process of spiritual self-discovery. Regardless of this changing context of yagé-drinking, Delfín sided with his father in describing it as a knowledge process, aimed at understanding the world and the composition of the cosmos (Payaguaje 1994; see also Kopenawa and Albert 2013). By 'getting to know' these beings and their capabilities through bodily metamorphosis, he and other shamans are able to know who is causing what action, in order to cure illnesses, but also to steer certain social relations.

What was most striking in the account was how the *yëi-watí* appeared to Delfín as white people wearing hats like the *Runa* (Kichwa). After returning home and while we were sitting on the porch outside his house, he explained in more detail about the plantation and about how the capabilities of the *watí* are comparable to those of human beings:

> The watí have power *tutu kë'i* or *tutu kë'watí*, but the power is of the forest. It is like a spider web, thin invisible threads that the spirits leave behind when moving through the forest. If someone then walks through the forest, it can stick like a spider web. We say that is the sweat of the spirit. When the shaman talks to the spirit [in the process of healing] it will say that the sick person 'has caught my sweat'.

The Sieko-pai use the same word for the power of spirits as the power of human persons. The prefix *tutu kë'* means capability while the suffix *'i'* or *'watí'* refers to the bodily form (human persons and spirit beings, respectively). As already alluded to above, these beings may interfere in human lives, but if their capabilities should have any non-incidental effect in the world – beyond inflicting sweat (fever) due to people accidentally crossing their path, for example – the being must stand in relation to a shaman. The shaman becomes the 'owner' of spirits and steers the actions of the *watí* by talking to it, convincing it to use its capabilities for desired ends. Apart from being essential to cure illnesses, Delfin said that the *yëi-watí* of the *ceiba* tree can, for example, also influence human physical wellbeing and sense of bodily strength, or even guide persons to find their path in life. In this sense, humans and spirits have interconnected social lives – they are part of the relational fabric of the forest – but they have different bodily capabilities. The power of slow-growing trees thus goes beyond their role both as symbol (see Rival 1993, 1998; Reichel-Dolmatoff 1996) and as index, rather compelling human people to pursue a particular course of action (Kohn 2013). In *How Forests Think* (2013), Kohn situates representation in a broader non-human world and describes the forest as 'an ecology of selves' where all beings are capable of creating and interpreting signs (ibid.: 7–9). However, the reduction of individual trees to indexical signs bypasses their agentive complexity (Herrera and Pálsson 2014: 240), especially on the extractive frontier.

The spirit or being of the *ceiba* tree – the appearance of the *yëi-watí* as whites that resemble highland Kichwa (Runa) through the hats they wear – suggests that the ontological being of the *ceiba* involves a process of 'bodily' incorporation of alterity, through which they become relationally controlled and owned. In the colonial taming of the Amazonian frontier, the Runa were brokers in inter-ethnic relations, which included an active role in slave raiding and trading, as workers at the Jesuit missionary *reducciones* along the Napo River, and as the right hand of the rubber patrons during the 1880–1914 rubber boom (Muratorio 1998; Cipolletti 2017). In the eyes of the Sieko-pai, this has always given them a position closer to powerful outsiders and persons superior to themselves in the colonial hierarchy. Over the two generations that have passed since Delfín's grandfather fled the Algodón River, a tributary of the Putumayo in the heart of the area controlled by the infamous rubber cartel Casa Arana (Taussig 1987; Hvalkof 2000; Santos-Granero and Barclay 2002; Cipolletti 2017), the Runa have become the largest indigenous group in lowland Ecuador, settling primarily along the main rivers. Over several centuries, the Runa were enemies of the Sieko-pai, as well as other small groups of indigenous people in the Ecuadorian lowland, but in the past twenty years they have also become the preferred partner in interethnic marriages (see also High 2015), being seen as more educated and civilised and better at doing business. Several anthropologists before me have described the desire to make marriage arrangements with former enemies (Viveiros de Castro 2001, 2004; High 2015) which, among the Sieko-pai, also implied the incorporation of the Runa into their social world as affinal kin.

Delfín's description of the *yëi-watí* as Runa and Runa-like thus seems to suggest that their alterity has become incorporated into the spiritual world of the Sieko-pai, in a way analogous to what is done today with Runa affinal kin. The being of the *ceiba* tree encompasses the power of the Sieko-pai's principal 'other', but it is an 'internal alterity', so to speak, which is familiar to the old shaman-leader. In a context of colonial memories of oppression, as Michael Taussig has noted, the shamanic visions become a way to restore order (Taussig 1987: 329) and transform exterior power into an animate controllable force. In this sense, the *ceiba* tree is alterity brought under control by becoming incorporated and mastered.

It is important to note that the resulting familiarity, in Delfín's view, is not the outcome of a historical process. The tree beings have not changed with time because, as he expressed it in response to my continuous questioning, 'the *watí* can transform, but always remain the same'. The key seems to be that their transformability – their change of bodily appearance, hats (!) and capabilities – is exactly what effects the continuity of their (superior) power. The shamanic relation to the auxiliary spirits is 'affinity all the way down' (Viveiros de Castro 2001), being less a restoration of order on the colonial extractive frontier than an appropriation and control of relations of alterity through logics of master-ownership (Fausto 2008). Throughout Amazonia, master-ownership is a form of relation known from the spirit-masters of animals and plants, and found between warrior and captive, in relation to adopted children and pets, and between shamans and their spirits. It is also an asymmetrical relation that involves both control and care, enclosure or incorporation (ibid.: 323–333).

All this suggests that the substitution of a known cultural forest with an agro-industrial palm oil plantation renders colonial relations 'visible in a form other than themselves' (Strathern 1988: 182), namely as various tree species and spirits. The *yëi-watí* of the ceiba tree suggests that the forest ecology is not only marked by colonial difference and alterity, but that this has quite literally been incorporated by forest beings. As a consequence, the forest is not a stable, external nature that is simply ascribed symbolic or cultural meaning; it is made of transformational, relational entities, which shamans can come to know and control. The ceiba tree is the first figure of environmental alterity – an incorporated and immanent one, but one that inevitably also reopens the question of how to think about the oil palms and their masters.

OIL PALMS AND EMPTINESS

Delfín found that the felling of the large slow-growing trees in particular was leaving the territory empty. The resulting *poe'say'yo* (empty space) was described by most members of the community as 'a long distance between trees and not many animals to hunt', for which reason the Sieko-pai found themselves increasingly unable to make a living off and in the forest. In Delfín's view, however, this emptiness essentially concerned the fact that the tree-spirits were moving away, as their houses – the large, slow-growing trees – were felled. The new oil palm plantation around the community simply voided the area of social relations that he was able to engage with and control: 'When we cut the forest and the large trees', he explained, 'the spirits have no place to live. They simply go someplace else'.

The emptiness of the forest reminded him of the barrenness that existed in mythical time, prior to the labour of *Wi-watí* (the spirit of growth) who, in ancient times, had made the Amazon tropical forest 'come into being'. Our frequent conversations about the current situation within the territory would compel him to relate the story of how the forest (*airo*), and what we would today call biodiversity, was first created in an encounter between *Nañë* (the Moon, and primary mover of events in Sieko-pai mythology) and *Wi-watí*:

> In the wind a person appears. Nañë [the moon, creator] recognises it as Wi-watí. Wi-watí is the spirit of growth; when he shouts, plants grow. On arriving, Wi-watí shouts 'wii-nooo' with force, and the forest grows. After the first cry, the forest only consists of hardwood trees. The trees are so hard that they are impossible to cut or fell. Nañë burns the forest; he destroys it. Then Wi-watí shouts again, but the same process repeats itself. When Wi-watí shouts for the third time, what we recognise as a forest starts to grow: hard and soft-wood trees, many different plants and beings. [...] The Amazon forest is limited by the force of Wi-watí's voice. The place where his voice was not heard is empty, a desert, and the home of other peoples.

The story concerns both the Sieko-pai as a forest people and the practice of shifting cultivation, and it assigns emptiness to the land of 'others'. Today, this barrenness formerly associated with the land of the other groups, and especially with white people, is emerging within the Sieko-pai's own territory and due to their own actions. The emptiness of these foreign lands as well as of the oil palm plantation is characterised as being 'without life', and hence deprived of *tutu kë' watí* (the power and capabilities of spirits), which Delfín and other shamans can relate to.

Analogous to Carlos Fausto's question in *Feasting on People* (2007) about how people can hunt and eat animals if they know they are persons, one may similarly wonder how the Sieko-pai can fell their trees if they know that they are *pai* (persons)? In light of the understanding that trees hold capabilities of their own, doing away with their potentially dangerous agentive qualities seems to be at least part of the answer, particularly when seen from the perspective of the Pentecostal members of the community. Recalling the eloquent ending of Esaias's statement during the visit to the oil palm plantation, about how he now only found himself 'at war with the grass', the agency of trees was not equally desirable to all community members.

Instead, caring for the plantation crops has become quite a chore for some of the 20 families, who find the weeding both extremely laborious and boring. Few had the same monetary means as Esaias in order to hire workers from the outside, nor his possibilities of cultivating a friendship with the manager of the plantation company. This brought two kinds of alterities and 'ownership' into tension. Esaias and his plantation are an index of a relationality dominated by capitalist ownership and exploitation, which through palm oil creates an emptiness (*po'say'yo*) that comes to exist alongside the encompassed alterity of the *yëi-watí*.

At the same time, the planting of oil palms has brought concerns that are more fundamental than questions about future income and the pending environmental fine. Several people in the village expressed the worry that the new oil palms could house alien spirits, or, in other words, that they permitted the entrance into the territory of new and potentially malicious beings. In Delfín's view, these new trees were unlikely spirit houses, but nonetheless he and others were beset by doubt as to whether they were causing harm. He wondered if he would ever 'be able to get to know them'. The lack of relations to this empty space of transcendental alterity implied that its powers were uncontrollable for the time being.

In this ambience, people carefully monitored the trees and the extent to which these alien beings were interfering in people's lives. On the most immediate level, of course, the toxicity of the chemicals used to control the weeds was causing the death of fish in a tributary of the Aguarico River, which for the past several years has been one of the community's only sources of freshwater fish. On a more speculative plane, perhaps, which nonetheless thrived in the community, a wave of thefts of outboard motors was ascribed to the actions of economically ambitious others – somebody entering the community from the outside bent on causing harm (see Krøijer 2018). The void left behind by the departing *watí* made these changes largely outside the shamans' control and subject of collective concern.

CONCLUSION

Nearly 30 years ago, Rival showed how among the Waorani, people and forests are experienced as holding interconnected social lives (Rival 1993; 2003). Kohn has continued this line of thinking about the tropical forest by defining it as 'an ecology of selves' that like human beings are involved in semiotic processes (Kohn 2013). According to the Sieko-pai, the first humans, such as the *Wi-watí*, were makers of the forests – and the *airo* (forest) is cultural, not natural, and hence at the core of an Amerindian perspectivist cosmology. A forest is not simply an object for humans to exploit, but rather filled with non-human persons to whom one must relate.

This article contributes to the vast literature on Amerindian groups, cosmology and nature by adding trees to the discussions of Amerindian perspectivism. Here I have outlined two forms of environmental alterity – the Runa-like alterity of the *yëi-wati*, which can be known and owned through bodily metamorphosis, and the transcendental alterity of the plantation. If we think along the lines suggested by Delfín, the plantation of African oil palms seems to entail the emergence of an empty space within Sieko-pai territory that is filled with unrelated or undomesticated others – invasive species/spirits, if you will, which are beyond human control.

When shamanic knowledge of the ecology is organised around knowing and controlling its transformability, beings that cannot be known and related to come to pose a problem. The process of substitution of forest landscapes, which the oil palm venture entailed, also occasioned a full reversal of the distinction between nature and culture. If the Amazonian tropical forest is indeed *culture*, inhabited by different kinds of *pai* (persons), who perceive themselves as human (see Viveiros de Castro 1998, 2012), the new palm oil plantation is alterity, *nature* in the Western transcendental sense of the term, whose exteriority is a challenge to continued self-determination. It is possible, obviously, that the distant and potential affinity of oil palms and other stranger-items will become encompassed and known in another form.

Historically, Amazonia has been looked upon from Europe as one of the planet's last wild and unknown places, but the story of the Sieko-pai and their forest suggests that transcendental environmental alterity is best associated with the plantation, its genetically manipulated crops, invasive species and mono-cultural mode of production. From this perspective, terms like the Plantationocene wrongly seem to suggest that plantations are spaces of absolute human mastery. Instead, continued attention to non-relationality – spaces, beings and entities that resist attempts at knowing and relating to them – has the potential to critically engage both the underlying tenets of the literature on the Anthropocene, as well as its assumption that human beings are having a fundamental and equally distributed impact on the planet.

This does not suggest that nature is of the same essence as the renderings of nature found since the Enlightenment in everything from early travellers' tales romanticising the wild unknown to the colonisation policies of countries like Ecuador, casting Amazonia as uncivilised empty land. In other parts of the world, such as Denmark, people are striving to re-establish wild nature through rewilding initiatives, seeking to orchestrate a space of transcendental alterity outside human control and resurrect an essentialist notion of nature, while new environmental alterities and emptiness are emerging in unexpected ways, even in Amazonia. We should take seriously how these alterities cut against a relational ontology.

NOTES

1   As Whitten has shown, whiteness was, in colonial times, associated with the nobility of Spanish descent, but after independence, it increasingly became a relational and processual term known as *blanqueamiento*, a process associated with civilisation and social mobility. The migrants colonising the empty lands in Amazonia were not necessarily 'white' in substantial terms – they were often of Kichwa (Runa) descent – but were identified as such either because of their lighter skin or their superior social and economic status.

2   The organisation OISSE was formed in 1976 and consisted of the members of the Siona and Secoya indigenous peoples, who after 1942–43 intermarried and lived together at the Cuyabeno River. In the 1990s, urged by the emerging indigenous movement promoting identification as indigenous 'nationalities', the organization split in two. The Secoya organisation first took the name OISE, Organisación Indigena Secoya de Ecuador, but later changed its name to NASIEPAI, Nacionalidad Sieko-pai (NASIEPAI 2014).

3   https://www.acnur.org/fileadmin/Documentos/BDL/2008/6716.pdf (accessed 1 March 2019)

4   This is in line with other recent scholarly work describing indigenous peoples' perception of their relationship to the state and other powerful outsiders as a predator-prey relationship (Fausto 2007; Viveiros de Castro 2012; Rival 2017). Viveiros de Castro argues that to Amerindian groups, dealing with alien and spirit beings is somehow analogous to dealing with such outsiders, both being dangerous endeavours; supernatural encounters in the forest are 'a kind of indigenous proto-experience of the State' (2012: 37). Encounters with jaguars, spirits – and states – involve a fear of being captured under an 'other' dominant 'point of view'. This fear, which corresponds to the fear of being prey to a jaguar that sees you before you see it, demands either 'incorporation of the other or by the other' (ibid.). This question of incorporation of the other quite unexpectedly also involved tree beings, as I shall return to in the following sections.

REFERENCES

Acosta, A., 'Towards the Universal Declaration of the Rights of Nature: Thoughts for Action' (2010) <https://therightsofnature.org/wp-content/uploads/pdfs/Toward-the-Universal-Declaration-of-Rights-of-Nature-Alberto-Acosta.pdf> [accessed 23 February 2019].

Blaser, M., 'The Threat of the Yrmo: The Political Ontology of a Sustainable Hunting Programme' *American Anthropologist*, 111. 1 (2009): 10–20.

Brightman, M., C. Fausto, and V. Grotti, *Ownership and Nurture: Studies in Native Amazonian Property Relations* (New York: Berghahn Books, 2016).

Casey, H., *Victims and Warriors: Violence, History and Memory in Amazonia* (Urbana, IL: University of Illinois Press, 2015).

Cipolletti, M. S., *Sociedades Indígenas de la Alta Amazonía: Fortunas y adversidades (Siglos XVII-XX)* (Quito: Ediciones Abya-Yala, 2017).

de la Cadena, M., 'Indigenous Cosmopolitics in the Andes: Conceptual Reflections beyond Politics', *Cultural Anthropology*, 25.2 (2010): 334–370.

——, *Earth Beings: Ecologies of Practice Across Andean Worlds* (Durham, NC: Duke University Press, 2015).

El Universo. Multa de $ 375.000 a secoyas por talar bosque por palma, (2011) <https://www.eluniverso.com/2011/07/31/1/1447/multa-375000-secoyas-talar-bosque-palma.html> [accessed 30 March 2019].

Escobar, A., 'After Nature: Steps to an Antiessentialist Political Ecology' *Current Anthropology*, 4.1 (1999): 1–30.

Fausto, C., 'Feasting on People: Eating Animals and Humans in Amazonía', *Currrent Anthropology*, 48.4 (2007): 497–530.

——, 'Too Many Owners: Mastery and Ownership in Amazonía', trans. by D. Rodgers from 'Donos Demais maestria e domínio na Amazônia', *Mana*, 14.2 (2008): 329–366.

Grandin, G., *Fordlandia: The Rise and Fall of Henry Ford's Forgotten Jungle City* (New York: Metropolitan Books, 2010).

Gudynas, E., *Derechos de la naturaleza. Ética biocéntrica y políticas ambientales* (Buenos Aires: Editorial Tinta Limón, 2015).

Haraway, D., 'Anthropocene, Capitalocene, Plantationocene, Chthulucene: Making Kin', *Environmental Humanities*, 6 (2015): 159–165.

Haraway, D., and others, 'Anthropologists Are Talking – About the Anthropocene', *Ethnos*, 81.1 (2016): 535–564.

Herrera, C., E. Giraldo, and G. Pálsson, 'The Forest and the Trees', *HAU: Journal of Ethnographic Theory*, 4.2 (2014): 237–243.

Hvalkof, S., 'Outrage in Rubber and Oil: Extractivism, Indigenous Peoples, and Justice in the Upper Amazon, in C. Zerner, ed., *People, Plants and Justice: The Politics of Nature Conservation* (New York: Columbia University Press, 2000), pp. 83–116.

Killick, E., 'Godparents and Trading Partners: Social and Economic Relations in Peruvian Amazonia', *Journal of Latin American Studies*, 40.2 (2008): 303–328.

Kohn, E., *How Forests Think: Towards an Anthropology beyond the Human* (Berkeley, CA: University of California Press, 2013).

Kopenawa, D., and B. Albert, *The Falling Sky: Words of a Yanomami Shaman* (Cambridge, MA: Harvard University Press, 2013).

Krøijer, S., *The Company and the Trickster.* Unpublished Master's Thesis. Copenhagen: University of Copenhagen, 2003.

——, '"Being Flexible": Reflections on How an Anthropological Theory Spills into the Contemporary Political Life of an Amazonian People', *Tipití: Journal of the Anthropological Society of Lowland South America*, 15.1 (2017): 46–61.

——, 'In the Spirit of Oil: Unintended Flows and Leaky Lives in Northeastern Ecuador', in C. V. Ødegaard and J. J. Rivera Andía, eds., *Indigenous Life Projects and Extractivism: Ethnographies from South America* (New York: Springer, 2018), pp. 95–118.

Muratorio, B., *Rucuyaya Alonso y la historia social y económica del Alto Napo, 1850–1950* (Quito: Abya Yala, 1998).

Nacionalidad Sieko-pai (NASIEPAI) and Gobierno Autónoma Provincial de Sucumbios. *Plan de Vida Siekopai 2014–2029*, unpublished document (Nueva Loja, 2014).

Payaguaje, F., *El bebedor de yagé* (Quito: CICAME, 2014).

Penfield, A., 'Maneuvering for Paper: Physical and Social Experiences of Bureaucracy in Venezuelan Amazonia', *The Journal of Latin American and Caribbean Anthropology*, 21.3 (2016): 457–477.

Reichel-Dolmatoff, G., *The Forest Within: The World-View of the Tukano Amazonian Indians* (Dartington: Themis Books, 1996).

Rival, L., 'The Growth of Family Trees: Understanding Huaorani Perceptions of the Forest', *Man* 28 (1993): 635–652.

——, *The Social Life of Trees: Anthropological Perspectives on Tree Symbolism* (Oxford: Berg, 1998).

——, *Trekking Through History: The Huaorani of Amazonia* (New York: Columbia University Press, 2003).

——, *Huaorani Transformations in Twenty-first Century Ecuador: Treks into the Future of Time* (Tucson: University of Arizona Press, 2016).

Santos-Granero, F., 'Of Fear and Friendship: Amazonian Sociality beyond Kinship and Affinity', *Journal of the Royal Anthropological Institute*, 13.1 (2007): 1–18.

Santos-Granero, F., and F. Barclay, *La frontera domesticada: historia económica y social de Loreto, 1850–2000* (Lima: Fondo Editorial de la Pontífica Universidad Católica de Peru, 2002).

Strathern, M., *The Gender of the Gift: Problems with Women and Problems with Society in Melanesia* (Berkeley, CA: University of California Press, 1988).

Taussig, M., *Shamanism, Colonialism, and the Wild Man: A Study in Terror and Healing* (Chicago, IL: University of Chicago Press, 1987).

Tsing, A., 'Unruly Edges: Mushrooms as Companion Species', *Environmental Humanities* 1 (2012): 141–54.

——, *The Mushroom at the End of the World: On the Possibility of Life in Capitalist Ruins* (Princeton: Princeton University Press, 2015).

Vickers, W. T., 'Ideation as Adaptation: Traditional Belief and Modern Intervention in Siona-Secoya Religion', in N. E. Whitten, ed., *Cultural Transformations and Ethnicity in Modern Ecuador* (Urbana: University of Illinois Press, 1981), pp. 705–730.

——, *Los Sionas y Secoyas: Su adaptación al medio ambiente* (Quito: Abya Yala, 1989a).

Vickers, W. T., 'Traditional Concepts of Power among the Siona-Secoya and the Advent of the Nation State', *The Journal of Latin American and Caribbean Anthropology*, 1.2 (1989b): 55–60.

Viveiros de Castro, E., 'Cosmological Deixis and Amerindian Perspectivism', *The Journal of the Royal Anthropological Institute*, 4.3 (1998): 469–488.

——, 'GUT Feelings about Amazonía: Potential Affinity and the Construction of Sociality', in L. Rival and N. Whitehead, eds., *Beyond the Visible and the Material: The Amerindianization of Society in the Work of Peter Rivière* (Oxford: Oxford University Press, 2001), pp. 19–44.

——, 'Exchanging Perspectives: The Transformation of Objects into Subjects in Amerindian Ontologies', *Common Knowledge*, 10.3 (2004): 463–484.

——, 'Immanence and Fear: Stranger-events and Subjects in Amazonia', *HAU: Journal of Ethnographic Theory*, 2.1 (2012): 27–43.

Wasserstrom, R., and D. Southgate, 'Deforestation, Agrarian Reform and Oil Development in Ecuador, 1964–1994', *Natural Resources*, 4 (2013): 31–44.

Whitten, N., 'Introduction', in N. Whitten, ed., *Cultural Transformations and Ethnicity in Modern Ecuador* (Urbana: IL University of Illinois Press, 1981).

THINKING IN FORESTS

Lys Alcayna-Stevens

INTRODUCTION

The seeds of this chapter grew from a kaleidoscope of contrasts made between 'field' and 'home' by fledgling field primatologists studying an endangered and elusive great ape (the bonobo) in the equatorial forests of the Democratic Republic of Congo. During both fieldwork and retrospective interviews, young scientists reminisced of 'a separate world' which was 'remote', 'isolated', 'pristine', 'undisturbed', 'interconnected', 'alive' and 'easier to breathe in'.

Initially, I was tempted to read these narratives alongside familiar global discourses of habitat loss and environmental crisis, an exoticising or fetishising of African wilderness, and a nostalgia for simplicity, authenticity and immediacy. And yet, as I thought more about their reflections, and my own experiences in those same forests, and as I pored over my notes and re-listened to interviews, I began to pay more attention to those moments in which researchers themselves punctuated their reflections with caveats; 'this sounds like a cliché' they would admit, insisting that they were unable to find the words to fully capture their experiences of the world around them (and beyond them), their own subjectivities and the passing of time in 'the field'.

What to make of these caveats? The apparent failure of language to capture experience has spurred me to reflect on the kinds of embodied 'edgework', or 'cuspwork', through which these neophyte field scientists navigate the known, the unknown and the inarticulable, as they come to appreciate the forests in which they live and work when searching for, following and studying elusive and itinerant bonobo communities. In using these terms, I am inspired by the invitation of feminist geographer Kathryn Yusoff (2013: 209), to 'think along the cusp' or 'the edge' of the insensible when attempting to apprehend issues such as biodiversity loss and climate change.

Feminist scholarship has long challenged the neutrality, rationality and disembodiment on which scientific objectivity rests (Barad 2007; Haraway 1988; Myers 2015; Myers & Dumit 2011). Many of these theorists have taken a phenomenological approach, privileging the body of the scientist in their analyses of scientific work. Seeking to capture not only scientists' narratives and impressions, but also the world with/in which those impressions are formed, they write within relational and materialist frameworks which allow them to challenge assumptions about the kinds of labour required to do scientific research, and reframe this work as premised on 'the capacities of a lively sensorium tethered to a lively world' (Myers 2015: 15).

These scholars have also explored the limits of knowing and understanding, including the ways in which such limits are stretched in the messy, fleshy-semiotic encounters between scientists and animals (Despret 2004, 2013; Haraway 2008). These encounters are perhaps at their messiest in 'the field'. STS scholars and ethnographers who have followed scientists to the field have examined the ways in which they attempt to stabilise their data and control for the vitality and excess which encroaches (Henke and Gieryn 2008; Walford 2015). Field primatologists themselves forgo the more systematic, reproducible and controlled nature of lab-based cognitive experiments, and I argue that an ethnographic exploration of their edgework in the forest can dovetail the limits of knowing and relating explored by feminist approaches to animal science, and feminist geographies which explore the indeterminacies of the contemporary environmental crisis.

The chapter draws on intensive ethnographic research at one bonobo field station, shorter visits to three other bonobo field stations (all in the Democratic Republic of Congo), and ongoing exchanges with the primatologists who work at these sites. In field primatology, there are many unknowns, and much remains unpredictable: where the primates will go, what they will do, whether it will even be possible to find them. The bonobos are free-ranging, sometimes travelling up to 10km in a day, and there are no tracking devices with which to find them in the dense forest. Researchers have very little equipment (a pen, a notebook, a pair of binoculars and a GPS), and must rely on their bodies to find and follow bonobos, and to collect data. The forest itself is often just as unpredictable as the bonobos; researchers are sometimes attacked by bees or wasps and can find themselves in parts of the forest which are almost unnavigable due to swamps, rivers or tangled vegetation.

'The field' is all the more compelling, in studies of science, because domestic and professional life are not as separate there, and the ethnographer has access to both. Junior research scientists often live at field sites for up to 9 or 12 months. While this chapter will not touch on researchers' more domestic activities, it will examine those interstitial moments in which field scientists cannot collect any data because they have 'lost' bonobos – in which bonobos have melted into the shadows of the forest and disappeared, sometimes for hours, sometimes for days or weeks. I am interested in what happens in those moments of waiting, searching and wondering. Indeed, it is often during those interstitial moments that the forest comes to the fore and begins to captivate the researchers' attention. This shift opens up the possibility for different kinds of thought – thoughts which are embodied, undirected, uncertain, introspective and indeterminate. That is, kinds of thought which are seldom associated with the neutrality, rationality and disembodiment of scientific objectivity.

Phenomenological approaches have allowed for a resolution of the mind-body problem in philosophy and social and psychological science, bridging the distinction made by Enlightenment philosophers between thinking (reason) and feeling (sentience). For phenomenologists, thought is felt. Nonetheless, thinking and feeling remain fairly exotic topics in anthropology, due to the discipline's focus on *social* patterns and dynamics. 'Psychological' or 'cognitive' matters, such as emotion, inner dialogue, mood, free association, reverie and imagination, have often appeared too unstable and too individuated to qualify as an object of social study. Unlike behaviour (in the form of ritual, exchange and performance) these experiential phenomena have little empirical ground.

Social scientists have made many attempts to grapple with emotion and experience, most of them engaging with debates in phenomenology and materialism.[1] Other approaches have prioritised semiosis. Rising to prominence with Geertz' interpretive anthropology and finding its most recent expression in Kohn's (2013) Peircean 'anthropology of life', semiotic approaches have emphasised communication, symbolism and shared meaning. In order to extend anthropology's reach, Kohn uses Peirce's triadic semiology to argue that all life forms engage in processes of signification. He argues that iconic signs and indexical signs must be brought into the anthropological agenda (heretofore dominated by symbolism), because icons and indexes are the signs that non-human organisms use to represent the world and communicate.

Kohn then makes a connection with thought, arguing that all beings are *thinking* beings, and that living environments are environments of *thought*. However, using the inspiration of the forest, and taking 'sylvan thinking' (Kohn 2014) in another direction – one inspired by feminist geographies and studies of science – I want to untether thought from communication and semiosis, and to linger on those moments when meaning fails to cohere and when understanding appears beyond one's grasp. Taking sylvan thinking in this direction necessitates 'staying with the trouble' (Haraway 2016) of alterity and lingering on the ways in which indeterminacy emerges as bodies flourish and as bodies die. I am interested in the echoes, traces and palimpsets of elsewheres and elsewhens which render thought simultaneously relational and beyond the relation. Thoughts appear then as tendrils reaching out to others (times, places, being), but seldom connecting.

Attention to thought in ethnographic writing perturbs both a commitment to the empirical and a commitment to the social. Thoughts are ephemeral and wayward, and others' thoughts are often opaque or only indirectly available to us. In an attempt to grasp the kinds of thinking which the forest facilitates, I will employ ethnographic fiction, and follow a composite character whose movements – both wandering and wondering – are based on formal interviews and informal conversations with scientists, and on my own experiences of living and working in the forest, alone and with others. There are many limitations to this approach, and this composition should be read as an experiment rather than an analysis. It is an experiment which allows me to linger on the mundane, the habitual, the non-event, and on the interstitial moments in which thought meanders and mutates and brings alterity and understanding in and out of one's grasp.

INDETERMINATE

Our field scientist methodically ticks off her mental checklist and packs the remaining objects (a satellite phone, her GPS and binoculars) into her backpack, making sure that her notepad, pencil and compass are securely tied to the belt loops on her waistband. Eager to leave camp, she wolfs down a bowl of rice and boiled cassava leaves prepared by the Congolese cook, and muses on where she might search in order to find the lost bonobos. She signs herself out in the 'daily book' and notes down the names of the trails she plans to walk this afternoon.

It is nearly noon as she walks quickly through the camp towards the forest path, and the sun is already beating down on the thatch roofs which provide shade for the researchers' tents. Sweat begins to bead on her forehead. She steps over the fallen tree which marks the entrance to the forest and is engulfed by the hum of insects and the cool shade of the dense canopy. The stale heat and exposure of the camp melt away and she picks up her pace, feeling purposeful.

She is aware of the forest beneath her feet, stepping over lines of driver ants and avoiding tree roots. Her lungs feel capacious, and her legs feel powerful as she side-steps and skips over uneven ground. Passing another fallen tree, she takes a deep breath, inhaling the smell of sap, bark and crushed foliage. She feels connected to the forest and kindled by the unseen activity around her. If she had been here six hours earlier, the beam of her headlamp would have bounced off the back of the retinæ – the tapetum lucidum – of hidden mammals and insects, alerting her to their presence. Now in the daylight, even if they are there, they remain unseen.

After some time walking and letting her thoughts unwind, her mental checklist replays itself and she begins to doubt that she put the second notebook in her backpack. She stops and takes the bag off her back, resting it against the buttress of a giant tree – she doesn't know the species. Her notebook is there.

She makes the most of the pause to take a swig of water and wipe her brow. Now that the breeze driven by her movement has stopped, heat emanates from her body and appears to coagulate beneath her shirt. She pulls at her collar to fan herself a little and licks the salt above her lip.

So much is unknown in the forest. A stream of light filtering from above and glinting off a russet leaf catches her attention. Behind it is a slim, moss-covered tree trunk,

FIG. 2.2 Tree trunk covered in intricate and staccato white markings – fungi 'glyphs' (Photograph by Lys Alcayna-Stevens, 2012)

bright green, and covered in intricate and staccato white markings. She assumes they must be some sort of fungi, even if, in that moment, they look to her like ancient or alien glyphs or simple drawings of antelope or birds. When they have talked about the markings in camp, others have suggested that they look like dancing figures.

She never ceases to be amazed by the forest. One can easily transform markings into hidden signs with one's imagination, just as one can easily miss or misinterpret other elements which could have been read as signs; the tracks which Congolese hunters follow with great skill, for example. Cycles of life and death render these signs even more ephemeral. She has seen insects camouflaged as sticks and stones, detectable only by their movement – if at all. When they die, they become invisible for ever more.

She is also amazed by the speed with which things grow and re-grow, Lazarus-like, in the forest. Even here, not far from the 'buttress tree' (as she calls it), is a fallen log. Its branches are bare and mostly disintegrated, indicating that it must have fallen several weeks or months before. And yet, growing out from the broken bark, vertically towards the sky, is a new branch. A sapling? The tree is still alive.

At times, she feels overwhelmed by the forest. By its magnitude and its majesty. It is an uncanny feeling. If anything, the forest emanates… indifference. As she touches the buttress tree's rough, mossy bark, she feels insignificant. The powerful feeling which comes from that realisation cannot be described as either good or bad. It feels like a kind of rejection, but one that leaves her winded rather than stinging. And grateful somehow... She grazes her fingertips lightly down and off the bark, takes a deep breath, swings her bag onto her back, and begins to walk again, picking up the pace.

Bonobos (*Pan paniscus*) exist only in the equatorial forests of the Democratic Republic of Congo and have been very little studied compared with their close evolutionary cousins, the chimpanzees.[2] The two ape species are separated by the Congo River, with bonobos encircled by the curve of the river along its left bank, and chimpanzees ranging beyond it, in forest and forest-savannah landscapes to the north, east and west, from Senegal to Tanzania.

Unlike evolutionary psychologists, who conduct lab-based experiments to explore the limits and potential of primate minds, field primatologists are committed to the principle that studying a species in the environment in which it evolved can provide the most insight into the factors which have shaped its body, mind, behaviour and social organisation. This issue is of particular relevance to questions of bonobo evolution, because current hypotheses suggest that some of the most significant differences between bonobo and chimpanzee social structures and behaviour lie in their different ecological niches. As the theory goes, while chimpanzee females often reside alone in a territory which has only enough fruiting trees to support them and their offspring, bonobo females live in forests abundant in 'fall-back foods' (terrestrial vegetation), and females are therefore able to travel together. In terms of social structure, this has led to the formation of male coalitions (and male dominance and violence against females) in chimpanzees, as groups of males patrol and control the territories of several females, and a more egalitarian and peaceful social life in bonobos, where females are able to form coalitions which limit male dominance and violence.

For field researchers, the forest is an essential component in their study of bonobo ecology, social structure and behaviour, and much of the data they collect is about seasonality in fruiting trees, bonobo feeding, travel and nest-making behaviour. However, the forest also 'gets in the way' of their research. Visibility is hampered by thick vegetation, and researchers' ability to follow bonobos is slowed by swamps and rivers, which bonobos are able to bypass by sticking to the canopy or making use of fallen logs too precarious for researchers to clamber over. Furthermore, hookworm infestations from walking through swamps, and allergic reactions to the stings inflicted when researchers disturb bee hives or wasp nests, can force researchers to spend days in camp recovering, and thus miss valuable data collection opportunities.

While researchers learn about the forest by following and even mimicking bonobos' movements within it (Alcayna-Stevens 2016), many of them have acknowledged retrospectively that it was in the hours and days spent searching for lost bonobos that they most appreciated the forest. Freed from the pressures of data collection, they had time to linger, to examine odd or unusual things in more detail, to revel in the forest and to drift into reverie.

It was in retrospective conversations that I had the opportunity to discuss these solitary moments with researchers in more depth. I think of the distinctions they would draw between 'home' and 'field' (often used interchangeably with 'forest') as a *kaleidoscope of contrasts* because the distinctions do not map neatly onto each other, and at times they even contradict, with the same terms being used to compare and highlight different differences. For example, an urban and 'artificial' home in which one is isolated and 'cooped up in a box with electric power all the time' was often contrasted with a 'verdant' forest in which one is 'connected' and 'very much in tune with what's happening around you'. At other times, however, constant connection was what characterised life at home, while the forest – using an electronic metaphor – was described as 'a place to recharge your batteries'.

Similarly, life in the field was often described as 'simplified', 'predictable' and 'limited', in contrast with an 'overwhelming' return home in which one would 'have to deal with hundreds of options'. At other times, it was the forest which was described as 'unpredictable' and with 'so much going on it's hard to keep track'. The passage of time was also conceptualised through a variety of contrasts. Some researchers described days in the forest as endless and full of events, while the 'outside world' was described as speeding by with very little happening. At other times, researchers described the changes and events (missed weddings, celebrations, newsworthy occurrences) which happened in what they also called the 'real world', while very little happened in the forest. In all cases, the contrasts served to capture the timbre and tenor of their experiences, if only partially.

One can read within these contrasts a nostalgia for simplicity, authenticity and immediacy, a desire for connection and an exoticising or fetishising of wilderness and nature. It is a familiar nostalgia. Scholarly and popular accounts of globalised late capitalism are often shot through with anxious and nostalgic notes (Stewart 2013): a 'disembedding' of social relations from 'local contexts' (Giddens 1990), and a disconnection from place, which was described by Said (1979: 18) as a 'generalized condition of homelessness'. But these are not simply narratives. Sensory regimes, like bodies, are shaped by the processes of capitalism, colonialism and biopower. Social scientists have examined the ways in which such processes leave bodies ruptured, exhausted and abandoned, afflicted by toxicity or obesogenic 'slow death' (Das 1996; Povinelli 2011; Chen 2011; Berlant 2007). Researchers' descriptions capture something less dramatic, but equally beyond narrative and representation. These simultaneously pedestrian and prodigious experiences of 'lethargy', isolation and oversaturation are captured powerfully in the words of one researcher:

> I felt more alive in the forest. I was very aware of this constant cycling process of life and death and regeneration. It's hard to explain, but you do have a feeling of connectedness. It's the level of solitude and nature that I need to feel normal. Here, sometimes I feel like I'm having trouble breathing, I feel more lethargic, I have more headaches. The best way to describe it is I just breathe better in the forest.

It is the caveats – 'it's hard to explain', 'I know it sounds silly', 'I'm having trouble expressing it', 'I can't articulate it', 'I know it isn't exactly true, but it feels like...' which interest me most here. These are not simply narratives drawing on established tropes of wilderness and disconnection. They are also attempts to express and verbalise vital, excessive and ineffable experiences.

The impression I have, from both informal and formal conversations, and from my own experiences in the forest, is not that language here fails to capture an intuitive *understanding* of the forest. If anything, what they appear to point to is that the forest is fundamentally other, and beyond one's grasp – and that this is one of the reasons it is so compelling. Researchers continuously come across plants, animals, fungi and other phenomena for which they have no name and no explanation. They sometimes search for the most striking of these lifeforms in the mouldy paperback field guides stored in a metal crate in the camp depot. But, as none of these guides address little-studied central African flora and fauna in detail, their efforts to identify are not always successful.

At times mysterious, the forest is also mercurial. Walking a few hundred meters, it can transform from a cool, open understorey, to a dense, hot and almost impenetrable overgrowth of terrestrial herbaceous vegetation. It is mercurial because it is multiple. The animals within it often attempt to evade discovery. 'Crypsis' is a term used by ecologists to describe an animal's ability to avoid detection by other animals. It can refer to strategies of concealment, including nocturnality, camouflage and mimicry. Phasmids – also known as stick insects, leaf insects, ghost insects or 'walking sticks' – offer one of the most striking forms of crypsis.[3] Many use 'motion camouflage' by swaying or rocking in the breeze like leaves or small branches, or, alternatively, entering a 'cataleptic state' in which they adopt a rigid, motionless posture which can be maintained for a long period, or 'thanatosis' in which they drop to the ground and play dead, becoming indistinguishable from the leaf litter of the forest floor.

Uncertainty and indeterminacy are anathema to the goal of science, which is to explain and to understand. And yet it is the imponderabilia, the unanswerable, the unfathomable and the indeterminate which research scientists find so compelling when thinking with and about the forest. After all, even if uncertainty and indeterminacy have no place in science's goals, wonder and curiosity are the seeds of the scientific endeavour. A brush with the innumerable other worlds which 'graze' our own (Yusoff 2013) is what appears to produce a feeling of connection in researchers to something larger than themselves, in all its multiplicity. Theories of affect and semiotic approaches are inadequate frameworks for capturing this indeterminacy because of their emphasis on the social, the shared and the communicative. Reading scientists' narratives with Yusoff's theory of 'cohabitation' in mind, they are not about what is shared or communicated, but about an acceptance of connection irrespective of asymmetry, non-rapport, nonrecognition and indifference.

INTROSPECTIVE

After walking for nearly an hour, our field scientist decides to stop. She has reached another large 'buttress tree', which marks the beginning of one of the most southerly trails. The bonobos were last seen near here two days before. While it seems unlikely to her that they would still be here after two days, she has been surprised before to find them close to where they were lost.

She plucks two large, broad, waxy leaves from a nearby arrowroot plant and places them between the buttresses. She sits on the leaves and drinks from her bottle. Bathed in the dappled light of the canopy, she looks languidly around, her knees up, elbows resting on them, her water bottle dangling from her index finger by its lanyard. After walking for so long, with her mind wandering along other paths, her head feels fresh and empty.

As the heat builds around her body, her thoughts too, seem to catch up with her. She can feel her heart beating, and her muscles hum like the insects in the undergrowth. She makes a mental note to walk more often when she returns home. To spend more time in nature. She takes another sip of water and tries to recall another mental note she had made to herself as she walked, but has momentarily forgotten. It was a question she had wanted to ask her parents next time a batch of emails would be sent out with the satellite radio system – ah yes! That was it: Are there native wild honey bees in Europe, or are they all feral?

She sits for a moment, lost in thought. Then she takes her second notebook from her backpack and notes the question down. As her pencil scratches along the paper, other thoughts come back to her – other people to email, belongings to organise or look for in camp, an article someone mentioned finding in the depot about bonobo language experiments, which would probably take a while to find, buried in a large metal crate, under other yellowed, wrinkled and mouldy papers. She scribbles down some of her other thoughts into lists. Lists of things to do in four months, once she gets back home, books to read, people to visit, recipes to experiment with…

She enjoys making these lists in the forest. The lists are all the more satisfying here because there is nothing she can do to complete them until she returns home. Here, she is in a kind of limbo, where lists can be conjured but not executed. She never has a to-do-list weighing on her mind the way she does back home, because everything she needs to do is almost always both pressing and immediately realisable. She wonders how long she will keep doing fieldwork, whether one day she will tire of this itinerant lifestyle and of the stresses which fieldwork can impose on personal relationships.

She muses on that 'home self', whose life and priorities are so different from her priorities here. She is a different person, inhabiting a different body, when she is in the field. When she first arrived in Kinshasa, she was hit by the hot, heavy, evening air of the runway and a smell of... not-home. She isn't sure how she would describe it. When the little bush plane dropped them off near the villages and she was finally able to enter the forest for the first time, it was this cool air, brimming with the scents of different vegetation that connected her to why she had come and what she was here for, and to all of the discomforts she was willing to endure in order to focus on and collect her data.

The thought of her data takes her mind back to the bonobos. Where might they be? They had been walking less in the days preceding their disappearance. Perhaps they were tired. Or, more likely, they had been sticking around one patch of forest, waiting for the large, mature Dialium trees to come into fruit. She decides to keep walking. She hasn't quite reached the part of the forest where she thinks they might actually be, and there are no signs that they are in this area anymore. She will walk to a large fruiting Dialium slightly further to the south. That will be the place to pause and wait for them – if they are not feeding there already...

Time spent in camp is usually time spent eating, washing, organising things or inputting data into the camp computer. When bonobos are lost, the forest offers researchers an opportunity for quiet reflection, for solitude, and for introspection and prospection – a moment to think, and to visualise thoughts, in the form of letters, diaries, notes, doodles or lists. In these moments, researchers 'lose themselves' in a very everyday and un-spectacular way.

Building on Barad's (2007) agential realism, according to which phenomena and objects do not precede their interaction, but emerge through encounters or 'intra-actions', Yusoff (2013: 210) asks 'how to understand the durability of intra-actions, beyond the intra-action itself?' She poses the question in order to think through enduring environmental harm, toxicity and degradation. Here, the question inspires me to linger instead on the ways in which subjects are connected to the world through the echoes, traces and palimpsests of elsewheres and elsewhens which emerge in thought.

While relatively marginalised as an object of anthropological examination until the 1980s, dreaming, and its relationship to ritual trance, spirit possession and oneiromancy, has received increased attention in the last few decades.[4] Galinier et al. (2010) argue that the relative anthropological neglect of dreaming is just one example of the ethnographic privileging of public, daytime experiences over private, night-time experiences. However, if dreams have received relatively little anthropological attention, *daydreams* and reverie have received even less.

I did not study the daydreams and reveries of research scientists in detail (to do so would have necessitated a different methodology). What I am interested in here is how reflecting on daydreaming in the forest can reveal something about researchers' relations with and within it, and offer a new dimension to sylvan thinking – or perhaps, to sylvan *thought*. The distinction between the verb and noun is significant. Where 'thinking' is often conceived as a cerebral manipulation of information, or a mental process which allows beings to model the world and to engage with it according to their goals and desires, a 'thought' appears to have agency of its own – it is something which occurs somewhat spontaneously in the mind.

Researchers spoke of feeling refreshed after an hour's walk in the forest had allowed their thoughts to wander – refreshed in the way one might feel after waking up from a restful dream. Reverie allows for a kind of 'wringing out' of accumulated perceptions and preoccupations – a chance for thoughts, ideas and observations to combine and recombine, and mutate, in myriad configurations. Imagination travels beyond immediate experience, and rather than abstracting a subject from the world, thoughts serve to tighten knots to other places, persons and times. They are imprints of an intra-action, which continue to have an effect even in their apparent absence.

In those moments of connecting with others – of reaching out tendrils of thought to those others – a temporally-stable self becomes difficult to pinpoint or hold on to. Researchers muse on their future selves – 'I wonder whether I'll be interested in that kind of thing at that point in my life?' – and even their past selves – 'I don't know what I was thinking back then'. Selves appear temporally extended, unknowable, multiple. Selves, conceived over time, appear as an internal other, or intimate alterity.[5]

A self is a term used in conjunction with terms which conjure vitality, wakefulness, perception and reflection, such as 'consciousness'. When considered the object of introspection or reflexive action, a self often remains beyond one's grasp. We often conceive of a 'sense of self'. This sense is distinguishable from other senses because, unlike them, it is proprioceptive and interoceptive, or inward-looking. The exteroceptive senses perceive the outside world, conceived of as 'other', while the 'sense of self' perceives the self – or, through introspection and reflection, *labours* to grasp the self. This is often edgework, especially when the self is conceived temporally.

In order to theorise a 'sense of self' across time, and to recognise its relationship to the forces of capitalism, colonialism and biopower, social scientists often work with the concept of subjectivity, which is as much a process of socialisation as it is a process of individuation. Taking a phenomenological approach to subjectivity, I find it useful to conceive of it with reference to 'emplacement', which suggests the sensuous interrelationship of body-mind-environment (Howes 2005: 7), and to the 'sensorium', which Jones (2006 in Myers 2015: 21) describes as 'the changing sensory envelope of the self'.

Researchers recognise their 'future selves' and 'past selves' as somehow absent and other, while simultaneously connecting their 'present selves' to other times and places. Sometimes, they conceive of this as a kind of oscillation between their 'field selves' and their 'at-home selves'. Several researchers described to me that they consider themselves to enter a kind of 'fieldwork mode' when they are in the field. This 'mode' comprised a 'very different state psychologically', one where people described being able to focus on one objective, and not having other distractions, or one in which they became more patient and resilient, less affected by discomfort and less disheartened by setbacks, even despite the blisters, insect bites, hunger and aching muscles that researchers describe. Entering this embodied and psychological mode was seen as essential to becoming a 'good fieldworker'; robust, single-minded and with a newly developed somatic awareness and muscular consciousness which enabled them to find, follow and identify bonobos (Alcayna-Stevens 2016).

In paying attention to descriptions of this 'mode', one can better appreciate the contrasts made between field/forest and home, which were not only about differences in the environment, but also differences within the researchers themselves. I find Bourdieu's (1977) concept of 'secondary habitus' illuminating for thinking about these newly acquired modes. While the primary habitus is the set of dispositions one acquires in early childhood through familial immersion, the secondary habitus is, in the words of Wacquant (2014: 7), 'any system of transposable schemata that becomes grafted subsequently, through specialized pedagogical labor that is typically shortened in duration, accelerated in pace, and explicit in organization'. The habitus which field scientists cultivate in pursuit of bonobos is embodied and all-consuming, but temporally and spatially bounded. Selves are tied to place and activity, both of which redefine the landscape of an embodied being and its 'sense of self'.

Introspection sits uneasily with the scientific method and has largely been discredited in favour of empiricism – and, in the human and animal sciences, behaviourism.[6] The deeper one looks into oneself, the logic goes, the further one recedes from external others, and from the world. According to much euroamerican conceptualisation, thoughts reach out to the world, but seldom connect with it – at least, not *symmetrically*. For example, when researchers think about friends or family, or when they think about bonobos, this shapes their thoughts and feelings about these others, but it has little impact on the ways in which these others think about them – even if it will ultimately have an impact on the relationship. And yet, within these meandering thoughts, researchers nonetheless knot themselves to other places, times and beings.

INDIRECT

Her thumbnails flat against the front of her shoulders, her thumbs holding the straps of her bag slightly away from her body, she almost jogs the final few hundred meters. Then, something catches her eye in the leaf litter, slightly up ahead and to the left. She trots over and squats down to examine the broken foliage: The blackened stems of an arrowroot plant.

During her first few weeks in the forest, it is unlikely she would have noticed the pale green stems among the foliage and leaf litter. Now, these and other signs jump out at her, strike her, even when she is not looking for them. Even when she is lost in her thoughts and not actively paying attention to the path ahead.

She turns the broken stem over in her hand, trying to assess how long it has been on the ground. It is the stem of an arrowroot plant of the genus Haumania, often grouped together with others of the Marantaceae family as 'terrestrial herbaceous vegetation' (THV) when primatologists note down bonobo feeding activities. Bonobos break open the stems with their teeth and eat the tender pith within, discarding the fibrous remains. The sap, visible now in its blackened end, turns both their teeth and their urine a dark shade of red.

The stem is flaccid and desiccated – it isn't fresh. It must be from at least a few days ago. It is unlikely that this 'trace' will lead her to the bonobos. She keeps walking.

Finally, she reaches a large fallen tree which runs alongside the path, its roots upturned, now sprawling and branching out like a toppled crown of antlers. She recognises the tree and takes out her GPS to orient herself relative to the Dialium tree she intends to visit. She must walk northeast at 32°. She orients the arrow on the compass and adjusts her position so that she is facing the same direction as the needle. She steps off the path and begins walking through the forest, stepping over and under tangled vines, and around saplings and larger foliage.

As she approaches the Dialium tree, she feels her heart sink a little. The bonobos are not here. She takes off her backpack and lies down on the ground, using it as a headrest. She lies back on the log, looks up at the canopy, glinting with movement in the afternoon light, and concentrates on what she can hear: insects, a bird, the sound of a branch cracking and leaves rustling in the distance. She focuses on that sound, turning her head, straining to hear through the hum of insects. She makes out the sound of chattering monkeys accompanying the rustle of leaves and branches. She turns back to the glimmering canopy.

Her mind begins to wander again. She is somewhere else, and the forest is present only when the faint breeze from an insect's wing grazes her cheek. Then, suddenly she hears a chorus of calls – 'high hoots' – in the distance, and sits bolt upright. She orients her compass. The bonobos are at least 700m away, but she may catch them if she is quick.

If a certain scientific single-mindedness characterises researchers' 'fieldwork mode', it cannot be said to characterise every moment spent in the forest. Much of that time is also spent in absent-minded reverie. I would like to linger on this absent-mindedness, in order to think both about the nature of scientific labour, and about the limits of knowing.

The researchers were seldom to be found anthropomorphising, 'egomorphising' (Milton 2005) or attempting to speculate on bonobo desires, intentions or thoughts during their data collection. Following their research protocol, they noted down observed feeding and social behaviours, without commenting on intent or emotion. They did, however, egomorphise indiscriminately when attempting to find lost bonobos. They would spend hours, both collectively and individually, speculating and hypothesising about where the bonobos could be, and why they might be there. Were they tired? Were they waiting for a 'preferred' fruit to ripen? Were they avoiding, or looking for, certain members of the community?

There was much debate about how best to find bonobos. Should one look simply in the area one last saw them? Or should one target fruiting trees and other areas which might interest bonobos? Should one move around the forest searching for them? Or should one wait in a single place? All researchers agreed that whatever strategy one chose, ultimately one would have to rely on the senses, and the secondary habitus one had developed while conducting fieldwork. Their eyes, ears and noses were ready to be 'caught' by bonobos and their traces. They had learned to be affected by the subtlest of signs, and this did not require focus, but rather a broad openness to the possibility of bonobos' presence, even in their absence.

Researchers did not find bonobos through pure chance. They would discuss strategies and fan out across the forest in the areas they felt (sometimes through reasoning, sometimes because they had a 'gut feeling') they were most likely to find bonobos. But these strategies just as often failed as succeeded, and in order to be open to bonobos and their traces, but not frustrated by the endeavour, researchers' gazes were often broad and undirected, relying on their senses to pick out what was considered important to attend to. To be undirected is to be counter to the scientific method. However, like introspection, it is a strategy which field scientists employ to greater or lesser effect when *searching* for their study subjects. Absent-mindedness emerges, then, as an important tool for sanity and success in the field.

Beyond this functionalist analysis however, absent-mindedness can also serve as a way of thinking about the kinds of labour entailed in 'edgework' or 'cuspwork'. Critical studies originating in psychoanalytic and feminist theory postulate the 'gaze' as a 'one-way event that denies the agency of the perceived object' (Kaplan 1999: 57). With their emphasis on embodied, material and relational approaches, feminist scholars have stressed the reciprocal adjustments and 'attunements' (Despret 2014) required of scientists and their animal 'subjects' or 'objects' during encounters and 'cohabitation' (Haraway 2003). What interests me here is not the stories of communication and 'copresence' in primate research from which Haraway (2008: 76) draws inspiration. In the *absence* of bonobos, field primatologists often search for, come across, and follow signs. However, these signs are not messages, they are indirect and noncommunicative: traces of vegetation, knuckle prints, faeces, abandoned nests. Like thoughts, they allow field scientists to reach out to bonobos. But while they entail a rapprochement, they do not always connect.

To conceptualise these asymmetries, I would like to pause on Haraway's (2016) suggestion that the insatiable hunger of living beings for each other often ends with indigestion. I am interested in the limits of knowledge and understanding, in asymmetry, non-rapport, nonrecognition and indifference. The gaze is a metaphor of agentive asymmetry. I would like to suggest another asymmetrical metaphor in order to explore scientists' relationships to the forest – one which moves away from the ocular and lingers on the embodied and the indeterminate.

'Grasp' is evocative for a number of reasons. Firstly, unlike the eye, which is not a specialised organ of perception (beyond being able to detect colour) in humans and other primates, the hand and its dexterity are perhaps the most significant adaptation which defines the primate order. To survive, young primates must be able to grasp their mothers. Almost everything a primate eats passes through her fingers, and much of what she touches (including when she grooms her friends and neighbours, solidifying their social bonds), she touches with her hands. Grasp, of course, has another meaning beyond seizing and holding something. It also refers to mental activity, to comprehending something firmly and fully. Grasp can be used to conceptualise the limits of knowledge and comprehension precisely because it allows something to sit within one's perceptual range, without being fully understood.

IN CONCLUSION

This chapter has focused not on conventional tools of scientific knowledge-making, but on the moments in which researchers search the forest for lost study subjects. It is during these interstitial moments that the background of field research, the forest, comes to the fore and captivates the researchers' attention, opening up the possibility for different kinds of thought. These modes of thought, which are embodied, undirected, uncertain, introspective and indeterminate, are typically overlooked in social studies of science.

An attention to thought perturbs both a commitment to the empirical and a commitment to the social. I have argued that attending to such thoughts can challenge assumptions about the kinds of labour required to do scientific research. The field is important here, because scientists cannot control as much as they might in the lab, and their study subjects are always at liberty to evade them. Indeed, labour in the field extends beyond data collection, cleaning and analysis, and involves the embodied and perceptive skills required to find and follow bonobos (Alcayna-Stevens 2016). It is in this context that introspection and absent-mindedness emerge as important tools for sanity and success in the field. Similarly, while uncertainty and indeterminacy may be anathema to the explanatory goal of science, wonder and curiosity are the seeds of the scientific endeavour.

Beyond this functionalist analysis, I have drawn inspiration from feminist geographies and studies of science and sought to untether thought from communication and semiosis. Using an 'absential logic', Kohn (2013: 74) expands the definition of a sign – typically an object, quality or event whose presence or occurrence indicates the presence or occurrence of something else – into an embodied framework in which the elongated snouts and tongues of anteaters can be described as interpretations of the geometry of ants' tunnels. Interested also in absences and traces but inspired by feminist approaches to 'indeterminate bodies' (Waterton and Yusoff 2017), I would argue that an 'ecology of selves' might best be conceived as an 'open whole' precisely because other selves cannot be determined from the outset (see Cadena 2014). Selves must be discovered. And even once discovered, they remain unstable (they can disappear or die) and unpredictable.

Where Kohn seeks a unifying theory, an embodied and emergentist understanding of semiosis which would move anthropology beyond the human, 'sylvan thinking' leads me to linger on those moments when meaning fails to cohere and when understanding appears beyond one's grasp. Yusoff (2013: 225) argues that 'that which makes us comfortable reinforces the boundaries of the human, rather than exposing them'. Tracing along the edges of scientific labour, of field scientists' wandering bodies and wondering thoughts, and the limits of ethnographic fiction, I have sought to argue that it is the imponderabilia, the unanswerable, the unfathomable and the indeterminate which is so compelling when thinking with and in the forest. It is significance without sign. The political and ethical dimensions of this argument point to the vital importance, in an era of environmental crisis, deforestation and mass extinction, of action not being premised on rapport and recognition, but on an appreciation and respect for alterity, asymmetry, indeterminacy and the unknowable.

NOTES

1 Most recently and prominently, attempts have been made to examine how 'feelings' are generated socially and in dialogue with the world through studies of affect (Ahmed 2004; Stewart 2007). Previous scholars who embraced the 'edgier' elements of emotion and experience include Rosaldo (1980), Obeyesekere (1981), and Jackson (1996).
2 Until the end of the Congo civil wars and the turn of the twenty-first century, there was only one long-term and productive bonobo field site. Two others had been completely abandoned during the wars. There are now five sites, compared with over 20 chimpanzee field sites, several of which have been running since the 1960s.

3 To appear more botanical, many forgo the symmetrical nature of animal bodies and have a missing internal organ. Their bodies may have ridges resembling leaf veins, bark-like tubercles, and other forms of camouflage, such as mossy or lichenous outgrowths.

4 A collection of anthropological works on dreaming, some of which draw on psychoanalysis or cognitive science, can be found in Bulkeley et al. (2016).

5 Stasch (2008) explores the ways in which the southeastern West Papua Korowai people similarly sometimes appear to be 'other to themselves'.

6 Feminist STS has challenged the alluring myth of objectivity and perspectivalism (Haraway 1988; Mol 2002). Furthermore, critical scholars of the animal sciences, such as Crist (2010), Despret (2014), and Milton (2005), have challenged mechanistic reasoning and suggested 'egomorphism' as a method for understanding animal selves.

REFERENCES

Ahmed, S., 'Affective Economies', *Social Text*, 22.2 (2004): 117–139.

Alcayna-Stevens, L., 'Habituating Field Scientists', *Social Studies of Science*, 46.6 (2016): 833–853.

Barad, K., *Meeting the Universe Halfway: Quantum Physics and the Entanglement of Matter and Meaning* (Durham, NC: Duke University Press, 2007).

Berlant, L., 'Slow Death (Sovereignty, Obesity, Lateral Agency)', *Critical Inquiry*, 33.4 (2007): 754–780.

Bourdieu, P., *Outline of a Theory of Practice* (Cambridge: Cambridge University Press, 1997).

Bulkeley, K., ed., *Dreams: A Reader on Religious, Cultural and Psychological Dimensions of Dreaming* (New York: Springer, 2016).

Chen, M. Y., 'Toxic Animacies, Inanimate Affections', *GLQ: A Journal of Lesbian and Gay Studies*, 17.2–3 (2011): 265–286.

Crist, E., *Images of Animals* (Pennsylvania, PA: Temple University Press, 2010).

Das, V., 'Language and Body: Transactions in the Construction of Pain', *Daedalus*, 125.1 (1996): 67–91.

De la Cadena, M., 'Runa: Human but not only', *HAU: Journal of Ethnographic Theory*, 4.2 (2014): 253–259.

Despret, V., 'The Body We Care for: Figures of Anthropo-zoo-genesis', *Body & Society*, 10.2–3 (2004): 111–134.

——, 'Responding Bodies and Partial Affinities in Human–Animal Worlds', *Theory, Culture & Society*, 30.7–8 (2013): 51–76.

Galinier, J., and others, 'Anthropology of the Night: Cross-Disciplinary Investigations', *Current Anthropology*, 51.6 (2010): 839.

Giddens, A., *The Consequences of Modernity* (Cambridge: Cambridge University Press, 1990).

Haraway, D., 'Situated Knowledges: The Science Question in Feminism and the Privilege of Partial Perspective', *Feminist Studies*, 14.3 (1988): 575–599.

——, *When Species Meet* (University of Minnesota Press, 2013).

——, *Staying with the Trouble: Making Kin in the Chthulucene* (Durham, NC: Duke University Press, 2016).

Henke, C., and T. Gieryn, 'Sites of Scientific Practice: The Enduring Importance of Place', in E. Hackett and others, eds., *New Handbook of Science and Technology Studies* (Cambridge, MA: MIT Press, 2008).

Howes, D., *Empire of the Senses* (Oxford, UK: Berg, 2005).

Jackson, M., ed., *Things As They Are: New Directions in Phenomenological Anthropology* (Washington, DC: Georgetown University Press, 1996).

Jones, C. A., ed., *Sensorium: Embodied Experience, Technology, and Contemporary Art* (Cambridge, MA: MIT Press, 2006).

Kaplan A., 'Looking for the Other: Feminist, Film and the Imperial', *Film Quarterly*, 52.3 (1999): 57–58.

Kohn, E., *How Forests Think: Toward an Anthropology beyond the Human* (Oakland, CA: University of California Press, 2013).

——, 'Further Thoughts on Sylvan Thinking', *HAU: Journal of Ethnographic Theory*, 4.2 (2014): 275–288.

Milton, K., 'Anthropomorphism or Egomorphism? The Perception of Non-Human Persons by Human Ones', in J. Knight, ed., *Animals in Person: Cultural Perspectives on Human-Animal Intimacy* (Oxford: Berg, 2005): pp. 255–271.

Mol, A., *The Body Multiple: Ontology in Medical Practice* (Durham, NC: Duke University Press, 2002).

Myers, N., *Rendering Life Molecular: Models, Modelers, and Excitable Matter* (Durham, NC: Duke University Press, 2015).

Myers, N., and J. Dumit, 'Haptic Creativity and the Mid-Embodiments of Experimental Life', in F. E. Mascia-Lees, ed., *A Companion to the Anthropology of the Body and Embodiment* (Hoboken, NJ: Wiley Blackwell, 2011), pp. 239–261.

Obeyesekere, G., 'An Essay on Personal Symbols and Religious Experience', in M. Lambek, ed., *A Reader in the Anthropology of Religion* (Hoboken, NJ: Wiley Blackwell, 1981), pp. 383–397.

Povinelli, E. A., *Economies of Abandonment: Social Belonging and Endurance in Late Liberalism* (Durham, NC: Duke University Press, 2011).

Rosaldo, M. Z., *Knowledge and Passion* (Cambridge: Cambridge University Press, 1980).

Said, E., *Orientalism* (New York: Vintage, 1979).

Stasch, R., *Society of Others: Kinship and Mourning in a West Papuan Place* (Oakland, CA: University of California Press, 2009).

Stewart, K., *Ordinary Affects* (Durham, NC: Duke University Press, 2007).

——, 'Regionality', *Geographical Review*, 103.2 (2013): 275–284.

Walford, A., 'Double Standards: Examples and Exceptions in Scientific Metrological Practices in Brazil', *Journal of the Royal Anthropological Institute*, 21.S1 (2015): 64–77.

Wacquant, L., '*Homines in Extremis*: What Fighting Scholars Teach Us about Habitus', *Body & Society*, 20.2 (2014): 3–17.

Waterton, C., and K. Yusoff, 'Indeterminate Bodies: Introduction', *Body & Society*, 23.3 (2017): 3–22.

Yusoff, K., 'Insensible Worlds: Postrelational Ethics, Indeterminacy and the (K) Nots of Relating', *Environment and Planning D: Society and Space*, 31.2 (2013): 208–226.

EASY GESTURING OR INVENTING POLITICS?

A conversation between Marisol de la Cadena and Casper Bruun Jensen

As a way to generate further reflections on the ideas proposed in Krøijer's and Alcayna-Stevens' chapters, but also seeking to avoid formats that might summarise or resolve the questions the chapters pose, we invited Marisol de la Cadena and Casper Bruun Jensen to have an open conversation about the chapters, in relation to the introduction to the book. We recorded the conversation, and then transcribed it verbatim. Afterwards we asked each scholar to edit the conversations, and only then did we lightly edit them ourselves – this in order to try to keep the stylistic effect of a conversational format, an exchange of ideas and a non-linear narrative. In so doing, rather than an ending, we hoped to provide readers with further open directions in which to think.

IN THE FOLLOWING CONVERSATION, DE LA CADENA AND BRUUN JENSEN explore how the concept of environmental alterities offers the possibility for creating ontological openings involving the transformations, and destabilisation, of the concept of the human. They discuss how complicating the figure-ground distinction might be a way to point to how the ground (environmental but also conceptual) is always fragmented, unreachable and unknown, thus making environmental relations a subject that needs to be continuously invented. They consider how this shift can be understood politically, and how environmental alterities, as an analytical tool, does not respond to, but rather suspends, the temporalities and urgency embedded in politics as usual, or in concrete political environmental problems that usually demand opposition to the state, capital profit practices, and so on. Without reaching definitive answers, the conversation problematises the relation and existing tension between the need to act, politically, but at the same time, to think about worlds that are 'not-yet'. Thus, the engagements with forests presented in these chapters are reflected upon through the political potentialities and limits that the concept of environmental alterities affords.

CASPER: To start, I really like the project of exploring environmental alterities. It's a great project and it speaks to so many things that many – our group here and far beyond – have been talking about, trying to comprehend for years already. In STS of course with the famous nature/culture divides, whether from Latour's or Haraway's side, with Anna Tsing's 'more than human worlds', with Marisol's 'more than human, excessive earth-being', with Stengers' cosmopolitics and so on. Not to mention the controversial ontological turn that we have all been involved with in different ways. To my mind, the 'alterities' enter primarily via the literature of this ontological turn, but the environmental aspect is an obvi- ous, urgent and poignant complement in the context of the Anthropocene. I'm sitting in Cambodia, which has one of the highest deforestation rates in the world and is also heavily hit already by climate change effects – and is in many ways a totally different place from Marisol's Peru or my Denmark, or the UK or Chile. So, environmental alterities, and the different kinds of problem-spaces they create – conceptual and practical and political – are extremely pertinent. So, I'm excited and happy to be part of it.

Now, to turn to your way of organising the book – the introduction is struc- tured around three kinds of engagement with environmental alterities. So, there's the 'outside', in which alterities are something that's basically a non-relational, untouchable, withdrawn space, resembling object-oriented ontology's ways of thinking – more or less. Then there's a series of reflections on other literature that has more affinity with the kinds of anthropology Marisol does, and the kind of STS-moving-into-anthropology that Latour does (and I do), which is about internal heterogeneities and how they are patterned. It raises immediate questions about how to think about what's internal and what's external to begin with, and how to separate them, to the extent that they can even be separated. But anyway, as a didactic device, that's how the introduction is done, and it speaks to different literatures.

And then, towards the end, there's another one which perplexes me more, a kind of Wagnerian figure/ground reversal in motion, which asks about the relation between the 'relational 'and the 'outside', which was previously said to be a 'non-relation'. What kind of conceptual implications might follow from thinking about such weird spaces? I affiliate that with Antonia (because I've known her for a long time), with Marilyn Strathern to an extent – or a certain version of her – and with Roy Wagner who is famous for these kinds of chiasmatic relations and movements. This is all exciting, and I think we can relate it to the chapters – not in equal measure, but in various interesting ways. And then I have a few particular thoughts; one I would like to pose as a question to the writers of the introduction, and the other maybe more of a rant (or, as academics are not supposed to rant, perhaps it is a 'provocation'. But since the subject is a hobbyhorse for me these days, rant is probably more precise).

So, early in the text, there is a recurrent theme of 'mundanity', the everyday, everyday entanglements. In some sense, there's nothing extraordinary about climate change; we are starting to see all sorts of mundane ramifications. Keiichi Omura and the other editors of *The World Multiple* characterised their idea of the 'world multiple' along very similar lines in their introduction: the world multiple is made up of everyday practices and so on. As for myself, I'm not a huge fan of the mundane. I don't know what it is, or what it means. Is the everyday, in fact, mundane? Maybe not. But maybe in these days particularly, things aren't actually normal at all! In any case, I'd like to push the idea that things aren't normal at all, that there's nothing mundane about the situations we are in. I think they are quite mad, and I sure hope there is nothing mundane about where we are today. Of course, we continue to make cups of coffee, or chop firewood or go fishing if that's what we need to do. We milk our cows. Of course, everybody has a sort of habitual practice, they do things every day. Yet all around us things are changing in very dramatic ways, which seems to me to be systematically minimised by those with a strong commitment to everyday practices in phenomenological life-worlds.

Obviously, some of that is a response to what is perceived to be the exoticising tendencies of the ontological turn. Nothing to see here: we are really all living mundane existences. But I personally think more is to be gained by pushing the idea further: the whole world is becoming more and more mad and exotic, even to itself. Of course, I don't intend anything remotely resembling conventional colonial, supremacist fantasies of the Other. I mean that the world is becoming ontologically more and more exotic to practically everyone, in the sense that nobody has the least idea what it is going to come.

So that was an observation and a bit of a question. Leading on from that, the rant is about how mundanity becomes coupled with a particular critique of the notion of the Anthropocene and collapse, in what I think is a bad way. I mean, you, the editors, state that looking at unfolding climate disruption through the lens of the Anthropocene is highly problematic – for all the various and by now well-known reasons that the Anthropocene concept itself is criticised. And you add that thinking in terms of collapse is problematic because it obscures various other things that aren't actually collapsing. Which of course it does. But then refusing to look at collapse also obscures other things. Concentrating on making visible all those things that are obscured by the Anthropocene, also obscures things. For one, it obscures the by now relatively established fact that things are really not normal. Many things are going downhill pretty rapidly and are indeed headed for many forms of… collapse. Which means that the invocation of the many possibilities of 'life in the ruins' – Anna Tsing's phrase of course – the possibilities of finding other ways of life and so on, well, it sounds good but what would it mean? I would prefer to believe it, but what are the possibilities of living on a planet that has warmed by 6°c? What are the possibilities for living once the Antarctic ice has melted and water levels increased by 5, 10 or 30 metres? They appear terribly slim. So, I understand the sentiment behind rejecting the Anthropocene as a universalising label, but the backlash against the term and the idea of collapse seems to me to very quickly drift into easy gesturing towards vague, unspecified possibilities.

Those two points strike me as a way of framing the question of environmental alterities: mundanity versus what is definitely not normal; and how such practices play into politics and political imagination depending on whether one approaches the issues via an idea of Anthropocene collapse or in terms of continual change as something that is always happening. Basically, I'm very worried – so in the last few years I have become more inclined to think with

Eduardo Viveiros de Castro in terms of rupture, which means, again, precisely that there is nothing normal about what's going on. In my view the continuing academic debate about exactly what terminology to adopt, and the proliferation of competing '-cenes' and counter- '-cenes' detract from the major issues.

MARISOL: So, I am not going to repeat the ways I like the project, because they are similar to what Casper has already said. I like the idea of environmental alterities, and I like the way in which those two words can implode each other. So, if 'alterities' implode 'environmental', some consequential fragmentation happens. And, if 'environmental' implodes 'alterities', something also happens that perhaps connects the fragmentation. I like the interplay of those two words, what those two words can do to each other which can also be fragmented (and connected!). The only thing I would add to what you are saying, is that I think what Antonia and Cristóbal have written is also a proposal for what I call 'onto-epistemic openings' – perhaps different from the ontological turn because it doesn't propose jettisoning a concept, it does not suggest a method for an alternative end, it just proposes an opening. And what is being opened are concepts, which I think are worlding practices. My tool to perform openings is 'not only', a refrain that suggests things are more than what they are (or 'not only' what they also are.) But that is my tool – onto-epistemic openings, however you do them, are about working-at-the-cusp, edge work, signalling the limit not as the end zone, but as a starting line. I think that the mutual implosion of 'environmental alterities, working at each other's limits, performs those openings.

Okay. Now, engaging with what you, Casper, have said, about what you feel and think about 'easy gesturing'. I would say that it depends. It depends because easy gesturing can also be a very difficult engagement. If you take 'living within the ruins' seriously – I also want to think, with Eduardo Viveiros, *whose* ruins – it's easy gesturing perhaps if we think about the possibility of us living within *our* ruins. But, if we think of ruins as that which *we have ruined*, and that now we have to live with the awareness of those ruins only because we are being ruined too, that is not an easy gesture. If we write with the awareness of having been and continuing to be the coloniser – that's not an easy gesture. It is not an easy gesture to think what you have said: the exoticising of the mundane to the point that we become exotic to ourselves, with all that that means. An equaliser that is not quite an equaliser. And here I would take some issue with figure/ground reversal. I think that figure/ground reversal is a great tool to think with, but one with very important limits too. There can be no figure/ground reversal when there's no ground to reverse – it's as if we are all figures now, figures in search of a ground that's completely unstable. That instability can become mundane and then we – those who always felt stable – may become exotic to ourselves, also because we would be with those others who now appear not so exotic. None of this is necessarily easy gesturing if we want to think ourselves with those that we never thought ourselves with; this is very difficult to achieve – even in this volume. I was wondering how much the idea of the collapse is itself effecting collapse. Making 'all' the same without even being able to consider what 'all' is – I repeat, even in this piece.

So, how do we talk about collapse while locating the place from which we are talking about collapse, and acknowledging the limit of the collapse? I think that Kathryn Yusoff's work is something to consider here. And that work is similar to Danowski and Viveiros de Castro's 'ends of the world', and their comment that 'Amerindians have lived through many ends of the world' or of their worlds. Engaging with those ends would not lend itself to collapsing histories, stories, places, worlds.

Anyway, that's one point. The other point is that I feel there is one important figure that remains unmoved, untouched, and that is the historical figure of the human. I think that when we say 'post-human' or 'beyond the human' we are talking about a historical form of *being a person* which we have not even begun to think about provincialising. And it may only be this historical form of being a person – the human – that allows us to perform the collapse, to make it happen, and allows us to talk about the outside and the inside, and about what lies always within, even while questioning divisions like outside/inside or nature/culture. For several decades now we have been undoing mono-nature, opening it up to what's not nature – and that has produced great work. But we have done all that without touching the figure of the human. We started and stopped with Foucault: the figure of 'the man' was an invention, he said, and we contented ourselves with that, the critique of modern man. But what about the figure of the human? The invention of 'man' that Foucault remarks on, needed the invention of the human. And that invention, that historical emergence, is ignored. At best it is a matter of paleontological inquiry. 'The human' usually appears as an unquestioned, ever-present figure.

So, there is that monolith that we have not touched, although some (like Eduardo Viveiros) have been talking about it in anthropology. Perhaps Wagner is the only one who makes a figure/ground reversal himself and becomes that which is not only human, through his acrobatic inventions – which I love, but which are more than figure/ground reversals when he becomes that which is not only human. So, the person that is the shaman who can become jaguar (*pause*) is not the human that we are if only because we cannot become jaguar! And of course, after centuries of colonisation, that person is also human, or as I would prefer to say 'human, and not only'. But I feel that the human remains a monolith. There. Unmoved. It is as if it was invented to not be touched, and resists centuries of all sorts of sacred and secular thought. Now it is the Anthropos of the (s)cene that collapses all scenes. I feel 'environmental alterities' can have room for nature that is not only such, and also for the person who can be jaguar: human and *not only.*

C: This is very interesting to consider from the point of view of the book's title –*Environmental Alterities* – because if you translate it [environment] into Danish [*omverden*, literally 'surrounding world'] or Germanic, the *Umwelt* – same meaning – it is different for each entity, *per definition*, right? This is something Viveiros de Castro also touches upon in his discussion of perspectival Amerindian ontologies, but it is immediately evident back to von Uexküll, that the *Umwelt* is fundamentally relative: the *Umwelt* of a Danish hog farmer, a Mexican urban intellectual, a penguin and a fruit fly do not have much, if anything, in common. They are definitionally 'uncommon'. So, once you recognise this, any change in *Umwelt* entails a reshuffling of environmental alterities, to the point of possible incompatibility. Maybe I am imputing, but this is what I hear you saying. If you don't have one figure of the human, but rather as Kathryn Yusoff writes, a billion black Anthropocene figures, then you're going to also have a billion alterities. This creates very interesting kaleidoscopes effects, which are not just conceptually but also politically and practically very important, because it means that divisions and hierarchies – of which there are always enough to go around – simultaneously proliferate and change patterns.

All of this is great and important. But those patterns and effects *include* the ones generated by scientists to give shape to environmental alterities *via* the figure of the Anthropocene. It was not constructed in the first place to think about politics, coloniality, race and so on – although it might have been – but rather with a view to dealing with *other things* that are nevertheless also very important and which are, indeed, the central concerns of those scientists. In other words, contrary to the impression one might get from reading the infinite set of heated critical rebuttals, the Anthropocene never came into the world with the hidden subtext to demolish colonial and capitalist history as well as most other important differences in the world. So – and I am no longer referring to Cristóbal and Antonia's introduction, but to my feeling about the discussion as a whole – in my view, a lot of critical scholarship is in fact reading the Anthropocene proposal in a poor, and in fact very dumb way, because they have decontextualised it. They have moved it out of its *Umwelt* and turned it into grist for the mill for the nth round of critiquing Western hegemonies – critiques which would have been no less vigorous had the Anthropocene never become a buzzword.

So, to use Marisol's own words, the Anthropocene has a universalising tendency but it is *not only* that. It was also an effort to articulate what these scientists perceived to be something brand new, a change of state in the world that is going to affect every – not human, then – let's say every person – human or non-human.

This is why the discussion *pro et contra* Anthropocene always reminds me of the Confucian proverb, 'When the wise man points to the moon, the fool looks at the finger'. Everybody wants to debate terminology: 'the Anthropocene is universalising and a-historical, so let's dust off Marx: clearly the Capitalocene is far more appropriate. But no, it remains imperfect … how about Plantationocene. No, Chthulucene. No, really AnthropoObscene'! As if which finger is doing the pointing matters more than what they are all, from different angles, attempting to point at. This is, of course, a game which academics enjoy and at which they are skilled, no matter how inconsequential it may be. But to me, anyway, it seems that there are presently far more important things to do than continue to flog the already severely injured Anthropocene horse. And many of those things can only be done by accepting that scientists formulated that concept to at least try to grasp something quite novel in our planetary experience.

M: I think that's what I meant when I asked, 'is talking about the collapse itself effecting the collapse?', and collapse as I am using it refers to the practice of 'making the same again'. This sameness may be (re)done by practising the term (Anthropocene) through geo-engineered solutions to the problems it creates, and also in critical opposition to the term Anthropocene and the forces that continue to create what it names. To avoid sameness a politics has to be reinvented, and that reinvention I want to say provocatively may even be post-political. The 'post' would be to politics as usual, perhaps unrecognisable to the latter, certainly in opposition to it and, in that very way, it would itself be especially political. And that reinvention, daring to even slightly imagine it, I would say, again, 'is not easy', Casper.

C: Yes, of course.

M: Of course. Inventing politics is not easy. It may be easy to talk about 'ruins' or 'the uncommons' academically. That can even be pleasant, a challenge to relish. It makes us think, it positions us at the limit, and opens – I'm talking about myself and how I relish doing it – obliges us to open concepts to what those concepts cannot grasp. Of course, this conceptual work needs to be done, but, again, not only. It has to be done along with a reinvention of politics, or as a practice of politics, perhaps starting with – in a sense – an initial figure/ground reversal, where if we are ground we become figure and vice-versa. But an initial one only, because then things would unfold that would make us reinvent ourselves: for example, if we become figure, we may discover that the ground is fragmented and does not hold as ground, or that our epistemic tools cannot know the ground, or that there is no ground. And we have to start relating to each other in ways that we do not have any idea about. We don't know what 'the relation' would be! Or, if we have been relational (using relations of any kind), what would we do if groundlessness – or the eccentricity of ground – places us in a non-relational condition?

C: This reminds me of the Wagnerian endpoint to the introduction, which evokes this wonderful figure – was it called the *tabapot*?

M: That is a great concept.

C: And then hearing you talking about this kind of reversal – which then reveals somehow that there isn't any ground to begin with, and then the space of environmental alterities is totally transformed as a consequence. After we've been in more or less a Deleuzian and Latourian space for twenty years, where everything became assemblages and relational networks, suddenly we are in a realm of *tabapots* and chiasmatic reversals that sound positively Derridean …

M: (*laughs*)

C: Roy Wagner actually reminds me quite a bit of Derrida – these undecidable, vibrating, ambivalent relations that won't stand still. It's interesting because in some sense it's so close to Latour and Deleuze and yet the momentum is totally different.

But, hey, maybe we should talk a little bit about the chapters? I think you should start that Marisol …

M: (*laughs*) I liked both papers and there were things that I disagreed with in both papers. I think that Stine Krøijer's paper offered a great ethnographic situation. The idea that the palm oil trees are to be engaged with in ways that are different, yet the same, and the ways in which the people Krøijer works with engage with the forest; yet these ways are also different because the trees are unknown. Are the trees going to be known? This question brings in the forest in a way that proposes symmetry and difference with the newcomer trees. Symmetry because knowing is a relation with the forest, and difference because palm oil trees are unknown. I like that a lot. I also liked how her analysis presents otherness without exoticisation – for example the shaman has a son who is just a guy, not a shaman. In the analysis 'others' and 'us' are family – like the shaman and his son. Another way of saying it, to extend it beyond 'the case', is that I like this analysis because it makes 'otherness' and 'sameness' familiar.

C: What I most enjoyed about the paper was quite similar. There's something neat about two sets of contrasts running in parallel, and they just keep running in parallel, but never really meet. On the one hand you have this jungle …

M: Jungle is a great image …

C: … and on the other hand, you have mono-crop palm trees. One appears man-made and the other is natural, the situation fully dual, and so it lends itself to this kind of classic environmentalist critique. Of course, you should not destroy the jungle for mono-cropping, and, anyway, almost nothing is worse than the damn palm trees. And then the problem is that it's not – for once – the nasty white people that have really 'done it'. It's the nice, local people. According to this …

M: Cliché …

C: …you know, the indigenous, and perhaps animist, 'relational people', must be contrasted with the dualist Western people. So, you have that standard normative and profoundly binary view of the new animism debates, where the white modern reductive dualist will do all the bad things, but then 'nature' or the environment will be protected by the loving, caring, relational locals. And that scenography is immediately ruined in this chapter because the locals decided 'well, sure there's a trade-off here but we're going to do it, it's probably better for us'. Up go the palm trees. There are of course internal disagreements, and not everybody even sees it as a question of the 'plantation versus a forest', so you have a second contrast – very Bruce Albert and Davi Kopenawa – that raises the question of what *is* even the problem here? We know we can't control the forest in any case, but we have some way of communicating with stuff in it, right? We know there are spirits, they build spirit houses, and we have some ways of getting in touch with them. The problem is, what are we going to do with this new palm tree quasi-forest? Probably it's like a spirit graveyard, probably there's nothing. But on the other hand, we don't know. So the scenographies of thought are totally incompatible. It doesn't have to do with palm trees or non-palm trees, or relational locals versus reductive Westerners, but it has everything to do with the inhabitation, or lack of habitation, of spirits. That's cool. I really enjoyed that the text plays a double track, where on the one hand, the plantation versus non-plantation resembles the kind of discussion you find in Anna Tsing and others, who take very seriously certain scientific modes of describing forests and other places and try to engage these ideas in new ways. It's like a new natural history, and it leads to questions about how to characterise and differentiate good and bad landscapes, and how they are inhabitable. But then, the chapter implicitly juxtaposes this type of approach with the completely different discussion of spirit cohabitation. That part originates in an Amazonian tradition – I'm thinking about Eduardo Viveiros de Castro and his colleagues – of perspectival forests, where the problems are entirely different. In this chapter, these incongruent forms are put right next to each other, which generates a very interesting double contrast for thinking about environmental alterities. The question then arises, of course, what are you going do with this scene of incommensurability and non-relation?

M: Yes, and where does the non-relation appear? Because I have a very hard time when what becomes the non-relational is a dualist relation or the absence of the 'traditional' relation –those are just different kinds of relation. The subject/object relation is also relational, right? So, when people talk about capitalism as non-relational, I have a huge problem. We started thinking critically about the subject/object binaries and then, I do not how it happened that we have ended up denying the relationality of subject/object rather than thinking that binary was not all that this relation could be, that it could also house complexities of its own. An analysis about relations between palm oil plantations and forest could, for example, highlight the trial of force between the (capitalist!) palm oil trees and the rest. For example, (and here I am just inventing a situation that is not in the chapter) plantations may effect an imposition of relations that makes impossible relations between human-person and tree-person, and this impossibility may occupy the forest even in the absence of deforestation. In that sense, deforestation would not be the absence of trees – of jungle, as Casper called it – but the absence of the forms of relations between human-persons and tree-persons. In that situation the force of the capitalist relation would have undone the possibility of symmetrical relations – if you want to call it something, I don't have the word right now – but symmetrical relations between tree- persons and human-persons.

c: I agree. And even if something is non-relational, why should that worry or excite me? How would or should the recognition change my orientation?

M: What you are also pointing at Casper, the evaluation of the non-relational as bad and the relational as good, is important too. That is the point when the relational is transformed from an epistemic tool, or a tool of analysis, into an ethical condition to be desired. And that type of commentary happens frequently, whether implicitly or explicitly. I have dear friends who think like that too; they desire the relational because it is good. And that's where we all become (*laughs*) positivists again: because then, the non-relational and the relational stop being analytical tools and become what is out there... But going back to the chapter: I liked that she opens it with one of her interlocutors being at home fighting the grass that might damage the plantation trees – not caring about the forest, but caring about the palm trees and their production, 'for now I'm only at war with the grass' – I loved that. It was as if he was mocking the anthropologist – not necessarily Krøijer, but any of us anthropologists, if we practise the 'other' and 'us' relation. I would also propose that this relation bothers him, and maybe that is why he repeats that he is at war only with the grass. This is also a relation; even if it cancels the possibility of relations (even his own relations) with forest tree-persons, killing the grass is a relation of care of the palm tree. Not a bad relation, not a good relation, although perhaps creating a non-relation with tree-persons – this guy is still relational.

A: I just want to explain that we actually asked our contributors to try to engage with this idea of the non-relational. The question was whether there is there any mileage in bringing a relational perspective together with a putatively non-relational one – with all the impossibilities and contradictions this implies? And that's where our *tabapot* comes in, as it does not allow us to settle on one nor the other – it's the movement *between* them that we are interested in. It would be good to maybe reflect on this in the second paper as well?

C: Sure. This is, in many ways, a very different piece. It is about thinking *in* forests, not *like* a forest, as for Eduardo Kohn. We are no longer in Ecuador but in Congo – if I remember correctly – situated amid scientists who are tracking troops of bonobos. And – in contrast with Matt Candea's ethnography of scientists studying meerkats – a significant part of the interest this holds for Alcayna-Stevens is that the bonobos disappear into the forest all the time. It is really nice, very enjoyable – its mode of execution is quite far from what I could do, but I really enjoyed it. Imagine being in your laboratory, and the experimental subjects just vanish, get the hell out of there, and you have to spend half of your precious research time tracking them down. And of course, the bonobos are far more mobile and know the forest far better than you do, so it's a big problem.

And so, in line with the anthropological conception of oneself as the instrument of knowledge, whether you like it or not you just cannot be a neutral, passive observer. You have got to get off your ass and move around in the jungle for large periods of time. And because you don't know it so well, you're basically located in a kind of twilight zone. Between your knowledge and ignorance, but also between activity and the passivity imposed on you by the bonobos, since you can't find them. You are surrounded by foliage, inside what Alcayna-Stevens quotes Myers as calling a 'lively sensorium', which puts you on edge, perceptually and bodily. You get tired, yet you must stay keen and alert. She describes the state as being on edge, doing 'edge work' or 'cusp work', a very fine idea. Interestingly, the focus is hardly on what the scientists do when they find the bonobos – we actually know almost nothing about that. We hardly even know anything about what the forest looks or smells like, you have to imagine it yourself. And yet, it's a very lively description of the feelings one must have fumbling around after vanished bonobos in a dense forest. On the one hand, you are upset about it, but on the other hand it is also exciting. To revive an old term, it is a liminal space; you're not really doing anything and yet at the same time you are doing everything. Your mind is roaming freely, and you are trying to focus. It is a scene of intensity. It evokes patterns emerging as scientists wander the jungle, trying to create relations with bonobos that continuously elude them. But meanwhile, having to negotiate relations with all kinds of other entities – insects, mud, or snakes, and getting exhausted or perhaps sick.

Now, I suppose one could also view the chapter as grappling with the relational and the non-relational, or even, given a certain interpretation, the non-relational, *per se*. So, one might observe that scientists are spending an awful lot of time not actually making any relations with the bonobos. The bonobos are doing their own thing, and meanwhile scientists are in fact continuously detaching from an enormous number of relations with various parts of the forest in order to try to trace them. From this point of view – and this is with a nod to Antonia's 'data as relation and non-relation' – the ethnographic scene is paradoxically full of relations that are continuously severed. This is part of a deeply Strathernian mode of thinking relations. For me, the problem with 'non-relation' has more to do with the object-oriented ontology of people like Graham Harman and Timothy Morton, and I think there is some confusion in the introduction because these versions are not sufficiently differentiated.

M: …right

C: For the object-oriented ontologists of the world, of course, the big error of anthropology and indeed all human sciences since Kant, is that they stopped believing in their ability to deal with things in themselves, or that there even *are* things in themselves. So, they affirm that the recognition of such things is in fact very important, because they are always there, even if inherently withdrawn from, or in excess of, relationality. But philosophically pertinent as the point may be, as soon as you have scientists frantically running around in the forest in search of missing bonobos, it just doesn't matter very much because the forest in fact interferes 'relationally' with you at every point…

M: (*laughs*)

C: …Whether the entities are in some sense truly withdrawn, disengaged and beyond correlation with anything in human experience is, anthropologically speaking, pretty much a moot point. It may be that climate change is a withdrawn 'hyperobject', for example, but only philosophically speaking. In any particular environmental context it has immediate relational and experiential dimensions. And that includes for scientists, whether they depend on satellite data, or whether they are chasing bonobos.

So, when Alcayna-Stevens is playing with these ideas it has very little to do with the object-oriented sense of non-relationality. It is much more like what you described, Marisol, where everything is a relation and a non-relation at the same time. Indeed, everything sounds Derridean, once again, doesn't it? Things will not stop being non-relational at the same time as they remain relational. You are severed from the bonobos, in the same go as you connect with them, like you are severed from your lover in the same moment as you are connected with them. Nothing is either purely relational or non-relational, because everything happens in some other weird topology. Alcayna-Stevens, I think, uses the term 'interstices', doesn't she? Like patterned 'gaps' and Strathernian fractals, this notion is very useful for thinking about these patterns of relations and non-relations. Again, perhaps we are not too far from the *tabapot*.

M: I also liked the way the chapter is written. I was very attracted to the way she invents the scientist as a knowledge chaser. This person is chasing knowledge, she is *after* the bonobos because she wants to know, she wants to know, she wants to know. She relentlessly chases her object of knowledge and is packed with gadgets to allow her to capture knowledge. The pen, the pencil, the backpack, everything... 'Do I have my notebook? Yes, do I have my second notebook?' All her tools are tools to capture knowledge, but knowledge escapes and keeps escaping. At the same time, she is surrounded by conditions that are intriguing to her, but she is not interested in those, even though they also present a knowledge challenge in a different way. She relates to those, but she's focused on her object of knowledge, which she keeps chasing. I found that figure extremely intriguing, along with the figure of the writer, or more precisely of the author as both the scientist and the writer of the chapter. Moving between them allows her to be both the scientist that chases knowledge and the writer that reflects on chasing knowledge. As the author looks at the chaser of knowledge and describes what she does, she releases what the scientist cannot capture: knowledge. I really liked that movement as an analytical method that yields through writing what it is after. The shift she achieved, the shift that Cristóbal and Antonia talk about in the introduction, as a method yields knowledge, and it is also a pleasant story achieved through good writing. A pleasant story that makes us know in a different way, in a way that is exacting of the inclination to think through engaging with fun reading. I feel that you, Casper, are saying something similar when you say, 'this is not the kind of writing that I would do, but I learned a lot through this'.

c: That's true (*laughs*).

CRISTÓBAL: I have the feeling that these three conceptual devices, or themes of concern we had in our introduction – the first, limits; the second, heterogeneities; and finally, the *tabapot* –, I have the impression that in our conversation today you're somehow bringing the *tabapot* into the second kind of alterity, 'heterogeneities'. It looks like now, in this conversation, we could work with two sections in the introduction, we have limits and heterogeneities, and within heterogeneities we have the *tabapot*. That's my feeling in this conversation. And what we were trying to do in the introduction is to put the *tabapot* in a third place, because we were also trying to think about how to encourage collaboration among scholars and the way we can make contrasts between different (epistemic?) understandings of politics, relationality, and its limits. In this respect it's interesting to note – this is a footnote – that every time you mentioned the *tabapot*, Marisol, you needed your hands to draw circles that allowed you to talk about this shift. And you as well, Casper – you were making other kinds of gestures with your hands, as if there was something, Derridean perhaps, you cannot reach. The shift itself is beyond any kind of epistemic possibility of being embraced or fully grasped, but there is a reason why we didn't put *that* in the heterogeneities section. There is an implicit concern in the book about how we think collaboration is not happening between scholars talking about limits and others talking about heterogeneities, and thus, building a dialectic between these domains. So, if we think seriously about the very force of the *tabapot*, do you both think it has any potentiality for rethinking politics and collaboration? Marisol, you made a contrast between what we do in academia and what we do at the limits of academia, how we engage in a kind of politics that goes beyond academia. Do you think that the *tabapot* can do something new? Or do we just need to embrace it as if it were a method of this ungraspable movement that we cannot fully embrace?

M: I think it's very difficult for me to think *tabapot* other than analytically – it is hard for me to practise *tabapot*, and even harder to *do* it politically. Perhaps I am being a realist – or am I? But I feel that there's a divorce, between the easiness that the *tabapot* offers to my analysis – it allows many thought possibilities, an important *movement* between possibilities – but it's harder for me to *want* to use *tabapot* to think *and* do politics – both practices: not only thinking politics but also doing politics. Not because it's impossible, but because what makes me feel the difficulty, and eventually makes me think about doing *tabapot* as impossible, is the 'stuff' that makes politics, its temporality for example: the now-ness that the need to act politically imposes, and that this now-ness prevents all shifts – which is precisely what the *tabapot* offers to thought. So, perhaps if we want to think about politics, we have to displace its demand of now-ness, suspend it as it were, to imagine politics (its thinking-doing) in a very *longue durée* that would allow us to open up politics to something like alterities, to possibilities that relate to the now-ness of – sorry I have to say it once again – not only. That *longue durée* would be very dense and unsmooth because it would also be emplaced, and perhaps 'change' would not be one of its main analytical motifs. The difficulty of coupling *tabapot* and politics is the quality of each of their temporalities: the stuff that makes the former enables agile shifting; its now-ness is dynamically acquired in that shift – I think that is not the case with politics. But of course, it depends on who is talking about politics and what we are talking about when we use that word. I can easily imagine a conversation about *tabapot* among academics talking political analysis – even if they are as different as Marxists or object-oriented ontologists. It would be a rough conversation, but it is not hard to imagine that conversation. However, when I think about the recognised politics that make our worlds (formal or informal, organised or not, against the state or by the state) and my (or our) conceptual thinking about politics, I feel a gap between both practices. The gap (which undoubtedly has to do with the now-ness of politics) is so tangible that I even bifurcate my practice into two kinds of activities. The one where I work with my politician friends and strategise concrete actions with them regarding allegedly pressing problems; and the other one – the politics that we are allowed to think when we suspend the urgency and imagine possibilities for a world that is not yet. So, how do we align thinking the world that's *not yet*, with political action in the world that *is*? I know it is doable, but it requires very specific circumstances, usually absent. That absence generates the question I just made and that I want to live as a problem that prevents complacency with my bifurcation of both practices. And that is probably why I search for thought partnerships with people like Mariano and Nazario Turpo or Davi Kopenawa – because, their worlds *are*, even against the history that decreed their impossibility. Through that mode of being (one that is but that cannot be) they participate in making worlds that are not yet, and clear space for thought. Those worlds practise a temporality that can ignore the urgency of politics, while also participating in this urgency, of course. Instead, the world of my friends from Lima is occupied by the temporality that makes those urgencies; more importantly (I think) it does not know how to not be. Maybe that is why my friends (and I) cannot dispel urgencies: would we risk not being? I think that that this politics requires not slowing down. So, 'slow down thinking' (the refrain that I use to think) doesn't work – over and over again, it does not work. And this is extremely depressing; the impossibility has to be slowed down or displaced. Caveat: when I say 'displace' – I have said it more than once now – I am conjuring Strathern, or my interpretation of her: not replace, but suspend the condition – in this case impossibility – or push it from centre-stage, make it be not the only option. So... perhaps instead of bifurcating my practice, I could practice *tabapot* through a constant shift between thinking a politics that is not yet and participating in the politics that wants to change the world that is. Thus, the *tabapot* would be both concept and practice, and I would not live in the divorce between these two possibilities. Moving between both in a way that also connects, without that connection undoing the separation and thus maintaining the need to shift. At this point I might have resolved the bifurcation, but the other side of the problem remains: how to lure my politician friends to seriously think without the pressure of the world that is? How to lure them to suspend the urges of this world and think worlds that are not yet and, of course, those that are in spite of their historically decreed impossibility? Perhaps if they think the latter, they may think their/our own 'not yet?'

C: What Marisol just said resonated with the point in the introduction where the editors say something like 'maybe it sounds counterintuitive, but really what is most important right now is slowing down our critical thoughts', and that's obviously with a view to opening up to new concepts, politics or practices, and... how could you disagree? There are, after all, lots of quick and easy analyses of everything, so you must slow down. But at the same time, the invocation of slowness – often via Stengers – is also driving me a bit crazy, because evidently for many purposes you should not slow down at all. In fact, you have to speed up to try to prevent all kinds of horrors even though you can't be sure what you are doing. Since we are talking about environmental alterities, it should be obvious that there are different temporalities. Why would we think that slowness is the one guiding value? Of course, politics has different contexts, and therefore different speeds, different types of urgency and different figures for opening thought and action. I don't think you need *tabapot* to impeach Donald Trump, and it needs to speed up.

M: (*laughs very hard*) I think you do!

C: Maybe that is, after all, the missing piece! (*laughs*). But anyway, there are many different contexts for thinking and action, and that goes for forests too, right? I mean, there are questions about indigenous lands within what are now nation states, questions about big shady logging operations; there's questions of the knowledge practices of forestry, and of collaborations and battles across the planet…

M: Yes, of course, Casper, of course. But the problem is that many different kinds of politics are *not*, also.

C: Yeah, but I think that is a really good question, right? The extent to which it is and is not, and how to 'measure' that in some sense, right? Marisol, I think we've talked about that before in terms of John Law's argument about the 'one-world world'. About the extent to which that characterisation of one single, massive division is helpful or not. And I think it is, mainly, not. In contrast, Stengers' insistence that 'we have to realise we are already quite different from what we think we are' is something I find extremely appealing, because it enables you to see that there are alterities even close to hand, and there are always many more things going on than you think.

M: Yes, I think you are right, and I think that we should end on the point that what we have to do is *assert* rather than propose – or propose assertively – that politics is not only what 'we' recognise as such. That many political practices *are* without recognition and do not even need recognition – they alter cognition. What I would change in what you said is the idea that there are different urgencies of different politics; I would say something like 'Now our proposals have to go beyond the assertion of ontological politics. Ontological politics *are*. Period'. How do we practise political ontology publicly? How do we make a public for politics that *are* beyond recognition? There are people who are making that politics … and that may make us realise that 'we are already quite different than what we think we are' – like the palm trees that are both like the forest trees and not.

C: This is perhaps a complementary point, but one of the things that strikes me – coming out of STS – is that forests are full of all kinds of stuff not touched upon in these chapters. This is not a criticism, because obviously nobody can cover everything, but it is nevertheless an observation. Forestry is a data science these days. You know stuff about forests from satellites and advanced technological equipment, as Antonia has written about. Acquiring knowledge about forests depends on distributed knowledge infrastructures. There are many people making forest knowledge in many, many other ways than searching for bonobos.

And the ability to roam the forests in search of monkeys in the first place is ena-bled by vast transport, financial and scientific networks and infrastructures that reach into the world's forests without always being immediately visible there. Conversely, the tentacles of palm plantations like the one described by Krøijer, stretch outwards in many directions. This sense of extended networks in and out of forests is missing in both chapters. Which is really a political issue too. Because if you ask how new 'problematic elements' enter places like the Amazon, the answer is that they do so via all kinds of infrastructural work.

Often, this does not take the form of high-level ontological politics of the kind you [Marisol] have analysed: should earth-beings be taken seriously or relegated to the status of primitive superstition – but rather as the banal onto-logical politics of infrastructure: 'are we going to build an extra stretch of road here? Are we going to allow the foreigners to cut this much further into our land?' This is ontological politics as silent infrastructural transformation. It is a realm of ontological politics that is often under the radar. It matters a great deal, but not in the same way as the struggles with earth-beings. So, I can't help thinking it would have been nice to include a third paper with an STS angle, articulating the infrastructures that produce forests as spaces of intervention and knowledge making. And I think that's not detached from the questions of political ontology that you raise either. But I guess we will have to save that for another time…

REFERENCES

Omura, K, G. Otsuki, S. Satsuka, and S. Morita, eds., *The World Multiple: Everyday Politics of Knowing and Generating Entangled Worlds* (New York: Routledge Advances in Sociology, 2019).

Yusoff, K. *A Billion Black Anthropocenes, or None* (Minneapolis, MN: University of Minnesota Press, 2018).

Danowski, D., and E. Viveiros de Castro, *The Ends of the World*, trans. Rodrigo Nunes. (Cambridge: Polity Press, 2017).

Kopenawa, D., and B. Albert, *The Falling Sky: Words of a Yanomami Shaman*, trans. by Nicholas Elliott and Alison Dundy (Cambridge, MA: Harvard University Press, 2015).

Kohn, E., *How Forests Think: Toward an Anthropology Beyond the Human* (Berkeley and Los Angeles, CA: University of California Press, 2013).

Candea, M., 'Habituating meerkats and redescribing animal behaviour science', *Theory, Culture & Society*, 30.7–8 (2013): 105–128.

Walford, A., 'Raw Data: Making Relations Matter', *Social Analysis*, 61.2 (2013): 65–80.

Harman, G., *'Object-Oriented Ontology: A New Theory of Everything* (London: Pelican, 2018).

Morton, T., *Hyperobjects: Philosophy and Ecology After the End of the World* (Minneapolis, MN: University of Minnesota Press, 2013).

Law, J., 'What's Wrong with a One-World World?', *Distinktion*, 16.1 (2015): 126–139.

COLLECTIVITIES

TO LIVE AND LEARN

NOTES ON ALTERITY AND TOGETHERNESS, OR: ON LIVING WITH DOGS

Marianne de Laet

'*companions are not here just to think with. They are here to live with*'.

— D. Haraway 2004: 298

FIDELITY

HOW TO BE TRUE TO THE EXPERIENCE OF LIVING TOGETHER WITH DOGS, when the language that is reserved for human-animal relations insists on describing such relations in terms of domestication, species-alterity and control? In this paper I tell three short stories about my life with dogs, each of which shifts the terms on which such 'living with' is possible, as well as the language in which to think of it. The stories give hands and feet to the theoretical musings about domestication, subjectivity, alterity and agency which they intersperse.

The first story introduces my canine counterparts Raylan and Kismet in an image; the story is about how this image was crafted and tells of what it produces. Thinking about the othering effect of photos as I try to do a photoshoot of my dogs, I list the work that it takes to be a subject, arguing that the dogs exert agency in this process, so asserting their subjectivity. The second story is about words. I take issue with a line of experimentation in animal science, where MRI scans of dogs' brains are used to 'show' that dogs 'understand' or 'know' words. Privileging language, which dogs are not supposed to 'have', the study on dogs-knowing-words banks on as well as affirms dogs' alterity. Depending on a protocol in which such alterity is assumed, the study meanwhile fuels the sensibility that dogs are not as alter as they seem. I submit that in their use or non-use of words dogs may not be as alter as the study presumes, nor as non-alter as it suggests; the urge to adjudicate alterity by way of understanding words may be a human preoccupation that has nothing to do with the dogs' life-worlds. The third story is about the walk. Diffusing the idea that the leash locates power and agency in the human, I relate the intricacies of going for a walk with and without the tether and describe how words, leash, human and dogs together craft fidelity to the practice of being a pack.

In these stories, or so I argue, the dogs have agency; it is from doing things together that fidelity – representational, practical, and relational fidelity – to their subjectivity arises.

WORRYING ALTERITY

1 May 2016. A video rolls by on Facebook, of the enormous head of a husky snuggled up to a baby who cannot be more than six months old. Barely able to sit up straight, the baby pets, pokes and bats at the dog's ears, nose and eyes; then it tumbles over, smothering the big head. This head, all that is visible of what must be a very large body, nuzzles the baby's face and 'grins' – a word used in dog training manuals to describe this particular canine facial expression which may or may not have anything to do with the bliss typically associated with its human version. The head rolls over to expose the dog's throat, and the video's final frame shows it lying, paws-up, on its back. The appeal of the image lies in the play of opposites: power and vulnerability, tenderness and indifference, dog and child. It rests also in a blending of alters that creates new contrasts: the powerful dog is tender; the vulnerable child is untamed. Domestication, or so the image suggests, resolves alterity.

As anyone who has read a bit of ethology – the study of non-human behaviour – knows, for a dog to roll over and show a human its throat is the ultimate signal of… and here I hesitate. What is this meaning that 'anyone … knows'? Of what *is* the throat-revealing act a sign? Of hierarchy, submission, control? Of domestication? Which is the word I am looking for? As Filippo Bertoni suggests in his dissertation *Living with Worms* (2016), the term domestication as a descriptor of relations with nature truncates the potentialities of what such relations might entail; the term implies a relationship of hierarchy and control, of domination and submission, denoting an *alterity* of the tamed and the wild. When relations among animals – humans included – are so framed it is difficult to imagine them in any other way. And so, I hesitate. For there must be a term that describes the husky-baby moment with greater fidelity to the agents involved.

This paper takes up the volume's concern with a central ethnographic dilemma: how to seriously account for one's informants when those informants' life-worlds do not affirm the intellectual and practical commitments that as a responsive and responsible thinker one knows to be true (or believes to be valid or thinks to be right).[1] In other words, what to do when *alterity* bursts onto the scene; when, as in the context of this volume, the ethnographer's intellectual and political attachments to a post-nature ontology are not borne out by constituents' practices – and when, as interlocutors, we must relate their business in our terms. The question becomes differently pressing when other-than-human animals are concerned. When, as in my case, those constituents are dogs, how to speak of and for their *Umwelt*[2], if I have little access, or none at all, to their ontological commitments?

In what follows I describe some of the domestic arrangements that allow me and my dogs to live together; I think through the life-world of a pack of which I myself am a member. I am cautious about how to represent these arrangements; my argument is inspired, again, by Bertoni's theorising of textual excess – that is to say, by the realisation that 'things are already engaged in multiple life formations and constellations, and these always do exceed the textual' (personal communication). But if, as Bertoni asserts, language is insufficient for grasping such life-worlds, it also fixes them as soon as they are described. While I share the volume editors' appeal to non-essentialist language as a potential way out of this dilemma, it seems to me that the term alterity may itself point to an essentialist practice: as soon as difference is articulated, it exists. So, I experiment with Haraway's suggestion, above, that 'living with' might be an extension of, but also a radical alternative to, 'thinking with'. I am interested in the circularity between thinking and living that is implied here: to frame being with dogs in terms other than domestication affords different ways of knowing and enables other ways of … being with dogs.

TOGETHERNESS: THE PACK AS METHOD

What form can 'living in/as a member of a pack' possibly take? Any dog obedience manual will instruct the 'dog owner' to assume the position of 'leader of the pack'[3]; in this stipulation, hierarchy, dominance and domestication are inscribed, and it is not what I am after when I figure myself a member of the pack. While I resort to such manuals when I try to learn about how to be with my dogs, I am also wary of the particular conception of leadership that is inscribed in them. According to these texts a dog owner must be a steadfast, directive and charismatic leader of the pack. Positioned as I am – a woman anthropologist in a STEM environment; steeped in feminist, critical and actor-network theory, and by inclination and conviction bent towards collaborative forms rather than directive organisation, that doesn't sit too well.

'Being a pack member' does not mean that I am one with the dogs, however. After all, I do not sleep with the new puppy in his crate. I do not eat out of bowls on the floor. I clean up the dogs' poop and their vomit; they do not return the favour, or go shopping when I am sick. They would rather chew than read my library; they eat my shoes, carry off my socks, and this paper-in-the-making is not their friend. I control their food and their snacks and in order to feed them, I set aside my vegetarian care for other animals and buy them processed-into-kibble meat. It would seem that the agency is all mine. And yet, my stories about living together tell a different tale.

While thinking in terms of a pack does not mean setting aside asymmetries among us, it does allow for different observations than a framing in terms of domestication would afford. Rather than suggesting that the pack is the whole that subsumes and renders equal its elements, I propose it as an analytical and methodological tool – a way to imagine human-animal collaborations as exceeding alterity while still denying that there exists some sort of generic, natural intra- or inter-species harmony. 'Pack-membership' does not make me a dog, nor does it make the dogs human – but if the pack is understood as an empirical object, to be engaged ethnographically, the collaboration of agencies and the collection of instantiations that hold it together begin to unfold. Observing the pack of which I am one, then, points to an auto-ethnographic effort to un-modestly witness shifting relations, and to recognise all three animals' subjectivities and concerns, as these emerge in our living together.[4]

As I attend to the ways in which the pack entails a shaping of each other's practices, I argue that boundaries delineating self from Other shift as these practices unfold. While this volume's concern is with how to maintain authors' and ethnographers' commitment to theorising 'after nature' when for their constituents' nature is assumed, I am interested in how to do togetherness in the face of such chasms. The 'othering' that occurs in ethnographic accounts, where one party speaks for or about another's ontology is, as we know, an effect of precisely the act of speaking for or about. I take our editors' concern with alterity, then, as an invitation to think about alterity *itself* – considering the project of *living together* as a commentary upon it.

Pertaining to the nature-culture space of living with dogs, this paper tells stories of living with domestic canines for whom nature may be long past but is all too present, nonetheless. After all, for my dogs nature is my rug, our car, the dog park, the prepared experience of the 'nature-trail', the leash that enables excursions on that trail – while for their cousins elsewhere it may be a landfill in Corum, Turkey; a dog house or a chain in the sub-Arctic where they are kept outside despite the freezing cold; a dog-meat farm in Asia; or the Iditarod, an annual long-distance Alaskan sled-dog race. While it may be true, as Haraway (2003) argues, that humans' and dogs' natures – in the sense of environment, character and bodily matter – are mediated by each other, it is also true that *our* designation of alterity prescribes *their* potentialities: where 'we' draw the line – which we do by way of the word *species* – has world-shaping consequences for them. This paper, then, comes out of an impatience with both the limits and the effects of such representations. The words that we-who-write offer, form at best partial understandings – meanwhile shaping the natures and the range of action and motion of our others. Rethinking alterity, then, in terms of living together, is a path towards framing different worlds.

STORY 1. SUBJECTS AND PHOTOGRAPHS: SUBJECTS OF PHOTOGRAPHS

FIG. 3.1 The ethnographer in her backyard, with laptop and research subjects (Photograph by the author, 2016)

Rather than discuss this pack in words, let's allow an image to do the work of representing. Anthropologists will recognise this photo; even if one has never seen this particular one before, it is nevertheless familiar – from Bronislaw Malinowski's rendering of the 'subjects' of his treatise on the Trobianders, or from the cover of George Stocking Jr.'s *Observers Observed* (1983). *A photo of the ethnographer in her backyard, with laptop and research subjects* shows the (here absent) but nevertheless iconic ethnographer together with attentive 'native' interlocutors; it suggests, at once, being-there, authority, and *her* license and ability to speak of and for *them*. And it is precisely this license and ability to *speak of and for*, and the suggestion that speaking of and for represents understanding, that is at issue here.

Being a research subject is not as easy as it seems; one is not positioned as a research subject 'naturally'. Preceding this picture was a half hour of negotiations, four treats, seven takes, a crushed snail, efforts to place, sit and stay, much mutual incomprehension and three (four, if we count the snail) unhappy persons. Raylan (left) and Kismet (right) clearly do not want to be there; you can see it in their postures and on their faces. Well... maybe you can't, but – and this is the point, perhaps, of this paper – I can. For the animals look back. Subject-ness cannot be un-mediated; it must be relational. And that applies to being the subject of a photo, the subject of an MRI (which is at the heart of my second story), or/ and the subject of another's understanding. Being a subject is predicated on with-ness (Haraway 2016); it requires at least two subjects, in relation. And so taking a photo of my dogs both calls out and asserts their subjectivity.[5]

Being a subject is also material, and it has limitations. The other subject of this photo (and of my query), the author – third member of the pack – cannot in this moment be subject, object and photographer all at the same time. Choosing, for now, to be photographer rather than delegating the task to another human or a selfie-stick, the author is absent from the photo but present as its medium; it is I who calls the picture into being. Being absent is not what it is cracked up to be either: one has to be present in order to witness and report, and in this case the dogs appear to be more present than I can be. So, while being a research subject is not as natural as it seems, being a researcher, ditto; in ethnographic research, one is rarely where 'it' happens, where one imagines one ought to be or – learns later – should have been. 'Being there', then, is an impossible imposition, as (I am stealing from the best, twice) there is no there, there.[6] Or at least, there is no a priori there; the situation is entirely made up. And yet in this made-up situation the subjectivity of Raylan and Kismet shows up.

I submit, then, that as I 'live with' them, I craft – continuously, on-goingly, inescapably and unwittingly – fidelity to the subjectivity of my dogs; a fidelity that is closer than what I might gain from scanning their brains with an MRI (which, again, is the conceit of the animal researchers in my second story). I take up and take seriously Haraway's suggestion that 'living with' might be an extension of, and an alternative to, 'thinking with' or 'speaking of'; I ask how to live with dogs – whom I both propose and problematise as my environmental other. Words cannot suffice as representational vehicles for human – let alone canine – understanding and yet one must put into words what offering a non-representational understanding might entail. The answer to this conundrum may be to experiment with modes of relating to what it is one seeks to understand; to engage rather than probe. It is, perhaps, to seek to accept that it is in living together in wonder, rather than in examining to understand, that an approximation to grasping the other's life world may be found.

This story, then, does two things: it demonstrates that being a member of the pack is not automatic; it takes work. But while in the moment of making the picture relations in the pack are not harmonious, that moment – and this is the second point – offers an opportunity to show off the dogs' subjectivity. That subjectivity manifests itself in their gaze, in their recalcitrance, in their faces, in their dissent and in their agency, which determines whether there will be a photo or not.[7] Recognising the dogs as subjects of my life-world is a first step in acknowledging that they are both other and (like) myself.

ANIMAL STORIES

Prompted by the admonishment that dogs are not here just to think but to live with, I wonder what kinds of thinking may yet be learned from living with them. Vinciane Despret's stories in *What Would Animals Say If We Asked the Right Questions?* (2016), about animal-human relationships in animal research, point a way. Despret – according to Bruno Latour (Latour 2016: ix) an 'additive' rather than 'subtractive' empirical philosopher – offers a steady stream of 'scientific fables' (vii) that fill and enrich animal studies practices with the relationships that such practices necessitate and forge. While 'interested in objective facts and grounded claims', Despret likes, in Latour's words, 'to add, to complicate, to specify, and, whenever possible, to slow down … above all, [to] hesitate so as to multiply the voices that can be heard' (ibid). Hesitation here is a key methodological moment, resonating with Viveiros de Castro's (2004) advice to 'equivocate' – equivocation being 'the condition of possibility of anthropological discourse'. Her hesitation allows a suspension of judgment, and as she sits with the stories, Despret not only reframes but also respects and values the animal science that her work is about – instead of dismissing what it has to offer.

So, when she describes how the notorious ethologist Konrad Lorenz, as he studies the jackdaw, becomes 'human-with-jackdaw' as much as the bird becomes 'jackdaw-with-human', Despret infuses his behaviourist account with Whitehead's (1920/2004) notion that being (and knowing) can only be in relating. And this notion applies as much to the ethologist as it applies to the bird: in their collaboration bird and ethologist learn to be affected by the other. Their study binds them, *producing* as much as *banking on* their togetherness; as Despret observes, they shape each other's life-worlds. Exemplifying Haraway's imperative, then, the story demonstrates how animal-human collaborations exceed 'thinking with' each other: the practice of 'living with' has world-shaping effects for which an animal study bent on producing knowledge has no eye.

When I take a picture of Raylan and Kismet at the back of my house, the three of us enter into a collaboration that turns each of us into a slightly different subject than we were before. In recognising their subjectivity, I am at odds with the practices of animal studies, where the term species denotes a *prima facie* self/others distinction between humans and animals. The alterity inscribed in that term would suggest that there is me (the ethographer and subject of the auto-ethographic stories I tell) and there is them (my canine companions and the objects of my accounts). If dogs are other-than-self in their other-species-ness, our alterity is marked in at least three ways: I am subject, and they are not; I use words and they do not; and I am in charge of the strategies for navigating life that enable our togetherness. While my first story disrupts the idea that dogs have no subjectivity, the next story homes in on their use of words.

STORY 2. UNDERSTANDING WORDS

On 31 August 31, 2016, a major Dutch newspaper, *de Volkskrant*, reported a breakthrough scientific study suggesting that dogs understand words. The report infuriates me quite unreasonably. Not only, or so the report goes, can members of our companion species respond to intonation and inflexion: they actually *know*, the study unreflexively suggests, what certain words *mean*. MRI scans in experimental situations show that both left and right sides of the subject-dogs' brains light up when certain words are spoken. Previously, animal researchers had thought that only the left side – that registers affect – would fire, but it turns out that the right side – which houses cognition – is equally involved.

Forget for a moment the complex of assuming, processing and decision-making that allows MRI's to 'prove' anything at all[8], and imagine that the scans do indeed tell us something salient about the brain. Forget also the philosophical difficulties to do with 'knowing', 'meaning' and 'knowing meaning'; let's follow empirically how the researchers propose to extend our prior understanding of the understanding of dogs. It had been thought, earlier, that dogs are sensitive to the affect with which words are spoken and, more recently, that they do not respond to affect alone; a 'well-trained dog' will offer the 'intended behaviour' even when her person gives certain 'commands' in a neutral tone. But that is not enough, or so the argument goes, to decide that the dog actually *understands*; after all, the behaviour may be no more than a Pavlovian response to a sound – a routed association between word and deed. The MRI study represents a 'breakthrough' in that it proves that more (whatever more is) is going on. The dog both 'knows' the *word* and, as the activity in the cognitive part of the brain suggests, 'understands' the *content*. Thus, with a big leap the newspaper report concludes, the distance between humans and dogs – a difference between species that seems to ultimately be at stake here – shrinks a little bit, yet again.

The study, then, at least according to the newspaper, offers a commentary on *alterity*. Dogs are not as different from humans as (to some) they may seem. But humans who are in a relationship with a dog know that dogs are not as alien to humans as our body shapes might suggest. We marvel at the dogs 'human-ness'; our dogs are with us, and they 'get' us, 'naturally', all the way – or so we like to imagine. So, how to account for *both* the attachment to alterity – dogs are so different from humans that we should be surprised that they understand words – *and* the attachment to non-alterity – dogs are so similar to humans that they understand their persons implicitly?

I choose to take this, again, as a question about fidelity: it is in living and doing that some sort of fidelity to circumstance and experience arises. And I propose as an alternative to an epistemic variety of fidelity – where it matters that dogs understand what words represent, and in which the wonder about their understanding is premised upon human-dog *alterity* – a relational version of fidelity, where understanding arises from togetherness, in which it matters that dogs act as our (environmental) match. In developing this notion, I am aided by the sensibility of the pack. To take the pack seriously – as an operational and an analytical term – is to find a language for togetherness, but it is also to push back against the fantasy that dogs are with us, naturally, all the way. For it is only in the *practice* of togetherness that a mutual sensibility can arise.

AGENCY

Some would argue that the dogs are 'other' in more ways yet: in ways to do with what one might call power. In our pack, it is after all I who decides when we travel; I decide when food appears, and when we go for walks. But while others may press me to own up to my powers as 'leader of the pack', I maintain that I cannot be sure that I – nor do I generally strive to – call the shots. I concede gleefully that I am not always everywhere 'the leader of the pack.'[9]

It is precisely the assumption of human agency and control that is at stake, here and in the broader conversation about human-animal relations; in order to modulate it, it is necessary to rethink what actors are and do. Not only is it imperative to distribute the possibility of agency among organisms – as in, for instance, Michel Callon's work on sociologies of translation, which locates agency in both fishermen and endangered scallops as they bring about an ecological disaster in Normandy's St Brieuc's Bay; it is also useful to reimagine agency itself. Being with animals requires what Gomart and Hennion (1999) describe as an 'active opening oneself to being affected'. Exploring the practices of music amateurs and drug users, the authors argue that in the day-to-day engagements with their habits, practitioners subject themselves to what objects (in their case music and drugs) do to and with them. Allowing oneself to be affected requires an active doing; surrendering oneself is not a passive move. I suggest that in living with dogs, too, all members of the pack engage in such what the authors call *faire-faire*.

My understanding of such *faire-faire* is informed, too, by the strategies, practices and sensibilities of sensory ethnography (Pink 2009), where the ability to say something salient about the state of the world rests in one's sensory as much as in one's vocabulary skills. Rather than trying to interpret the dogs' meaning or thought, rather than ventriloquising what goes on inside them, I attend to the sensory materiality of their actions and their effects. Who barks, how, where and, importantly, in what voice – and what does that prompt me to do? Where does their sniffing lead us as we wander about the town; how does one's sniffing tell me that I need to take the other to the vet to treat an infected ear? How do I know from their behaviour that a squirrel is laughing at us from the fence, that in the middle of the night a skunk is about to do its business in the yard, that the mail is about to arrive, that I am happy or sad? And how to speak of all this?

As the volume's editors suggest, the refusal to reify alterity demands working around essentialist language. But speaking about animals in non-essentialist language invites the allegation of unreflective anthropomorphism; in speaking of animals, essentialist, behaviourist language is the norm. Animal stories that attend to animals' life-worlds, according to this critique, invite lazy projections of human characteristics, thus thwarting the rigour that scientific study demands. Following Daston and Mitman's (2010) collection of essays in defence of anthropomorphism, I take issue with the idea that anthropomorphism is a 'scientific sin' – suggesting, rather, that an anthropomorphic attitude offers the grounds for engaging animals seriously to begin with. As it polices the boundaries between species, the allegation of anthropomorphism maligns the possibility that humans and animals might shape each other as they live together and mix.

What animates my argument, then, is an anti-anti-anthropomorphic position, which I adopt for two reasons: in the first place, as I-the-author am located in a human body, not to be anthropo-centric or -morphic is a pipe-dream – which is, in a nutshell, Daston and Mitman's point. But more important, anti-anti-anthropomorphism is a commentary on the term 'species', and on the alterity of humans and animals that the term suggests. Rethinking animal-human relations as a matter of mixing and togetherness destabilises the divisions inherent in that term. And the critique of anthropomorphism – that attributing human characteristics to animals is a philosophical fallacy – is moot, as it rests on the idea that species do not mix. My beef is with precisely this contention that human and animal characteristics – or, rather, humans and animals – do not mix; it is after all their mixing that has my interest. For, as Lorentz's, Despret's, Haraway's, Callon's, and Daston and Mitman's stories about living with animals attest, mixing is what we humans and animals *do*.

STORY 3. ON (TAKING) THE LEAD

When Kismet, Raylan and I walk out the door, it takes us a moment to establish an understanding of how we will arrange things, this time. For it is different every time. Forty kilos each, with eight firmly anchored feet between them and two bodies consisting of pure muscle, if they were to combine forces, they'd have me, again and again. But they don't. Or, I should say, they rarely do. Sure, they impose their collective and individual wills upon me, but they don't do it by force. It is, rather a pack decision – a matter of togetherness – that determines where we go, what we do, and when and how we do it.

Minutes before we leave the house, even if no preparations have been made, we all know that we are about to leave the house. I may be at my desk, working, when they decide from one moment to the next that it is time to go. All of a sudden, tails wag wildly, toys are brought, paws are placed on the very arm I am using right now. Right now. Invariably, I will say 'Wait, I have to finish this' – where 'this' can be the sentence I am writing, a chapter I am reading, a cup of coffee; between the agency of their restlessness and the agency of my voice, the three of us know that we are about to leave but not quite yet. And then I put on my shoes, and they are at the door, looking at the hallway closet where the leashes are kept. I have to remind them – with quiet voice, otherwise they think I am joining in the (fun of) loudness – not to bark; to tell Kismet not to yell at me and Raylan to calm down. As soon as they are harnessed, we are out the door. Sometimes in all this mayhem I forget my keys.

Tied together and looped around my back, a dog on each side, the leashes make us one three-headed body. It is not smooth; it takes this body a while to become one, to get in sync. But once we have adjusted to the actuality that we are not three, but one, we can move in the same direction. Or, once we move in the same direction, we adjust to the actuality that we are not three, but one; as usual, it is not clear in which direction the causal arrow goes. What is clear, however, is that the leash leads; it *makes* – in all senses of the word: enabling, achieving, assembling, forcing, creating, causing, managing, and rendering – our connection. It transmits Raylan's movements to my part of our body, and on to Kismet's; mine to theirs; hers to his via mine. This is what the lead does for us: it does the work of making us one. It is perhaps not knowledge that we share as we are walking, tethered by our leash. But we share something. Struggle. Pleasure. Direction. Companionship. Being a pack. Understanding. Togetherness.

The leash – and togetherness – are assisted by my words. When we practise using my voice as a lead of sorts, coming and staying and sitting and going, that reinforces our togetherness as a pack. Here, my words are not representations; they do not mean things. They are actions and they mean activity.[10] They do things; they affect and effect; they are an act. Sometimes, in moments of great tightness between the three of us, these words do substitute for the leash. This happens, for instance, when we walk back from the park, and I keep Raylan on the leash but talk Kismet home without it. I can't just say 'Kismet, heel', however, and consider the job done; even if I say that many times, it is not enough to keep her by my side. Only if I focus my attention on her presence and keep letting her know that we are one with my voice, does she remain tethered. It is tempting to say that she follows my commands, that I order her to stay by my side and that she submits. But I rather think that I cross the space between us with my voice; I reach out and she reaches back, following as if she were on a lead. She could break this connection at any time. But just like me, she has a stake in maintaining our togetherness. If she didn't, she would bolt.

And then there is our joint and separate sensibility. For togetherness, we don't always need the leash. For this togetherness includes a distributed Sense of Something – not necessarily understanding in a representational sense but, rather, understanding relationally. It occurs when, for instance, a new person enters our house, and the dogs have to decide how to greet them. Bark? Act excited? Jump up and down? Sniff? Give a hug? They do as I do. They kiss my mom, sniff my little nephews, bark at strangers, and settle as soon as all are ok with being in each other's presence. And I follow their cues, too. If they don't bark, greeting the newcomer enthusiastically with body slams and presents and toys, I know this person is ok. When they know someone may be trusted to enter the house, so do I – and vice versa. This is what I have learned from my dogs: to attend to each other's presence. To respect that there are distributed somethings – maybe knowledge, maybe not; sometimes knowing, sometimes not, that move across and between our bodies. That togetherness is not always smooth, and it requires work – it needs to be done again on each walk, at each visit, at each moment one of us takes the lead. And the intricacies of going on a walk help diffuse agency and control. Words, leash, human and dogs together craft fidelity to the practice of being a pack.

CONCLUSION

I am interested here in the notion of alterity. When ethnography concerns human counterparts, perhaps alterity resides in a non-sharing of cosmologies, and lines between one way of framing and practising the world and another may be drawn with some clarity. Early on, ethnography knew three positions regarding the dilemma of rendering 'other' cosmologies: 1. Their terms are inadequate, so let's describe them in ours. 2. Our terms are inadequate, so let's describe them (and perhaps us) in theirs. 3. Different worlds are fundamentally incommensurable; translation is by definition inadequate – *'traduction est trahison'* – and correlation is the best we can hope or strive for. One might say that in each of these modes the production of alterity resides in the power-ful act of 'rendering': capturing the subject's life-world in another's language makes the subject strange. It is precisely this altering effect of rendering that was at issue in ethnography's critical, literary turn of the 1980s – its result a rethinking of the political stakes of ethnographic discourse (Clifford; Clifford & Marcus; Marcus & Fisher; Taussig; and others) and a set of experiments with the limits of language whose, sometimes deliberately non-transparent, products wonder rather than worry about alterity's effects.

This paper wrestles with the essentialist perspective on species that infuses animal science. It proposes, as an alternative take on human-animal relations, to recognise all manner of agencies in the wildly asymmetric situations which are so readily understood in terms of 'humans calling the shots'. That requires eschewing representational language that frames alterity as a given, and which banks on a reflexive dualism between self and other while it is precisely this dualism that requires examining.[11] So I question taken-for-granted notions of species, nature, agency and power that seem to me rooted in the words 'we' anthropologists use but are belied by the practices by which we craft fidelity to the environments of enquiry that we engage; throughout, my question is how to achieve such fidelity. Here I again borrow from Bertoni (2016) the notions of togetherness and excess. What we know and think to be true or real is both under-determined and over-determined by language: it cannot be fully captured in representational terms, but it is precisely those terms that dictate how to frame and understand life-worlds. It is in the practices of living together with and among heterogeneous entities that reality emerges and can be known.

It seems to me that in this volume – in our STS-, critical ethnography-, and theory-infused neck of the woods – we are after something else. As Walford and Bonelli suggest in the introduction to this volume, a line of scholars – from Derrida to Haraway to Latour, from critical ethnography to feminist epistemology to thinking with agency and relationality – engage precisely the question of how *from this position* to account for ethnographic material that seems to *exceed this position*. While perhaps in that very articulation the altering is already done, I'd say that what binds this work, and separates it from what came before, is that it decentres alterity at the same time. If there is a temporality to these theoretical strands, perhaps the present moment offers a new-ish attention to local imbroglios in which opportunistic, strategic, spontaneous, but meanwhile serious, structured and rooted practices reign.

We are all other – and non-otherness is a fleeting, crafted, event that is more of shared moments than it is of shared sensibilities. My aim is not to produce *narratives* that 'hold' or 'capture' or 'explain' alterity; the task at hand is rather to frame and acknowledge *situations* that 'hold' or 'capture' both alterity and togetherness and whose very existence 'explains' itself. In other words, I am hoping to achieve some sort of *fidelity* with my field that exceeds representation, and that mobilises my interlocutors' subjective agency, my own truthfulness, and an explicit normative position *vis-a-vis* the attachments that I hold dear. If there is an enemy to this approach – and if there is an alter to my own thinking – it may be precisely that idea of alterity, itself.

NOTES

1 For another framing of this question see Cristóbal Bonelli (2015), who asks what happens to academic writing 'when we are invited by our interactants to realise that what is serious for one situated set of practices' might not be quite as serious in and for another?

2 With the term *Umwelt* the early twentieth-century Estonian biologist Jakob von Uexküll refers to a being's perceptual life-world; the concrete or lived milieu of the organism, whose potentialities are directly related to its perceptive apparatus – without reducing those potentialities to perception alone.

3 Cesar Millan's books and tv presentations are a case in point, but so are the much milder handbooks written by the monks of New Skete. See for instance Millan (2006); *Monks of New Skete* (2011: 19).

4 Aside from Donna Haraway's essential work on dogs in STS (2003, 2008) and Vinciane Despret's studies of animal scientists (for instance 2016), an emerging body of work in animal studies itself explicitly or implicitly deploys the methods of (sensory) ethnography (Pink 2009), 'following the animal' so as to offer a non-human-centred perspective on the animal's world (see Horowitz 2011, 2017; Grandin 2009; Mayeri 2007, 2012) offers cinema for primates in which the human is an instrument for facilitating apes' subjectivities.

5 For the making of subjectivity through photography see Barthes 1981.

6 Gertrude Stein, unrecognised ethnographer of her times, suggests that, like time, place is elusive – an artefact of one's framing. And another unrecognised ethnographer, Chauncey Gardener, subject in Jerzy Kosinsky's *Being There*, immortalised by Peter Sellers, suggests that being is all there is.

7 To Uexküll, too, animals are the *subjects* of their life-world: 'Each environment forms a self-enclosed unit, which is governed in all its parts by its meaning for the subject' (1934/2010:144); such worlds are many and varied. For an ant, a cow, and a little girl picking flowers, a square metre of meadow will hold very different meaning but, more important, open up a range of different opportunities for action. Uexküll's, then, is a commitment to multiple ontologies, as for each of these beings this piece of the world is a different thing; the biologist's 'thick description' of an animal's life-world aims to bring into relief its scope, infer its meanings, describe its potentialities and realise its constraints.

8 For an analysis of the operations and the work invested in producing an MRI scan, see Dumit 2004.

9 I should also note that this is a dangerous proposition: in certain circumstances it is unsafe for the dogs if I do not take the lead and so I must exert agency in deciding when to insist and when to let go.

10 For words as actions see Austin 1963.

11 For a critique of reflexive dualist schemes, see for instance Latour 1993.

REFERENCES

Austin, J. L., *How to Do Things with Words?* (Oxford: Oxford University Press, 1962).

Barthes, R., *Camera Lucida* (New York: Farrar, Straus and Giroux, 1981).

Bertoni, F., 'Living with Worms' (PhD Thesis, University of Amsterdam, 2016).

Bonelli, C., 'Eating One's Wor(l)ds. On Foods, Metabolic Writing, and Ethnographic Humor', *Subjectivity*, 8.3 (2015): 181–200.

Callon, M., 'Some Elements of a Sociology of Translation: Domestication of the Scallops and the Fishermen of St Brieuc's Bay', in J. Law, and J. Hassard, eds., *Actor Network Theory and After* (Oxford: Blackwell, 1999), pp. 196–223.

Clifford, J., *The Predicament of Culture: Twentieth-Century Ethnography, Literature, and Art* (Berkeley, CA: University of California Press, 1986).

Clifford, J., and G. Marcus, *Writing Culture. The Poetics and Politics of Ethnography* (Berkeley, CA: University of California Press, 1986).

Daston, L., and G. Mitman, *Thinking with Animals: New Perspectives on Anthropomorphism* (New York: Columbia University Press, 2005).

Deleuze, G., and F. Guattari, *A Thousand Plateaus. Capitalism and Schizophrenia* (Minneapolis, MN: University of Minnesota Press, 1987).

Derrida, J., *The Animal That Therefore I Am* (New York: Fordham University Press, 2008).

Despret, V., *What Would Animals Say If We Asked the Right Questions?* (Minneapolis, MN: University of Minnesota Press, 2016).

Dumit, J., *Picturing Personhood* (Princeton: Princeton University Press, 2004).

Gomart, E., and A. Hennion, 'A Sociology of Attachment. Music, Amateurs, Drug Users', in J. Law, and J. Hassard, eds., *Actor Network Theory and After* (Oxford: Blackwell, 1999), pp. 220–247.

Grandin, T., *Animals Make Us Human* (New York: Houghton Mifflin, 2009).

Haraway, D., *Primate Visions. Gender, Race, and Nature in the World of Modern Science* (New York: Routledge, 1989).

——, *The Companion Species Manifesto: Dogs, People, and Significant Otherness* (Chicago: Prickly Paradigm Press, 2003).

——, *When Species Meet (Posthumanities)* (Minneapolis: University of Minnesota Press, 2008).

Hennion, A., *Comment La Musique Vient-elle Aux Enfants?* (Paris: Economica, 1990).

——, 'Those Things That Hold Us Together. Taste and Sociology', in *Cultural Sociology*, 1.1 (2007): 97–114.

Horowitz, A., 'Theory of Mind in Dogs?', *Learning and Behaviour* 39 (2011): 314–317.

——, 'Smelling themselves: Dogs investigate their odours longer when modified in an "olfactory mirror" test', *Behavioral Processes* 143 (2017): 17–24.

Latour, B., *We Have Never Been Modern* (Cambridge: Harvard University Press, 1993).

Marcus, G., and M. Fisher, eds., *Anthropology as Cultural Critique: An Experimental Moment in the Human Sciences* (Chicago, IL: University of Chicago Press, 1988).

Mayeri, R., *Primate Cinema Series* (http://www.vdb.org/titles/primate-cinema-apes-family, 2007, 2012) [acessed 1 January 2020].

Millan, C., *Cesar's Way: The Natural, Everyday Guide to Understanding & Correcting Common Dog Problems* (New York: Random House, 2006).

Mitman, G., *Reel Nature. America's Romance with Nature on Film* (Cambridge: Cambridge University Press, 1999).

Mol, A., *The Body Multiple: Ontology in Medical Practice* (Durham, NC: Duke University Press, 2003).

Monks of New Skete, *The Art of Raising a Puppy* (New York: Little, Brown, and Company, 2011).

Stocking, G., *Observers, Observed: Essays on Ethnographic Fieldwork* (Chicago: University of Chicago Press, 1985).

Taussig, M., *Mimesis and Alterity. A Particular History of the Senses* (New York: Routledge, 1993).

Tsing, A. L., *The Mushroom at the End of the World. On the Possibility of Life in Capitalist Ruins* (Princeton: Princeton University Press, 2017).

Uexküll, J. von, *A Foray into the Worlds of Animals and Humans. With a Theory of Meaning* (Minneapolis, MN: University of Minnesota Press, 1934/2010).

Viveiros de Castro, E., 'Perspectival Anthropology and the Method of Controlled Equivocation', *Tipiti. Journal of the Society for the Anthropology of Lowland South America*, 2.1 (2004): 3–22.

Whitehead, A. N., *The Concept of Nature* (Amherst, MA: Prometheus Books, 1920/2004).

Wolfe, C., *What is Posthumanism?* (Minneapolis, MN: University of Minnesota Press, 2009).

PLANETARY ALTERITY, SOLAR COSMOPOLITICS AND THE PARLIAMENT OF PLANETS

Bronislaw Szerszynski

INTRODUCTION: HOW TO GAIN AND LOSE A PLANET

On 18 February 1930, our solar system gained a planet. Clyde Tombaugh, a 24-year-old amateur astronomer and son of a farmer from Illinois, had started work at the Lowell Observatory in Flagstaff, Arizona just a month before. The observatory had recruited him to help in the search for a hypothesised planet that had been going on since Percival Lowell had calculated in 1905 that only the existence of a distant, unseen 'Planet X' could explain observed perturbations in the orbits of Neptune and Uranus. Tombaugh had been given the task of using a blink comparison technique to detect any differences between pairs of photographic plates taken on different nights of the same area of the night sky (Schindler et al. 2018: 64–68). His successful blinking, by discovering a point of light that had changed position between 23 and 29 January, thus took the complement of planets in the system from eight to nine.

But then in 2006 the number of planets in our system fell back down from nine to eight again. The International Astronomical Union finally agreed a new definition of a planet, in an accommodation between competing scientific 'ways of knowing' in the astrophysics community – between a 'structuralist' focus on what a planet is made of and a 'dynamicist' focus on how planets move and interact with other bodies (Messeri 2010:190). The new definition was 'Aristotelean' in form, in that it consisted of a list of necessary and sufficient conditions for something to be classed as a planet (ibid.: 191). Thus, the IAU agreed that a planet is a body (i) that is big enough to have made itself spherical through its own gravity (i.e. achieved hydrostatic equilibrium), (ii) that orbits a star, and (iii) that dominates that orbit (Soter 2006, 2007). Pluto passed the first two criteria but failed the third, since it moves in an elliptical orbit that crosses that of Neptune – and is not even the largest body in that region of the solar system. Pluto was thus demoted to the status of a 'dwarf planet' or 'Kuiper Belt object', a decision that raised much controversy – not least among the wider public, who had got used to the idea of Pluto as part of the complement of planets.

What is 'due process' in the process of deciding what planets are and how many we have in our solar system? And how might exploring that question help to inform our thinking about alterity in non-human realms? In this chapter I will explore these questions by drawing on the cosmopolitical proposals of Isabelle Stengers and Bruno Latour: proposals for ways to determine what things exist in the world, and how they should coexist, which do not prematurely foreclose or divide questions of fact and value. I will repeatedly return to the two core cosmopolitical questions that Latour poses in *Politics of Nature* (2004a): how many are we? how shall we live together? I will explore the idea that deciding, reckoning, counting and accommodating might be operations that can be carried out by matter itself.

In doing so I will draw a great deal on planetary science, but also on the thought of Henri Bergson, Gilles Deleuze, Felix Guattari and Gilbert Simondon, which will help us develop a geophilosophical understanding of the modes of alterity exhibited by matter under planetary conditions. We will see that the concrete, individual planet that presents to us is a mere effect or phase in a wider ongoing process of ontogenesis, and that the material isolation of planets never wholly sunders them from immanence and possibility. We will also see that each planet exhibits alterity and multiplicity not just in relation to others, but internally, in that planets are always out of step with themselves, which is what enables their becoming. And we will see that the way that planets become, endure and interact involves various modalities of alterity, difference and multiplicity, modalities that are inextricably bound up with planetarity itself: with the particular mode of existence of planets.

GEOPHILOSOPHY, TRANSDUCTION AND PLANETARY BEING

This chapter is an exercise in 'geophilosophy', a term that originates with Deleuze and Guattari (1994). By analogy with Annales historian Fernand Braudel's argument that all history is geohistory (ibid.: 95), Deleuze and Guattari regard geophilosophy not as a particular branch of philosophy, but as a way of doing philosophy that pays attention to the Earth 'as a milieu that determines philosophy from within, an earth that intrinsically belongs to philosophy, an earth that is the turf of philosophical thought' (Gasché 2014:16). Geophilosophy is thus thinking not *about* but *through* the Earth, reflecting on how being for us is conditioned by planetarity.[1]

Although my account will draw a lot on the empirical findings and theoretical understandings of the natural sciences, the planet that Deleuze and Guattari's geophilosophy summons for us is not simply the planet as known to science. Deleuze and Guattari argue that the sciences approach entities such as planets on what they call the 'plane of reference', cataloguing the lawful behaviour of the 'actual', of already constituted entities (Deleuze and Guattari 1994: 118). By contrast, they argue, philosophy – and I would say specifically *geophilosophy* – approaches entities on the 'plane of immanence', because it is concerned with the intuition of a 'Whole' that is full of the 'virtual', multiple possible states that may never actualise. Thus, for example, whereas the sciences employ the logic of exclusive disjunctions and the excluded middle (in which things are either this or that but not both), geophilosophy, for Deleuze and Guattari, employs a logic of the inclusive disjunction (things can be 'both-and'). In this chapter I suggest, however, that planets even as understood by the natural sciences are entities that require us to think of them on the plane of immanence, of the virtual. And crucial to this is one important aspect of planetarity: that of *multi*planetarity, that planets exhibit multiplicity – they are other, different, alterior.

In particular, first, planets are multiple in multiple ways: they manifest numerical difference (they are countable), but also qualitative difference and forms of 'internal' difference, which bring them into relation with each other. Second, planets exhibit multiplicity in a way that is distinctive to planetary (and other astronomical) bodies; even numerical difference means something different to planets. Third, each planet as it forms and develops has, in a sense, to discover and invent planetary alterity anew. Fourth, we as human thinkers about planets have to follow an analogous process to the becoming of planets.

To expand on that last point, we can draw on the work of Simondon.[2] Simondon (1992) criticises the categories of conventional logic for the way that they deal with the 'already constituted individual', treating the process of individuation through which it came into being as not important, and dividing the individual entity from its milieu. He argues that we should 'understand the individual from the perspective of the process of individuation rather than the process of individuation by means of the individual' (ibid.: 300). To help us to grasp this, Simondon uses the concept of 'transduction', an idea that points in two directions. First, transduction is a 'psychic process' and a 'logical procedure' that occurs within the analyst of a phenomenon; but in contrast to the standard logical procedures of deduction and induction, it occurs as a continuous process of discovering 'the dimensions according to which a problematic can be defined'. However, second, transduction is also the process through which an entity itself individuates from the pre-individual state, and out of which emerges not only the individual itself (always only a partial resolution of the latent potentials of the pre-individual state) but also the structures and dimensions within the individual that will determine its development and the individual-milieu relation (ibid.: 313). So, as well as us as thinkers being engaged in transduction in thinking about them, planets themselves can be understood as being engaged in transduction in coming into being. Planets as they develop *compose themselves* into certain kinds of individuals, and then into different categories, and do a kind of accounting or reckoning with each other.

DUE PROCESS IN THE HEAVENS

How do we understand what happened in the two cases discussed in my introduction? What happened to the number of planets in our solar system in 1930 and 2016? I want to start to address this question through the idea of cosmopolitics, as developed by Isabelle Stengers. Stengers takes the concept of cosmopolitics from Kant (1903) but develops it in a decidedly un-Kantian direction: for Stengers, adding 'cosmo' to 'politics' does not point to a kind of universality, and nor is cosmopolitics beyond politics; instead, it is a recognition that there is something in politics that exceeds the human will (Stengers 2011: 351–62). As Latour puts it, in Stengers' redefinition of 'cosmopolitics' 'the strength of one element checks any dulling in the strength of the other. The presence of 'cosmos' in cosmopolitics resists the tendency of 'politics' to mean the give-and-take in an exclusive human club. The presence of 'politics' in cosmopolitics resists the tendency of 'cosmos' to mean a finite list of entities that must be taken into account. *Cosmos* protects against the premature closure of *politics*, and *politics* against the premature closure of *cosmos*' (Latour 2004b:454).

In *Politics of Nature* (2004a), Latour develops a particular cosmopolitical proposal, and we can use this to distinguish three possible ways of treating 'how many planets are there' as a cosmopolitical question. The first would be to consider it within the frame of what Latour (1993) had called the 'modern constitution', an understanding of the world that makes a sharp distinction between nature and fact on the one hand, and politics and value on the other.[3] A modern would locate the two changes in the numbers of planets described above – from eight to nine and then back to eight again – purely in the realm of 'culture' rather than 'nature'. Such a position would be to say that Pluto as an astronomical body did not 'blink' into existence on February 1930; the only thing that blinked was Clyde Tombaugh himself. Pluto, the 'thing in itself', had been there for billions of years, although unknown to humans; however, over time, technology and science developed so that by 1930 we humans were able to perceive it and incorporate it into our model of the solar system. In this version of solar cosmopolitics, it was only our *model* of the solar system that changed, not the solar system itself. Then, we might say that the more recent change downwards was merely the result of change in a human classificatory system, as this was adjusted to reflect improvements in human understanding. Out there, in space, once again nothing had really changed.

But this is to enact a disguised cosmopolitics, to hide the political aspects of planetary designation. In *Politics of Nature* (2004a), Latour suggests how we might assemble a cosmos of humans and non-humans in a way that accords with what he argues would be 'due process' rather than arbitrary power. He proposes a modern, cosmopolitical constitution that would require the setting-up of a more-than-human 'Parliament of Things' in which politics and science were not seen as separated powers but were done together. However, Latour's parliament would have its own distinctive separation of powers. The first, upper house would have 'the power to take into account', be oriented to the question 'how many are we?', and obligated to keep as open as possible questions of truth, consistent with the due process rules of 'perplexity' and 'consultation'. The second, lower house with 'the power to arrange in rank order' would be about closing things down again, guided by the question 'can we live together?' and involving procedures and norms of 'hierarchization' and 'institution' (Latour 2004a: 109).

Asking about planets in the more transparently cosmopolitical way described by Latour would involve a multi-disciplinary speculative planetology that kept as open as possible the question of how we think about planets. This view would ask whether the decision about Pluto followed 'due process'. Following Latour, the question of 'how many are we' would need to involve skills from the humanities as well as the sciences, and to involve wide consultation with publics to open up the widest set of questions about what planets are, how many there are, what they might do, and what their significance is for the cosmos. Then, the processes of hierarchisation and institution would also involve diverse skills and conversations in order to come to a shared agreement – and crucially, the process would never be regarded as completed once and for all. As Latour insists, 'all Republics are badly formed, all are built on sand. They hold up only if they are rebuilt at once and if the parties excluded from the lower house come back the next morning, knock at the doors of the upper house, and demand to participate in the common world' (Latour 2004a: 183).

But in this chapter, I want to suggest a third option, one that radicalises Latour's idea of the Parliament of Things in a way that is even more open to the agency of the non-human. One limitation of Latour's parliament is that it is less a parliament of things than a parliament of people who can represent things – as if things can only be lively if they are enrolled into networks with humans. Elsewhere Latour makes it clear that he is very happy for the world to be doing things when we are not there. In 'Irreductions', for example, he writes that '[h]ermeneutics is not a privilege of humans but, so to speak, a property of the world itself' (Latour 1988: 245).[4] So how can we be more Latourian than Latour when it comes to convening our planetary system? What if we were to ask, not 'what human skills and knowledge do we need to gather together to open up and then close down the question of what is a planet, and thereby how many planets we have', but instead, 'how do planets *themselves* decide "how many are we?" and "how should we live together?"' Is it really only humans that 'make planets count', or do planets do it themselves – make themselves countable things? And do planets decide how to live together, and if so, how? Can we speak of the solar system as itself a solar Parliament of Things – and one that does not have to pass through the minds of human beings to constitute itself? And what is the role of alterity in the countability and coexistence of planets?

THE CHANGING COUNTABILITY OF PLANETS

Of course, when Bruno Latour asked, 'how many are we?' he was not simply thinking about the sheer number of beings admitted to the collective. But let us start by thinking about numerical alterity – about how planets may be counted. We will see later that the question of what it means to say that planets or anything else are countable is not so simple, but let us start with a simple working definition, with two parts. First, countable things have to be sufficiently individuated that they can be counted – they have to be other to each other. Second, they need to belong to a boundable class of things – so that we know when to stop counting: as a class they need to be other to the things that we don't want to include in our count. Thus, to speak of Earth and Mars being two planets is to speak of two separate members of the class of things that are planets. And in some ways planets seem eminently countable, as they are objects that are materially isolated and thus 'other to each other' to an extent that is never found with entities on Earth.

Planets have not always been seen as such clearly demarcated things. Defined initially as lights in the sky that seem to move slowly against the fixed stellar background, it was nevertheless not always obvious that different lights seen in the sky on different occasions were in fact the same celestial body. The Mesopotamians seem to have known that 'the morning star' sometimes seen before sunrise in the east, and the 'evening star' sometimes seen after sunset in the west, are the same entity (the planet that we now call 'Venus'). The Sumerian myth of the goddess Inana's disappearance from the sky and her sojourn in the underworld is at least partly a narration of the synodic movement of Venus in the sky as seen from the Earth, by which it spends eight months visible in the east, then disappears for about two months when it goes behind the sun, then reappears in the west (Cooley 2008). But in ancient Greece these two celestial lights were still regarded as different things, named Phosphoros and Hesper or Hesperus respectively. Book XXII of Homer's *Iliad* is full of astronomical allusions; the glint of Achilles' spear as he prepares to slay the giant Hektor is likened to Hesper, the evening star heralding the onset of night (Genuth 1992: 295). The recognition in ancient Greece that they were the same entity is traditionally credited to Pythagoras around 500 BCE (Dreyer 1953: 48).[5]

Then, in the ancient cosmos of Ptolemy's second-century *Almagest*, the planets became a group of seven lights in the heavens, including the sun and the moon, that were all understood to circle the Earth (Ptolemy 1984). The Ptolemaic universe defined dominant elite views of the heavens in Europe for centuries to come, and implies that the planets are a 'closed class', closed in a similar way to that in which some word classes are closed, in the sense that it is difficult to add new members to them (Dixon 2004). The class of all of planets was not seen as being capable of being expanded by discovery or fiat; the seven-ness of the planets was not accidental but somehow essential to the concept of planet.

Copernicus famously displaced the Earth from the centre of the universe and set it on the move. A planet was now defined not as a body that moved against the star field as seen from the Earth, but as one that orbited the sun. In the Copernican system the sun and moon were removed from the list of planets – but the Earth was added, to make six in all. In the longer term, the work of Copernicus was to signal a revolution in thought which turned the closed world into an infinite universe. Alexander Koyré describes this revolution thus: 'the disappearance, from philosophically and scientifically valid concepts, of the conception of the world as a finite, closed, and hierarchically ordered whole ... and its replacement by an indefinite and even infinite universe which is bound together by the identity of its fundamental components and laws, and in which all these components are placed on the same level of being' (Koyré 1957: 2). In this new 'infinite universe', the sun became a star, a mere member of an open class of 'suns' with potentially infinite membership.

But was the class of planets around the sun also an open class? Was the six-ness of the planets an empirical fact, that could be overturned by new discoveries, or an a priori truth? In 1596 Johannes Kepler noted that the ratios of the orbits of the six planets seemed to correspond to what would be the case if the five Platonic solids (tetrahedron, cube, octahedron, and so on) were nested between each pair of orbits in turn; he called this the 'Mysterium Cosmographicum' – the secret of the cosmos (Kepler 1981). This seemed to imply that the convening of the planets around the sun followed some kind of logic of necessity – not just regarding their arrangement (how shall we live together?) but also their number (how many are we?). For in three-dimensional Euclidean space there can only be five Platonic solids, so if each gap between planetary orbits can be uniquely assigned to one of them, there can a priori only be six planets. Such thinking also resurfaces in later post-Copernican thought – for example the Titius-Bode Law of 1772, that observed that the semi-major axes of the planets are of the form $a = 4 + x$, where $x = 0, 3, 6, 12, 24, 48$ etc., which was apparently confirmed by the discovery of Uranus in 1781 (Jaki 1972).

The Titius-Bode law also seemed to predict that there should be a planet between Mars and Jupiter, where instead there seemed to be an empty space. Between 1801 and 1845 the hunt for this apparently necessary planet resulted in the discovery of first one, then many objects orbiting the sun, classed first as the missing planet, then downgraded to asteroids (Hilton 2017). Once the huge difference in size between asteroids and planets was determined, a formal definition was not seen as socially necessary. The definition of 'planet' was pro-totypical (e.g. a planet is something like the Earth), and took a loose, 'family resemblance' approach, able to accommodate the different ways of knowing of different communities of natural philosophers, then scientists and the wider public (Messeri 2010). It was this informal definition that was to last until 2006.[6]

PLANETS AND NUMEROSITY

Counting (form the Latin 'com-putare', reckoning together) is not the only way that planets might relate to number. Cognitive psychologists and anthropologists tell us that, for humans and other animals, 'number' is not really a single system or phenomenon, but a collection of separate numerosity systems with quite different logics (Dehaene 1992: 34–35). Counting is just one of these – a particular form of numerosity which is closely linked to verbal ability and relates as much to *parole* (specific embodied performances of language) as to *langue* (language as an abstract system of relations); counting is at core an embodied action, linked to recitation, rhythm, cadence, one that is often gestural and indexical, involving pointing towards countable things (Maurer 2010). This is most clear when people count on fingers, knuckles or other body parts – or when shepherds use sheep-counting rhymes, or children use counting-out rhymes to generate remainders to choose people and items (Bolton 1888). Counting is linked to *ordinal* numbers, which are semantic (they denote – e.g. we say 'the third planet') and paradigmatic (are potentially interchangeable with other predicates that also denote the same entity, such as names) (Crump 1990: 39).

As we have seen, humans can count the planets. Doing so can be described as making a one-to-one correspondence between the planets and the first eight members of the set of natural numbers – 1, 2, 3, 4 etc. – or with sets of other 'numerons' such as tokens, words or body parts (Crump 1990: 32). Because of the way that planets 'live together', in near-circular concentric orbits, it might feel more natural to count them ordinally – 'first', 'second', 'third from the sun'; or we could even count them without numbers – we could recite the names of the planets, perhaps aided by a mnemonic. But planets themselves do not count – the lack of language or an articulated body would make it hard (though maybe they could be said to have counted themselves if they each were able to attract only a single moon as a numeron). However, planets can certainly be interested in some features of ordinality – if you are a planet that has a big planet near you, whether the orbit of that planet is inside or outside your own can make a big difference to how you live with them.

A second form of numerosity is *absolute* number, about which planets seem less interested. Dehaene identifies *arithmetic* or calculation as a distinctive system of numerosity. Like counting, the process of calculating seems dependent on language but goes beyond finding the number that corresponds to a collection of items to the manipulation, combination and application of *abstract* numbers – numbers as concepts that are detachable from any particular manifestation (Dehaene 1992; Pica et al. 2004). If counting is related to *ordinal* numbers, calculation is more tied to the *cardinal* numbers, which are inherently abstract, syntactic, operational and ready for manipulation (Crump 1990: 39). Indeed, when we count a class of objects we turn the last number in the count into the number that represents the whole set – we make it cardinal, ready for calculation (Dehaene 1999: 119).

But we can relate planetarity to certain other forms of numerosity that allow some forms of calculation but resist absolute number. One way to do this is by *approximate numerosity*, which is available to animals and preverbal infants as well as adult, verbal humans. This involves processes such as 'subitising' (recognising the numerosity of small numbers of items by eye) or 'estimation' (judging the size of larger groups). Planetary systems can be said to estimate. Like all non-linear self-organising systems, if they can be said to be computing, they do so using analogue computation, based on continuous physical quantities such as speed, mass and distance, rather than distinct natural numbers (Pickering 2009). When a planetary system forms, there will be an approximate number of planets that the system is 'trying' to form, as the interactions among the planets 'estimate' a reasonable number of planets for their system.

But ethnomathematics can help suggest other ways to think about planets calculating without absolute number. In many number systems, numerosity – for example 'threeness' or 'fourness' – is not seen as an abstract concept that can be transferred between different classes of entities: the 'threeness' of one class of thing, for example, might be seen as quite distinct from the 'threeness' of another. For example, Helen Verran argues that whereas in English numbers are simply a subset of qualities or predicates that can be applied to any kind of spatiotemporal particular (objects, places and so on), in West African languages like Yoruba numbers are modal terms (i.e. modes of presentation) that are applied to *sortal* particulars (things which are defined as inherently possessing certain qualities). As she summarises, '[a]n English speaker who talks of spatiotemporal particulars might say these particulars have qualities. A Yoruba speaker, however, talks of sortal particulars, and since these particulars have been defined by categorisation around sets of characteristics, these objects cannot be said to have qualities, but they can be said to have modalities, or modes' (Verran 2001: 137). Numbers in Yoruba work less like adjectives than adverbs; they describe *how* things appear, whether as a group or as a collection of individuals, and also as a collection of how many (Verran 2001: 67). Another feature of number in many languages that breaks with the logic of abstract number is that of 'numeral classifiers' – terms that are included when numbers are attached to nouns and are specific to that class of noun. Sometimes there are only two sets of numerical classifiers, for animate and inanimate things respectively – as if the three-ness of 'three rocks' and of 'three cows' are different, but other languages have dozens (Ascher 1991: 11–13).

Such features of non-Western number systems have been taken to mean that non-literate peoples simply do not understand abstract number; however, treating numbers as adverbial modes of presentation or using numerical classifiers can be read as a recognition that quantity can be meaningless without quality – that it is not always reasonable to abstract numerosity from the specific qualities of the type of entity in question. Indeed, with the adoption of the 2006 definition, planets in Western scientific thought became something much more like one of Verran's 'sortal particulars', a kind of entity that inherently has a particular set of relational properties. Just as a living thing's interactions with its environment is not accidental but constitutive of its status as a living thing, similarly what makes something a planet includes the role it plays in a wider assemblage and set of processes.

MODES OF PLANETARY ALTERITY

In the last section we focused on planetary alterity as involving numerical and quantitative difference. But in order to develop a fuller geophilosophical account of how planets live together we also need to attend to different modes of alterity. Firstly, planets are alterior, other to each other, not just because they are materially separated and countable, but also because they take different forms. When we talk about Earth and Mars, we are not just talking about two numerically distinct things, like two electrons; they also look different and behave differently – they exhibit *qualitative* difference. But secondly, in order to understand this qualitative difference geophilosophically – not just as a statement of fact, but as something that binds them in ontogenetic relations – we also need a notion of alterity that does not just involve contrasting a thing with something else. We thus need to mobilise concepts of 'internal multiplicity' – 'non-oppositional difference', or 'difference in itself' (Deleuze 1994: 28–69). This further complicates the idea of multiplanetarity and planetary alterity as I have developed it above; we will see that, on the dimension of internal difference, the 'multi' in multiplanetarity does not simply divide planets from *each other* but also divides them *from themselves*.

This internal difference within planets is not simply a descriptive state of affairs: it is a dynamic, active force. We can develop this idea using three concepts developed by Deleuze – 'multiplicity', 'the virtual' and 'the intensive'. In his *Bergsonism* (1988), Deleuze takes from the philosopher of vitalism a particular idea of 'multiplicity' as the differential ground of existence. Bergson insists on looking at difference not as a secondary property derived from a metaphysically prior 'identity' but as itself originary. For Bergson (1921), difference is an explosive force within things that creatively and inventively generates novelty. Deleuze also takes from Bergson the idea of the 'virtual' as a way to understand the genesis of new forms. Unlike 'the possible', which we think of as imagined counterfactuals with no reality, the virtual is no less real than the actual. Virtualities are already present in the world, real but latent, and simply may or may not be actualised. Finally, the distinction between the 'intensive' and the 'extensive', discussed by Deleuze in his later work *Difference and Repetition* (1994), was first posed by the physicist Richard Chase Tolman (1917). 'Extensive' properties are divisible properties such as length, volume and mass that together comprise the stable, actual, completed form of an object. 'Intensive' properties such as temperature, pressure and density, by contrast, cannot be divided or altered without introducing asymmetries and qualitative change. Deleuze links Chase's concept of the intensive closely to Bergson's concepts of multiplicity and the virtual.

We can use these concepts, combined with Simondon's focus on ontogenesis as a continuous process of individuation, to understand the role of alterity in planetary becoming – including the emergence of the numerical alterity discussed above. Before there are any countable planets orbiting around a given star, there is a smeared, immanent solar nebula, a spinning protoplanetary disc of hydrogen, helium and metals. Then, fluctuations, generated largely by the dynamics of the rotating disc itself, disrupt the latter's homogeneity, triggering a process whereby intensive forces starts to generate extensive form, and the disc organises itself into separate clusters of matter. Initially these are simply areas of greater densities of particles, but some of these will clump into 'planetesimals', some of which then combine into 'planetary embryos', which either separately or through combination form the cores of a number of planets circling around the central star, made variously of rock, ices and captured liquids and gases.[7] So planets *fall into being*, self-assemble, create their own gravity wells, forming dense, approximately spherical bodies orbiting in stable near-circular orbits separated by empty space.[8] They *turn themselves* into countable things.

But by such processes of ontogenesis, planets also come to have qualitative alterity, because of the specific intensive conditions under which their emergence takes place. Such conditions include the type of star and the metallicity of the accretion disc; how far from the sun the planets form; and the presence of other planets that might affect the process of formation or their movement. Analyses of the distribution of the mass and size of known exoplanets (planets around other stars) suggest that planets tend to fall into three groups: rocky planets (like Earth) with at most a thin atmosphere; middle sized planets (like Neptune) with a solid rocky or icy core and massive, thick atmospheres; and gas giants (like Jupiter) with metallic cores (Buchhave et al. 2014; Chen and

Kipping 2017). These qualitative groupings are a product of emergent (we might say with Simondon 'transductive') patterns in their ontogenesis. If a planet is in – indeed *is* – a constant process of becoming, of taking form, then it is a form that it generates 'on the fly' from its own internal inconsistencies.

Here the work of Simondon is useful again. For Simondon, individuation is 'a partial and relative resolution manifested in a system that contains latent potentials and harbors a certain incompatibility with itself' (1992: 300). Becoming is thus 'a capacity beings possess of falling out of step with themselves ..., of resolving themselves by the very act of falling out of step' (ibid.: 300–1). Viewed this way, a planet's becoming is determined on the virtual plane by its internal incompatibilities or 'singularities', non-linear thresholds which act as attractors or tipping points in the dynamics of the system.[9] The trifurcation of planets into Terran, Neptunian and Jovian worlds suggests that there are singularities around 2.0 Earth masses and 0.41 Jupiter masses, unstable saddle points that divide the possible futures of emerging worlds. In theory, all planets contain the same virtual structure of singularities and possibilities and are simply separate 'actual' instantiations of it. But because of the way that planets in their forming diverge into these different classes of planet, and then follow a particular developmental course within that class, while increasingly isolated in the vacuum, it is truer to say that they each instantiate a particular subset of that common virtual structure.[10]

Planets, once formed and kept 'out of step with themselves', are constantly involved in generating new forms of otherness within themselves. For example, diverse forms of immanent, intensive alterity are constantly being generated in their vast, extended regions of solid, liquid or gaseous 'continuous matter', without clear borders or interfaces, crosscut by intensive gradients of pressure and temperature, and in constant motion on different timescales. In fluids in particular, the 'actual' and the 'extensive' is also full of 'intensity' and 'virtual' possibility. Fluids are constantly generating and dissolving form (Schwenk 1965). This kind of planetary alterity has three distinctive characteristics: rather than being transcendent, absolute and completed, it is immanent (internal to the region of the planet), gradual (it manifests as gradients) and generative (it is constantly producing form and new gradients).

But planets are qualitatively other to each other not just because of conditions which they are subjected to in their formation, but also because to some extent they can *take hold of their conditions* as they 'fall into being'. This point can be seen as a generalised version of Gaia theory (Lenton and Wilkinson 2003), one that sees the significant shaping powers that biological life can have over a planet's fate as merely a specific example of a wider set of planetary powers of self-organisation. Planets can do this because of certain specific features of planetary being: planets are assemblages of baryonic matter, chemically diverse, intermediary in temperature between stars and interstellar space, and gravitationally differentiated into different strata and compartments. As they orbit their star they are also subjected over long timescales to metastable flows of energy from the star as well as from their hot cores, with patterns of heating and cooling. They are thus maintained away from equilibrium, bringing their parts into active relation with each other, and able to do work on themselves (Kleidon 2016).

Thus, the concatenating internal differences within planets mean that they divide internally into different 'spheres' and substances and entities with different properties, which are maintained in dynamic relation. So, planets become *historical entities*, other to each other in a more than numerical way; their characteristics cannot be simply understood as the working out of universal laws; they are qualitatively unique, path-dependent entities, whose powers and possibilities are dependent on the particular course of development through which they have passed. Planets bifurcate, go through revolutions (Lenton and Watson 2011), and thus become other to themselves in a diachronic sense. Terrestrial planets in particular can retain the power to evolve and change, and they do so at their own pace. The divisions between the four great aeons of Earth's geohistory – the Hadean, Archean, Proterozoic and Phanerozoic – are identified first of all by the signs left in the geological record that a significant transition in the Earth has taken place, and only secondarily assigned chronological dates. These are thus internally generated forms of time (Adam 2004), as planets develop in unique, path-dependent ways, as they undergo Simondon's 'transduction' and themselves discover the way that the general laws of planetarity will be true in their domain. Planets are never solely at the mercy of external forces; even the effect on them of a collision with another astronomical body or a change in the brightness of their star will depend on how the planet has developed so far.[11]

Planets also react gravitationally to each other's presence, which can shape how many planets there are and where they position themselves in the planetary system. This is particularly significant in the early stages of a planetary system's life, when planets have formed but the disc has not yet been cleared of gas and planetesimals. During this time, larger planets interact gravitationally with the remaining protoplanetary disk, creating spiral density waves that have the effect of pulling the planets inwards towards their star (Morbidelli and Raymond 2016: 1967–1969). This migration is likely to destabilise the orbits of other planets and potential planets, especially smaller ones, which may be forced to merge, to become minor planets or 'trojan satellites' within the orbits of larger planets or be lost from the system altogether. But the remaining larger planets will tend to lock each other into orbits characterised by mean motion resonances between immediate neighbours in the ordinal sequence (for example, with the inner planet orbiting three times for every two orbits of the next planet outside it), and then be shuffled into new positions as the resonance starts to disrupt itself (Levison et al. 2011). Through this and other dynamic processes, the planets of a system arrive at a long-term arrangement of how they will share the space around their sun.

CONCLUSION: HOW MANY WORLDS ARE WE? HOW SHALL WE LIVE TOGETHER?

In *Order out of Chaos*, Prigogine and Stengers (1984: 305–306) suggested that a complex shift of cosmopolitics happened in early modern science, one in which the direction of modern science swerved as consequentially as any giant planet engaged in a 'grand tack' across its planetary system. For the classical science of Aristotle, pure mathematical descriptions had only been applicable to the incorruptible 'superlunary' world of the heavens and the gods; Earthly, 'sublunary' nature, by contrast, was regarded as a world of becoming, life, change and decay that did not admit of mathematical or deterministic understanding.

The original intention of many early modern scientists seems to have been to extend the logic of the sublunary sphere to include the heavens: to show that celestial bodies were in principle no different to bodies on the Earth. Galileo thus caused controversy by arguing that the spots revealed by his telescope on the surface of the sun were not bodies orbiting in front of it, but actual spots or imperfections on the Sun itself (Galilei and Scheiner 2010). Yet the focus of Galileo and Newton on the dynamics of pendulums and planetary orbits had the effect of *reversing* this trajectory: instead of extending the sublunary realm of impermanence and change into the cosmos, they extended the time-less perfection of Aristotle's heavens to include earthly things, with the ideas of lawful predictability, reversible (and thus timeless) change, and a detached, objective observer.

However, Prigogine and Stengers argue that with the rise of new sciences such as non-equilibrium thermodynamics another shift is happening, one that places the observer within a world characterised by inherently unpredictable change and emergent order. These new sciences, Stengers argues in a later book, are 'open to a dialogue with a nature that cannot be dominated by a theoretical gaze, but must be explored, with an open world to which we belong, in whose construction we participate' (Stengers 1997: 39). The idea of solar cosmopolitics developed in this article can be seen as illustrating and expanding on this claim, by showing how we can approach the findings of planetary science through the lens of geophilosophy, thereby revealing the heavens to be a realm of becoming, of negotiation and accommodation – and thus, by 'resisting the tendency of *cosmos* to mean a finite list of entities that must be taken into account', bringing a kind of politics into the cosmos (Latour 2004b: 454).

We have seen how the ethnomathematical findings of Crump, Verran and Ascher and others can help us clarify that the ways in which planets *are* indi-vidual countable, estimable or calculable entities, and also the ways that planets themselves *do* numerosity – counting, estimating, calculating – are specific to the mode of existence that is planetarity. Even bare numerical difference takes a particular form when it comes to planets; and each planet, in interaction with the planets and protoplanetary disc around it, has to discover planetarity and individuality for itself, and in its own way. The contemporary planetary sciences, when approached geophilosophically, further suggest that, while we no longer think that the number of planets in the solar system is an a priori, necessary fact in the way that it was for Ptolemy, neither is it simply a contingent one, as would be suggested by Newtonian, 'classical' physics. How many planets inhabit a given planetary system, and how they live together, are questions that have to be worked out by the planets themselves, jointly and severally, as they explore the virtual structure of singularities and possibilities that they inherit from the protoplanetary cloud out of which they form and seek a regularised mutual accommodation.

Drawing on the geophilosophical thought of Bergson, Deleuze and Guattari, we have also seen that different modalities of planetary alterity are a central part of planetary being and becoming – and that it is non-oppositional or 'internal' alterity that is more fundamental to shaping the emergence and character of numerical and qualitative alterity in planets. A planet is not just actual (the state of affairs at any one time) but virtual, in that it inherits a virtual structure of singularities and potentialities that may remain latent at any one time. And this virtuality of a planet, its power of becoming, creativity and historiality, derives from the way it manages to keep incompatible with itself, particularly in terms of its intensive properties, kept away from equilibrium by flows of energy.

We have also seen that planetarity weaves together alterity and relationality in distinctive ways. I drew on the ideas of Simondon to suggest that a planet is not simply the more-or-less completed solid ball of matter that is its clearest presentation to us, but a *process* of individuation, stretching back to the pre-individual stage before the planets were distinguishable from each other, and involving its milieu even after it has differentiated itself from it. Planets continue to interact through gravitational – and occasionally collisional – encounters, in ways that enable a 'parliament of planets' to answer the questions 'how many are we' and 'how shall we live together' for themselves.

But we also know that planets have the potential to encounter each other in other ways than the gravitational and collisional. As materially isolated bodies that can transductively take hold of their own development and pass through creative bifurcations, planets are able to carry out separate, diverse experiments in the self-organisation of matter. In the case of the Earth, this particular experiment has resulted in the emergence of organic life, the power of sight, and now the interplanetary movement of machines and potentially living things – all of which offer new ways in which the independent material experiments carried out by planets can start to interact with each other. It is surely the case that other planets will have produced very different new material powers and possibilities for interplanetary relationality, made possible by their own working-through of planetary alterity. However, thinking through the wider possibility space of how the being and becoming of different planets might weave together in radically different ways, activating new singularities and generating forms of alterity not available to single worlds alone, is a project for another day.

NOTES

1 In this chapter, however, I generalise the 'geo' in 'geophilosophy' from the Earth to planets in general and am also thinking *through* planets in order to also think *about* them.

2 Simondon's work on individuation was a great influence on Deleuze, although the latter only rarely references him directly – see Iliadis (2013)

3 In a sense, what Latour is describing as the modern constitution is a very non-cosmopolitical way of composing a common world – but in another it is a disguised cosmopolitics.

4 See also Harman (2009: 122-127).

5 Though the Greeks and Romans, even while recognising the evening and morning stars as the same planet, continued to worship them as two separate gods or divine aspects.

6 The class of planets that belong to our solar system is of course bounded not just by the distinction between different objects orbiting the Sun – planets, asteroids, comets, Kuiper objects etc. – but also by that between our sun's planets and those of other stars.

7 For a discussion of the uncertain state of knowledge about planetary formation, see Morbidelli et al. (2016).

8 The material isolation of planets is not absolute, and can be overstated (Clark 2005). However, it is still hugely significant: the density of the interplanetary medium around the Earth is about 23 orders of magnitude less than that of the solid Earth (Mann et al. 2010: 3), and the raining of cosmic dust onto the Earth would at the current rate of approximately 30,000 tons per year take about 200 quadrillion years to double the mass of the Earth – more than 14 million times the estimated age of the universe to date.

9 On singularities, see also DeLanda (2002: 14–16).

10 As Deleuze puts it, within a given virtual structure, individual entities 'select and envelop a finite number of the singularities of the system. They combine them with the singularities that their own body incarnates' (1990: 109).

11 See for example Kring (2003).

REFERENCES

Adam, B., *Time* (Cambridge: Polity, 2004).

Ascher, M., *Ethnomathematics: A Multicultural View of Mathematical Ideas* (Pacific Grove, CA: Brooks/Cole Pub. Co., 1991).

Bergson, H., *Creative Evolution*, trans. by Arthur Mitchell (London: Macmillan, 1921).

Bolton, H. C., *The Counting Out Rhymes of Children: Their Antiquity, Origin, and Wide Distribution* (New York: D. Appleton & Company, 1888).

Buchhave, L. A., and others, 'Three Regimes of Extrasolar Planet Radius Inferred from Host Star Metallicities', *Nature*, 509 (2014): 593–596.

Chen, J., and D. Kipping, 'Probabilistic Forecasting of the Masses and Radii of Other Worlds', *Astrophysical Journal Letters*, 834.17 (2017): 1–13

Clark, N., 'Ex-Orbitant Globality', *Theory, Culture & Society*, 22.5 (2005): 165–185.

Cooley, J. L., 'Inana and Šukaletuda: a Sumerian Astral Myth', *Kaskal*, 5 (2008): 161–172.

Crump, T., *The Anthropology of Numbers* (Cambridge: Cambridge University Press, 1990).

Dehaene, S., 'Varieties of Numerical Abilities', *Cognition*, 44.1–2 (1992): 1–42.

——, *The Number Sense: How the Mind Creates Mathematics* (Oxford: Oxford University Press, 1999).

DeLanda, M., *Intensive Science and Virtual Philosophy* (London: Continuum, 2002).

Deleuze, G., *Bergsonism*, trans. by Hugh Tomlinson (New York: Zone, 1988).

——, *The Logic of Sense*, trans. by Mark Lester with Charles Stivale (New York: Columbia University Press, 1990).

——, *Difference and Repetition*, trans. by Paul Patton (London: Athlone Press, 1994).

Deleuze, G., and F. Guattari, *What Is Philosophy?*, trans. by H. Tomlinson and G. Burchell (New York: Columbia University Press, 1994).

Dixon, R. M. W., 'Adjective Classes in Typological Perspective', in Robert M. W. Dixon and Alexandra Y. Aïkhenvald, eds., *Adjective Classes: A Cross-Linguistic Typology* (Oxford: Oxford University Press, 2004), pp. 1–49.

Dreyer, J. L. E., *A History of Astronomy from Thales to Kepler*, 2nd edn (New York: Dover, 1953).

Galilei, G., and C. Scheiner, *On Sunspots*, trans. by Eileen Reeves and Albert Van Helden (Chicago: University of Chicago Press, 2010).

Gasché, R., *Geophilosophy: On Gilles Deleuze and Felix Guattari's What is Philosophy?* (Evanston, IL: Northwestern University Press, 2014).

Genuth, S. S., 'Astronomical Imagery in a Passage of Homer', *Journal for the History of Astronomy*, 23 (1992): 293–298.

Harman, G., *Prince of Networks: Bruno Latour and Metaphysics* (Melbourne: re-press, 2009).

Hilton, J. L., 'When Did the Asteroids Become Minor Planets?' (2017), <https://aa.usno.navy.mil/faq/docs/minorplanets.php> [accessed 1 January 2020].

Iliadis, A., 'A New Individuation: Deleuze's Simondon Connection', *MediaTropes*, 4.1 (2013): 83–100.

Jaki, S. L., 'The Early History of the Titius-Bode Law', *American Journal of Physics*, 40 (1972): 1014-1023.

Kant, I., *Perpetual Peace: A Philosophical Essay*, trans. by Mary Campbell Smith (London: George Allen & Unwin Ltd, 1903).

Kepler, J., *Mysterium Cosmographicum: The Secret of the Universe*, trans. by A. M. Duncan (New York: Abaris Books, 1981).

Kleidon, A., *Thermodynamic Foundations of the Earth System* (Cambridge: Cambridge University Press, 2016).

Koyré, A., *From the Closed World to the Infinite Universe* (Baltimore: Johns Hopkins Press, 1957).

Kring, D. A., 'Environmental Consequences of Impact Cratering Events as a Function of Ambient Conditions on Earth', *Astrobiology*, 3.1 (2003): 133–152.

Latour, B., 'Irreductions', in B. Latour, ed., *The Pasteurization of France* (Cambridge, MA: Harvard University Press, 1988), pp. 151–236.

——, *We Have Never Been Modern*, trans. by Catherine Porter (Hemel Hempstead: Harvester Wheatsheaf, 1993).

——, *Politics of Nature: How to Bring the Sciences into Democracy*, trans. by Catherine Porter (Cambridge, MA: Harvard University Press, 2004a).

——, 'Whose Cosmos, Which Cosmopolitics? Comments on the Peace Terms of Ulrich Beck', *Common Knowledge*, 10.3 (2004b): 450–462.

Lenton, T. M., and A. J. Watson, *Revolutions that Made the Earth* (Oxford: Oxford University Press, 2011).

Lenton, T. M., and D. M. Wilkinson, 'Developing the Gaia Theory. A Response to the Criticisms of Kirchner and Volk', *Climatic Change*, 58 (2003): 1–12.

Levison, H. F., A. Morbidelli, K. Tsiganis, D. Nesvorný, and R. Gomes, 'Late Orbital Instabilities in the Outer Planets Induced by Interaction with a Self-Gravitating Planetesimal Disk', *The Astronomical Journal*, 142.152 (2011): 1–11.

Mann, I., A. Czechowski, N. Meyer-Vernet, A. Zaslavsky, and H. Lamy, 'Dust in the Interplanetary Medium', *Plasma Physics and Controlled Fusion*, 52.124012 (2010): 1–12.

Maurer, B., 'Finger Counting Money', *Anthropological Theory*, 10.1–2 (2010): 179-85.

Messeri, L. R., 'The Problem with Pluto: Conflicting Cosmologies and the Classification of Planets', *Social Studies of Science*, 40.2 (2010): 187–214.

Morbidelli, A., and S. N. Raymond, 'Challenges in Planet Formation', *Journal of Geophysical Research: Planets*, 121.10 (2016): 1962–1980.

Pica, P., C. Lemer, V. Izard, and S. Dehaene, 'Exact and Approximate Arithmetic in an Amazonian Indigene Group', *Science*, 306.5695 (2004): 499.

Pickering, A., 'Beyond Design: Cybernetics, Biological Computers and Hylozoism', *Synthese*, 168 (2009): 469–491.

Prigogine, I., and I. Stengers, *Order Out of Chaos: Man's New Dialogue with Nature* (Toronto: Bantam Books, 1984).

Ptolemy, *Almagest*, trans. by G. J. Toomer (London: Duckworth, 1984).

Schindler, K., W. Grundy, A. Tombaugh, and A. Tombaugh, *Pluto and Lowell Observatory: A History of Discovery at Flagstaff* (Charleston, SC: The History Press, 2018).

Schwenk, T., *Sensitive Chaos: The Creation of Flowing Forms in Water and Air*, trans. by Olive Whicher and Johanna Wrigley (London: Rudolf Steiner Press, 1965).

Simondon, G., 'The genesis of the individual', trans. by Mark Cohen and Sanford Kwinter, in Jonathan Crary and Sanford Kwinter, eds., *Zone 6: Incorporations* (New York: Urzone, 1992), pp. 297–319.

Soter, S., 'What is a Planet?', *Astronomical Journal*, 132 (2006): 2513–9.

——, 'What is a Planet?', *Scientific American*, 296 (2007): 34–41.

Stengers, I., *Power and Invention: Situating Science* (Minneapolis, MN: University of Minnesota Press, 1997).

——, *Cosmopolitics II*, trans. by Robert Bononno (Minneapolis, MN: University of Minnesota Press, 2011).

Tolman, R. C., 'The Measurable Quantities of Physics', *Physical Review*, 9.3 (1917): 237–253.

Verran, H., *Science and an African Logic* (Chicago, IL: University of Chicago Press, 2001).

RELATING TO RESISTANCES, CURATING ANTAGONISMS

A conversation between Dehlia Hannah and Manuel Tironi

As a way to generate further reflections on the ideas proposed in de Laet's and Szerszynski's chapters, but also seeking to avoid formats that might summarise or resolve the questions the chapters pose, we invited Dehlia Hannah and Manuel Tironi to have an open conversation about the chapters, in relation to the introduction to the book. We recorded the conversation, and then transcribed it verbatim. Afterwards we asked each scholar to edit the conversations, and only then did we lightly edit them ourselves – this in order to try to keep the stylistic effect of a conversational format, an exchange of ideas and a non-linear narrative. In so doing, rather than an ending, we hoped to provide readers with further open directions in which to think.

IN THE FOLLOWING CONVERSATION, MANUEL TIRONI AND DEHLIA HANNAH discuss the potential value of the tabapot figure not only as an aid to academic experimentation, but also as a generative heuristic that might do work in, and learn from, real political struggles taking place in different parts of the world. The idea of 'limits', as presented in the introduction, is extended by thinking about situated political resistances as establishing limits through refusal, thus creating new possibilities for collaboration, and new possibilities to craft collectives that are always transforming themselves. The conversation also dwells on the potential of interdisciplinarity, a key trope in the Anthropocence literature, and the allies forged through knowledge, as well as the limits of this. Implicitly inspired by the chapters of this section and the ways the chapters portray collectives through engagements with dogs and speculation with planets, Manuel and Dehlia further explore how environmental alterities allows us to think about the composition of a world which is always transforming, and so demands continuous coordination and critical discussion between antagonistic positions.

MANUEL: I just want to start with a disclaimer for this conversation. I'm not sure if you know that for the last month (October 2019) we have had a huge social mobilisation against neoliberalism, and against what has happened over the last decades here in Chile. It has been a very intense moment for a lot of us. For me, particularly, it has been a truly shocking moment in which I have been rethinking a lot of things in my own intellectual practice, and in my own affective economy as well – it has had a lot of affective reverberations for me. I feel like what is asked of me now is not to *speak*. I don't know if that makes sense, but this compulsion to constantly be articulate and vocal and intelligent, having one idea after the other, this dramaturgy of being opinionated, that whole epistemology of thought, has been quite destabilised these few weeks – for me at least. So, I'm very sorry if I'm not very articulate, I will probably play the role of the follower in this conversation.

CRISTÓBAL: Thanks for this, Manuel. This is a space for experimentation, and we welcome the things you have to say, as well as the things you want to keep silent about. Even if I am in the Netherlands, I have also been thinking about why we do what we do, why we think the way we think, why we write academic papers, and for whom. It is interesting, maybe, to allow yourself, Manuel (and also myself)[1], to speak from another place when engaging in this kind of conversation, because the concern of the book is also, in a sense, about 'crisis', or how to think in situations like the ones we are going through in Chile, which represents the collapse, and a radical crisis of the wider neoliberal, ontological, project we both grew up in.

DEHLIA: I would like to know more about what is going on in Chile, but I should also start off with the disclaimer of being a bit withdrawn from my own usual subjects of interest: I am a philosopher of science and art. That is my background, and my work over the last few years has focused on the cultural imagination of climate change – how this is manifested in the visual arts and in a broader space that takes up, sometimes tacitly or experientially, both scientific knowledge that circulates through media, and also changing perceptual experiences of our environments. The latter experiences differ quite radically, depending on where we are and who we are, and what background knowledge we bring. So, my approach to these Anthropocene topics is always fundamentally aesthetic and partially motivated by the perspectives that I have encountered through the arts and in the course of my research.

There is a lot to say. I have just had a baby, and it has really changed my relationship to my subject matter. Last autumn, when I was pregnant, I attended a conference of psychologists and psychoanalysts, in London, on the topic of psychoanalysis and climate change. It was certainly the most personal and involved conference that I have ever attended concerning climate change. I have been to quite a few in an academic context, but at this conference there were tears, there was anger, there were children running around, and there was guilt. Not just abstract academic guilt, but actual antagonism between the participants, which I found somewhat incredible. At the time, there was a lot of talk about what climate change means to *you*, personally, and I was still at an academic remove. After having a child, things have suddenly changed: I often find myself staring into my son's eyes and thinking 'shall I talk to you, or shall I go back to working on my book about this future that I am trying to improve in some way?' In the broader political scope of things, my attention has been focused on the crisis in Hong Kong (because that's where my partner is from), but these political crises are certainly very entangled with environmental crises and, of course, financial crises. So, I wonder if this feeling of withdrawal from the topic – since it happens to be a point of departure that we share – is actually quite interesting, in the spirit, as you suggest in the introduction, of a turn away from a holistic perspective offered by modernist aspirations, or this totalising idea of the Anthropocene. What becomes of this when we ourselves, as scholars, are fractured into our very particular relationships to the topic and our investments in it? I think this is a good place to start, even though it is uncomfortable.

c: In the other two conversations that we have had there was a tendency to divide our discussion into two parts: a first part concerned with the concept of environmental alterities, what it does and how it does what it does, and on the other hand, a discussion about politics. And today, in this conversation, this division appears as a very strange one, as an awkward divide, no?

M: It's great that you've mentioned the issue of politics Cristóbal, because that was actually one of the key questions that your absolutely brilliant introduction provoked in me. I don't think it is necessary to say how good the introduction is – although I have to say that it connected in so many ways with my own reflections, my own adventures into these partial connections, or into these tensions between relationality and what you call 'limits', which are crucial in my own work. You assembled that discussion so beautifully. But it was also interesting because in your third alterity, what you called the '*taba-pot*', you mentioned the issue of experimentation: How can we create, invent, experiment, in such a way that we don't oppose different framings, so that we don't enact an agonistic struggle between different positions but, rather, try to allow for a generative tension? So I wonder what experiments or experimental practices might bring forward this generative conversation between different, diverse, but connected bodies or sensibilities. And I actually thought, why shouldn't we think about this *politically*? Or at least consider whether this question of experimentation has a political dimension as well – if we should go to politics, actual politics as deployed in specific territories, to find these clues. Not only in ethnographic accounts, but actually in real practices. Can we find some clues, some inspiration, in actual struggles, in actual political commitments that you can see in diverse territories? Everywhere, not only in Chile or in Hong Kong, but in England or in Brazil, or elsewhere. Your introduction got me thinking about agro-ecological movements around seeds, for example, and indigenous struggles against extractivism, and even feminist movements in specific territories – how they can expand our imagination to invent experiments or experimental moments, and to think about this genera-tive tension between relationality and limits. Actually, I started thinking that, from a political perspective, maybe the tension is not between relationality and limits, but between relationality and *resistances*, right? I mean the actual practice of un-doing, of resisting, of saying no. Geology might be thought as a resistance in itself; sometimes the Earth is not friendly to 'us', I mean, that is one kind of limit. But there is also a political limit, when a community or a collective just says 'no, no more', or 'I won't do this', or 'I'm going to resist, no matter how important collaboration is, no matter how important consensus is, no matter how important making connections and relations is, I won't accept this'. I think that that moment is really interesting; it is another form of limit, that is not geological, but which is so important in thinking about environmental alterities.

D: For me, what was most interesting – also as a framing device for the chapters – was the proposition that it is not a contest between limits and heterogeneity, or relationality, but rather, the idea that the tension generated between the two ends up doing interesting work around the concept of the Anthropocene. Some of the topics that were raised in connection with that dialectic I have encountered before. Too often, I feel frustrated with efforts to resolve the tension in one direction or in the other, maybe beginning with the question of whether the Anthropocene is ultimately a turn away from the human, of the rendering of the human geological, eliding any kind of human particularity and political difference in favour of a flattening of the idea of our species' activity into a kind of geological force. Or, conversely, whether it's the height of anthropocentrism and the extension of the human and human logics to every part of the world. I think such a tension has been playing out; it has been very generative for science and technology studies, for the humanities and also for the arts. It does a lot of work, but I was quite taken by the idea that it is in some way irresolvable. You mentioned [in the introduction] something about a kind of undoing of the modern which then becomes an end in itself, posing for us the question of what comes after after-nature. The question that this left me with, and I think it is quite a challenging one, is where does this search for experimental or alternative modalities – ways of turning away from a dominant epistemological, political logic that got us into this situation in the first place – take us? And how do we move beyond the idea of experimentation as an end in itself? What is so pressing in moments like these, refreshing actually, is talking about this in the context of real struggles. We could talk about them in the abstract, as experiments in political transformation and new struggles for sovereignty, but they are very real. They are not experiments in the laboratory or in the art gallery. They are organic experiments in contexts where the stakes are extremely high, and they are not experimentation for its own sake at all. From a step removed, experimentation can generate so many different options and varieties of outcome that are welcome – but the experiments that count politically are often not at all looking for a variety of outcomes. They are looking for a very concrete outcome, and looking for it fast and furious, and there is an enormous amount at stake in getting the experiment right. I mean, how do we move past this attachment – as scholars, but also politically – to what sometimes seems like an endless search for new possibilities in the hope that we will find a kind of exemplary mode of living, or a model for how else we might live on the damaged planet, so to speak?

M: I actually have a question related to that for Antonia and Cristóbal. It is a very concrete question, and it is genuine. Why did you choose the *tabapot* figure to think about this third option – which I love – in which tensions are not resolved, but enter into a generative interaction between what are supposed to be opposed solutions? I'm interested how you got into the figure of the *tabapot*.

A: Hmmm, this means we [the editors] are going to have to appear more in the conversation…!

C: A way to answer this is with another question, or a request. We needed a figure in order to get rid of this reification of binaries and non-voluntary declaration of a sort of anti-collaboration in debates, that we saw as strongly connected with the potentiality to collaborate, right? Scholars engaged in a misleading debate. The *tabapot* was a figure that we came up with in order to think through that. So, maybe you can think about figures that are useful in your own work? Dehlia, you said that figures can be an invitation to think beyond experimentation, ways of living, or a world we want to create together. What kind of figures are available in your own work, in the intersection between arts and philosophy of science? Or which figures, Manuel, in your work, can maybe render better the idea that resistance is a generative movement?

D: I might offer that we return to ecological disasters, or what once went by the name of natural disasters. They have certainly been important figures for me, and I wonder if they have also been for you, Manuel? By way of an aside, I also want to say that it is quite in keeping with the spirit of this topic that we would entrap and entangle you, Antonia and Cristóbal, into this conversation a little, against your prescription. It is hard to toggle between a fresh conversation and a kind of meta conversation, and all of us STS scholars are just too acutely aware of this to put it aside! So, if we have entangled you in the web a bit, it is probably partly your own fault for articulating so clearly in your own text how and why we should embrace this kind of imbrication and entanglement. So, this could be a figure; or we could also turn back to disasters because I am curious about what kind of issues you have been working on, Manuel, and if you think of them as figures perhaps in this way for producing changes or swerves, or ways of reorganising your thought.

M: It's a great question I think, both Cristóbal's and yours, Dehlia. So, other figures… The question in itself is interesting, beyond the answer, right? How can we figure, how can we represent, how can we even create an aesthetics around the question, without necessarily having to answer it? So, for example, in the last couple of years I have been working in the highlands in the Salar de Atacama, in the Atacama salt flats, and I think that there are concrete objects that in themselves can concentrate the tension the introduction tries to foreground. I'm not being very innovative here, but I think that, for example, water in itself is a thing that entails this tension between relationality or heterogeneity on one hand, and the limits and the withdrawnness of matter, of earthly matter, on the other. So, at the same time, water is something that is ecologically related with everything, especially from an ancestral perspective but also from a scientific perspective. All these hydrogeological studies on aquifers in the salt flats, for example, show precisely this kind of flourishing relationality of underground water. But at the same time, they show how this water is completely indifferent and sovereign, materially independent. I guess that when you really look carefully at these objects or things that are implied in environmental crises or natural disasters, they show precisely their *tabapot* condition, this conversation in tension, a relation in divergence. In the case of my fieldwork, it is really interesting how this is something put forward and discussed and recognised, not only by Indigenous knowledge but also by scientific knowledge, Western scientific knowledge.

D: It is worth tracking the way that the Anthropocene, as you so eloquently explained in your introduction, collapses these kinds of antagonistic discourses. There is certainly a critical perspective you can take on it, but it is arguably a place in which the sciences have collapsed or internalised so many of what we have been taking to be the critiques of human physical activities, as well as a kind of epistemological perspective of the sciences. Within the discourse of the stratigraphic society and the debate concerning the Anthropocene, it becomes very clear that things which have seemed obvious to STS scholars for a long time seem to be new for geologists. The Anthropocene as a geological epoch maps onto a discursive space and a particular historical moment – in the history of science as much as a moment in the history of the planet. The Anthropocene becomes a kind of supervening figure through which we might seek to have these conversations on a very broad scale – despite the fact that it is the generalising, overly broad aspirations of concepts that are often the problem. I wonder if it is the figure of the Anthropocene, and the problematic figure of the Anthropos itself, that crystallises this problem, because all of these tensions and heterogeneous manifestations are part and parcel of what the Anthropocene discourse is about: where is the Anthropocene, what is the Anthropocene, who is and who has been Anthropos, what should the Anthropocene become? Even within the scope of the International Stratigraphic Union – one of the most arcane geophysical corners of the sciences for a very long time – all of a sudden, they are grappling (in a way) with the very same kinds of questions as come up in discussions that we have been having within a very theoretical space. Even the question of where and when the Anthropocene began, which seems to be at least a plausibly physicalist question –you know, let's find a rock somewhere, or part of the ground that would reflect our inscription the most clearly – becomes a very political decision because it's clear that whatever kind of scientific choices are made, they will be moments in political history. This is as clear from a scientific perspective as it is from a critical STS perspective. The inextricability of the criticism of the Anthropocene from its own internal discourses seems exemplary of the problematic that this book sets forth. I would offer this for our conversation: is the Anthropocene itself, or perhaps Anthropos, not the kind of figure that is becoming the one that we are looking to replace or refine in all of these appeals to *other* ways of thinking, other ways of being, living not in but *with* the world, or even with other planets?

M: I wanted to ask you, Dehlia. You are involved in that kind of hybrid space between STS and the arts. Because something that is really interesting in the introduction piece is how interdisciplinarity has emerged as a kind of… I wouldn't say the solution, but one avenue of exploration of what the Anthropocene, in all its complexities, is. Interdisciplinarity has become a very tempting way of thinking through the complexities and violences involved in the Anthropocene concept – through, and against, its homogenising and globalising gesture, of its figuration as an overarching and abstracted force. And in the introduction, I sensed a healthy pinch of irony around interdisciplinarity, I could sense a critique there, right? Of interdisciplinarity as the new epistemic lexicon or consensus to talk about the Anthropocene. So, Dehlia, I wonder how that has affected your own practice in that kind of hybrid space in which you are – this use and abuse of the interdisciplinarity grammar, how have you taken that?

D: As you rightly point out, interdisciplinarity has become in some contexts another hopeful area, if not a panacea. We look towards interdisciplinarity or collaboration to invite a relaxing of the old strictures and dusty old conventions of our own disciplines, which is to say, an openness to something other, to experimentation, to self-criticism of one discipline, as opposed to presupposing its own stability in relation to the other disciplines. But to a philosopher, I mean within philosophy, the discipline in which I was trained, philosophy is the queen of the sciences. A philosopher, very classically of course, aspires not so much to be on an equal footing with the other sciences, or the other fields, but to be in a supervening position – to comprehend them all. Of course, this is a grandiose aspiration. But I still think that there is something important in the perspective which philosophy brings to interdisciplinary conversations. My work has been very interdisciplinary: even as a grad student in philosophy I was very much involved in STS and going to STS conferences, and reading illicit magazines, you know, books by Bruno Latour, Michel Foucault and Donna Haraway, hidden away in the dark in the library toilets so other philosophers wouldn't see, and so on. I have come to realise that entering into an interdisciplinary space as a philosopher is very different than it is for every other discipline. One of my inspirations for what interdisciplinarity could look like comes from an early twentieth century philosopher of science, Otto Neurath, who was part of a leftist movement within what later became a very different kind of a philosophical project, namely, the radical origins of philosophy of science in its effort to produce an Encyclopedia of the Unity of Science.[2] At some point, this became the philosophical project that was the primary object of STS's consternation, namely this idea of a kind of grand unified project of knowledge of the sciences, in which everyone can talk to each other in the language of physics and there would be no political or social or even linguistic particularity that would compromise the status of that knowledge project. In its earlier manifestation, the unity of science project was much more practical and political. Neurath offered the example of a forest fire. Why do you need the unity of science? Well, think about it: what sort of sciences would be needed to deal with a forest fire? Neurath says it is obvious, if you take any kind of event like that, or practical thing in the world, then of course you need someone to assess how fast the leaves will burn. But you also need a sociologist to think about how to convince people to evacuate, rather than stay and watch their homes. And where will we get the water to put out the fire, etc.? So, coordinated action becomes the driver of coordinated knowledge production and the ability to speak across specialties, which later philosophers thought they could achieve by reducing everything to logic. But another way of taking that project forward would be to say that it is a kind of interdisciplinarity and ability to communicate across disciplines, sharing each other's assumptions, sharing each other's rhythms and habits of practice. These disciplines can even be subspecialties within the physical sciences themselves, which can have a very difficult time communicating with one another. I think this example is still very resonant today, because if we think about the Anthropocene and its myriad disastrous large or small causes, proximal or distant, by this or that set of historical factors, the Anthropocene forces us into an interdisciplinary or transdisciplinary kind of project – less by showing that there's no conceptual underpinning of the nature/culture distinction, than by creating problems that are very practical, inextricably scientific, environmental, political, social, economic, etc. – and we're forced to have these conversations if we are going to make any kind of meaningful progress. Of course, progress is very difficult to come by, certainly on a grand scale, but even in very local problems it is hard to achieve that kind of coordinated action and coordinated understanding. So I think interdisciplinarity, for me, comes about in the way that an event, a disaster or a set of needs forces people into conversation. I could say more about projects that have been developed in the sciences, but I will stop here… and open the talking space.

A: I'm going pick up on that too and ask Dehlia, and maybe Manuel can dive in: within a space where certain kinds of relations are prompted into being because of limits given by an event of some sort, what is the limit of a compromise? So, when it comes to this kind of conversation, what are the methods? I'm hoping with this question to lead into some discussion of the chapters themselves. How do you make the decisions about who to include, who not to include? I think that one interesting thing raised by some of the Anthropocene discussions I know of, is that they imply that some sciences are good, but some aren't good; you don't make relations with some, but you do with others. So, there is a sort of impetus from the world to create these interdisciplinary relational configurations, but there is also agency on your part in how you respond to that. And that is the question that we had in mind in bringing these two chapters together, which was that Latourian problem: how do you compose the 'common world'? I guess Manuel you could also talk about what is happening in Chile, because that's one way of thinking the question there as well: who become your allies? Who becomes your enemies? How do you negotiate that space in response to environmental and political upheaval? And if you can slip into any kind of reflections on the chapters themselves that would be really good.

M: That's a fascinating and complex question, which has also been quite present in my own work: how to treat the sciences, right? What is our engagement, how do we get involved? It's interesting how we are quite critical of the Anthropocene because of all the many reasons that we have talked about. But we are also quite ready to accept what science says about climate change, for example. Nobody is a climate denier, precisely because we accept what science has to say. So, we have quite an epistemologically ambivalent relation with the sciences, and maybe that's fine, maybe that's another *tabapot* figure right there. There is a very interesting genealogy of critical thought, which for example is where I think Donna Haraway comes from, that takes science as a backdrop to think about the real, even if that real is heterogeneous and always flourishing and always becoming. It is quite interesting to think, for example, that many really good thinkers – Haraway as I said, but also Whitehead or even Latour – take the sciences to be that which elicits the fundamental logics of reality; a mode of talking, a mode of representing and a mode of understanding the fundamental actuality of reality. And I'm thinking about these compromises and alliances that you were talking about, Antonia, at play in my own work. And it's a very tricky question. I don't want to make the classical STS gesture, but I think that these alliances are defined and implemented in practice, during and within fieldwork. I don't think there is one solution of how to deal with the sciences, how to manage your commitments with scientific collaborators and how to deal with what is outside and what is inside, which sciences are your ally, which sciences you're going to allow to say something legitimate about the real and which sciences you're going to deny that possibility to because they are colonial, for example. That's an exercise that is quite pragmatic and that you have to deal with in practice, I think. In Chile right now, for example, there is an issue with economics and with the mode of reasoning and the mode of rendering reality visible by economics, which is in a huge crisis, and not only in general terms but also particularly as regards environmental conflicts. The ideas of 'natural resources' or 'ecosystem services', abundant in liberal policy making, are in complete crisis right now. So, maybe it's time to resist economics. I am not denying economists the right to speak about the environment, but maybe in some specific situations, economics, or at least neoclassical economics, should keep quiet or should try to rehearse another political and epistemic position in the conversation with communities and collectives. In my own work I realise that geology, for example, has a very positive-realist way of understanding the earth, at times actually extremely colonial – given, among other things, that in Chile geology is a natural ally of the mining industry. Nonetheless, at the same time, working with geologists and geophysicists, I have seen in their practices truly inspiring ways of doing and thinking about the Earth that, I'm convinced, should be accounted for in our own discussions in the humanities and social sciences about the Anthropocene. Geologists rehearse a very interesting affective engagement with rocks, and magma, and volcanos and glaciers. So, while we are trying in the social sciences precisely to articulate these kinds of engagements, we deny what geologists say and do because they are immediately categorised as 'other', as being on the side of the Western/colonial sciences that have brought us into the situation that we are facing now.

D: I want to pick up on two points that you raised. First, I would point out that there is a sense in which the natural sciences or the physical sciences are posited as a kind of figurable alterity for STS, and I think maybe coming from a philosophical background this is less so in my discipline. For this reason, I don't assume that objective antagonism quite as much. But I think it's important that you raise the recognition that, within geology, and I would say within all the scientific fields I've looked at, there is this element of affective attunement of emotional connection, intuitive or aesthetic perception of the object of study. It is very central to epistemology, perhaps in a way that is underappreciated in a particular kind of characterisation of science, but in my experience, based on my background as a lab scientist, among scientists themselves this doesn't go into the articles, but it is absolutely present in their fieldwork. I was actually interviewing a glaciologist only yesterday, and he took out his violin and started playing some music that he plays when he thinks about the glaciers that he is working on. He was talking about the colours of the ice and… I mean, it was really very surprising to get that from a scientist. You expect it from an artist. But although I think that's certainly part of the epistemology, part of probably individual personalities, it doesn't necessarily add up to some kind of broader political or ethical relation.

So, I think that's something important to flag: that's also part of the hetero-geneity of the epistemological attitudes of the sciences, as it were: you can have all sorts of appealing or seemingly warm or fuzzier, intuitive or varied ways of knowing, but they don't necessarily coalesce into a better programme for living. And we have to be careful of that when we go in search of other ways of know-ing and being and other exemplars – different historical moments and varieties of practice in the present. It is interesting and problematic, because it suggests that the lines are not so easy to draw between a kind of oppositional attitude and ones that would be more promising. I mean that epistemologies do not *necessarily* drive us towards a better ethical or political relation to our objects of study. But to come back to the chapters… As we were talking, I was reminded of Marianne de Laet's discussion of the pack walk with her dogs, puzzling a bit about how to connect talking about dogs with Bronislaw Szerszynski talking about planets and how alterities are articulated, or manifested or worked out between figures – I wouldn't even say subjects or objects because it is precisely the point of both of these chapters that the boundaries of phenomena are constituted, they're lived out. Of course, this problem is a point of departure for the book, but it makes more sense when we think about these particular examples and how they can be articulated and distinguished from one another. Or, in an example closer to home, how to take a bunch of dogs for a walk? Who am I in a pack if I go out for a walk with my dogs? I consider it quite important that de Laet makes an objection early on in the essay to critics of anthropomorphism and those who would say she is critical of people, who say: 'well if you are going to have a dog, then you have to be the pack leader', like there is one way of running a multispecies social space that we share with animals.

At the same time, she is critical of people who want to reject anthropomorphism and overtly states that to think that we could escape an anthropomorphic perspective or even some kind of hierarchical power relation is really a pipe dream. This is a promising way of thinking about the collective, one that also takes us out of unfulfillable, unrealistic dreams of a harmonious collectivity in which all participants are equal and where there is always room for another chair at the table – because in the moment, in the situation, there is a kind of directionality, or a kind of value, or practical priority to what kind of collectivity is going to be able to function, what kind of pack can go for a walk, and how one needs to be in the pack in order to get to the park and then back home. I think it is the seemingly familiar quality of this example that makes it so useful.

So, if we think of the collection of interdisciplinary scholars or practitioners or emergency response crews as a kind of pack that needs to coordinate, it becomes very obvious that there is no standardised model that would allow us to distribute agency and distribute responsibility evenly, or even in the same way from one instance to the next. This is not to say that it is always going to work. Not every experiment will work and not every configuration of a pack will be successful in achieving certain kinds of goals. But it is that tension and that attunement and that ability to negotiate the tension that allows the pack to be functional. I wonder if this is also a suggestive analogy for ourselves as a pack of interdisciplinary scholars – I mean, I don't know, I feel I am pulling the leash here… (laughs)…maybe stopping to sniff a tree or something … and actually in the interdisciplinary projects that I orchestrate I usually use the term 'curate' – I really value, and even try to build in, some antagonisms between people who wouldn't usually talk to each other. Because I think, as in your volume, that it is in that space of tension and that kind of live negotiation that there are interesting results. It is productive, it is useful to see, basically, how far we can walk within that tension.

M: I think that there is this question about how to properly invite the non-human to a more extended collective without imposing human categories of what a collective is, or even what 'human' means – and I think this is a key question. How can we really recognise and invite others – *radical* others – without illuminating the world with our logics and our grammars and our humanity? But I think that what is interesting, following Isabelle Stengers, is the question itself; I think that that's beautifully put in your introduction. The key here is not to solve anything, but how can we invite the radically other, how can we invite the non-human in a way that is sensible to the political gesture at stake, to the divergence at the basis of the invitation? What is interesting here is the generative capacities of the question, both in itself and in the further questions that this question provokes when you take it seriously.

D: May I offer a way of concluding? I think this question is beautifully posed. It is true that the power of the question itself is really the force of this book. But I also think there is a certain irony in the very last part of this book, which is about planets and our ability to think of them in a way that captures their own way of differentiating themselves, according to their own logic. The question, for me, is why and how far should we try to escape our human – all-too-human and all-too-historically-specific – ways of thinking and being? How far should we go in trying to escape that? Because, as this discussion of planetarity suggests, there are so many ways of being and some of them are of immediate relevance and interest, and are perhaps very usefully corrective, and some of them are our own failings; and then there so many ways of being that could be comprehended, in some cases very much through the lens of one science or mode of reasoning or another. Do we really have to think of planets as the collective? I'm not sure. Are they very interesting to think of as their own collectivity? Is their own collectivity and their own differentiation, or subjectification, instructive for our own? Absolutely. But there is a certain irony in actually pushing the discussion that far, because if we think of the contexts of this discussion, of animals, and people, and our efforts to extend the collective, and we put it into that planetary scale, we kind of return ourselves exactly to the problematic of the Anthropocene, just a few little fleas dancing on the edge of one of these swirling masses of gases in the solar system, and it really pushes the question about how far our affinities, and epistemologies, and kind of forms of kinship and political affiliation really need to stretch. I think it's important to be responsible for the way that we open the door, but also the way we make circumstantial ways of setting the limits. And again, this tension between limits and heterogeneity that's central to the book, is present in the question of what sorts of heterogeneous communities we should be striving to be able to comprehend. So, I would just say, thank you for crystalising the productivity of that question; it has been quite interesting to think through.

Just to finish, I think that the context of these political crises or protests is hugely important. I think I lose sight of it when I focus on local politics, but it's often said that the proliferation of contemporary political crisis and the rise of the extremist right is a kind of supplemental effect of a broader environmental crisis. If we are wondering how people are aware of climate change… well maybe as a kind of generalised anxiety and self-protectiveness that leads to antagonism and the eruption of political crisis. So, I think that as a context for the book it is quite important to highlight these, in some ways related but in other ways very disjunctive, political discussions and protests in Hong Kong, Chile, and elsewhere that are happening at the moment.

NOTES

1 Cristóbal is also from Chile.
2 This story is told in George Reisch (2005).

REFERENCES

Reisch, G. *How the Cold War Transformed Philosophy of Science: To the Icy Slopes of Logic* (Cambridge/New York: Cambridge University Press, 2005).

MATTERING PRESS TITLES

Energy Worlds in Experiment

EDITED BY JAMES MAGUIRE, LAURA WATTS AND BRITT ROSS WINTHEREIK

Boxes: A Field Guide

EDITED BY SUSANNE BAUER, MARTINA SCHLÜNDER AND MARIA RENTETZI

An Anthropology of Common Ground: Awkward Encounters in Heritage Work

NATHALIA SOFIE BRICHET

Ghost-Managed Medicine: Big Pharma's Invisible Hands

SERGIO SISMONDO

Inventing the Social

EDITED BY NOORTJE MARRES, MICHAEL GUGGENHEIM, ALEX WILKIE

Energy Babble

ANDY BOUCHER, BILL GAVER, TOBIE KERRIDGE, MIKE MICHAEL,
LILIANA OVALLE, MATTHEW PLUMMER-FERNANDEZ AND ALEX WILKIE

The Ethnographic Case

EDITED BY EMILY YATES-DOERR AND CHRISTINE LABUSKI

On Curiosity: The Art of Market Seduction

FRANCK COCHOY

Practising Comparison: Logics, Relations, Collaborations

EDITED BY JOE DEVILLE, MICHAEL GUGGENHEIM AND ZUZANA HRDLIČKOVÁ

Modes of Knowing: Resources from the Baroque

EDITED BY JOHN LAW AND EVELYN RUPPERT

Imagining Classrooms: Stories of Children, Teaching and Ethnography

VICKI MACKNIGHT

www.ingramcontent.com/pod-product-compliance
Lightning Source LLC
Chambersburg PA
CBHW031428270326
41930CB00007B/608

* 9 7 8 1 9 1 2 7 2 9 1 4 2 *